EXCELLENT WOMEN

CONTENTS.

ELIZABETH FRY.
 BY JAMES MACAULAY, M.A., M.D. 9
SELINA, COUNTESS OF HUNTINGDON.
 BY REV. R. LOVETT, M.A. 45
RACHEL, LADY RUSSELL.
 BY JAMES MACAULAY, M.A., M.D. 78
FRANCES RIDLEY HAVERGAL.
 BY REV. J.P. HOBSON, M.A. 111
HANNAH MORE.
 BY HENRY JOHNSON. 149
SUSANNA WESLEY.
 BY REV. J. CUNNINGHAM, M.A. 176
MRS. HEMANS.
 BY REV. S.F. HARRIS, M.A., B.C.L. 209
MADAME GUYON.
 BY WILLIAM NICHOLS. 244
ANN JUDSON.
 BY FRED. A. MCKENZIE. 273
MARY LOUISA WHATELY.
 BY REV. W.R. BOWMAN. 302
AGNES JONES.
 BY ELLEN L. COURTENAY. 333
ELIZABETH, DUCHESS OF GORDON.
 BY REV. S.F. HARRIS, M.A., B.C.L. 363

ELIZABETH FRY.

I.

BIRTH AND EARLY YEARS.

Elizabeth Fry was born in Norwich, on the 21st of June, 1780. She was the third daughter of John Gurney, of Earlham, Norfolk, and Catherine Bell, daughter of Daniel Bell, merchant in London. Mrs. Bell was a descendant of the ancient family of the Barclays of Ury in Kincardineshire, and granddaughter of Robert Barclay, the well-known apologist of the Quakers.

John Gurney of Earlham, born in 1749, was educated in the principles of the Society of Friends, but as he advanced in life, and associated with persons of various Christian denominations, the strictness of his religious opinions was much relaxed, and he showed liberality of sentiment towards others, even if they were indifferent to all spiritual concerns. In fact, in those times there was throughout England, in all the churches, a decay of faith and a tendency to unbelief; against which a few men made noble protest, till the religious Revival, led by Whitefield and Wesley, inaugurated a happier era.

We are, therefore, not surprised to read that the daughters of John Gurney, deprived in early life of their mother's care, were accustomed to mingle with people entirely devoid of religion, although some of these were accomplished and talented in their way. The father continued formally to attend the Friends' Meeting; and the eldest daughter, Catherine, being of a thoughtful mind and with desire for instruction, was of use to her sisters in somewhat checking their love of worldly pleasure and amusements. Of Elizabeth, it is said that in her young days "she was singularly attractive; her figure tall, her countenance sweet and pleasing, and her person and manners dignified and lovely. She was gentle and quiet in temper, yet evinced a strong will." The visits of different Friends, especially her uncle Joseph Gurney, who always had much influence with her, both then and during her future life, helped to confirm the good teaching of her mother in childhood.

II.

BEGINS A PRIVATE JOURNAL: WITH RECORD OF HER EXPERIENCES.

In 1793, when in her seventeenth year, Elizabeth Gurney began to keep a private Journal.[1] In the early part of this record she frankly tells her proceedings day after day, and describes the long and gradual struggle that took place in her heart, which ended in her conversion by the power of the Holy Spirit, and in her thorough consecration to the service of the Lord Jesus Christ. It is a most instructive record, especially for the young.

Her father, a man popular on account of his genial ways and social disposition, making no objection, she joined, with some of her sisters, in all the gaieties of life in Norwich. Prince William Frederick, afterwards Duke of Gloucester, was then quartered with his regiment there, and there was an incessant round of pleasures—balls, concerts, and oratorios. Elizabeth Gurney entered into all the gaiety, but she was ill at ease. She says, "I see the folly of the world. My mind is very flat after this storm

---

1 This Journal was kept up by her till the close of her life, and contains not only a full account of events, but a personal record of her thoughts and experiences. It is preserved with pious care by members of the family. *A Memoir of Elizabeth Fry*, published by her daughters, in two volumes, was widely circulated after her decease. Innumerable biographies and memoirs have since appeared, the best of which, by Susanna Corder, contains selections from the private Journal.

of pleasure." "I do believe if I had a little true religion, I should have a greater support than I have now."

She had also before this time given expression to the better dispositions of her natural heart, saying, "I must do what I can to alleviate the sorrows of others; exert what power I have to increase happiness; try to govern my passions by reason; and adhere strictly to what I think right."

This condition of her mind, with alternate indulgence in vanity and resolutions after better things, lasted till she was twenty-two years of age, when she came to the settled conviction that "it is almost impossible to keep strictly to principle without religion. I don't feel any real religion; I should think those feelings impossible to obtain, for even if I thought all the Bible was true, I do not think I could make myself feel it: I think I never saw any person who appeared so totally destitute of it."

It was something to arrive at the conviction that she lacked the one thing needful; and that she felt that more than natural effort, even the power of the Holy Spirit, was necessary to awaken her to new life, and to change her heart. The arrival at Norwich of an American friend, William Savery, "a man who seemed to overflow with true religion, and to be humble, and yet a man of great abilities," confirmed her in her dissatisfaction with her own state, and strengthened her desires after a new life. Of him, she says, that "having been gay and disbelieving only a few years ago, makes him better acquainted with the heart of one in the same situation."

III.

FIRST VISIT TO LONDON.

While in this unsettled and partially awakened state of mind, Elizabeth's father proposed to take her to see London, an offer which she gladly closed with, without any thought beyond the excitement of new scenes and pleasures. He took her there, and left her for several weeks, under the care of a relative. It was a perilous trial for a young girl, but the result was for her happy. The effect was to disgust her more with the world and mere worldly amusements, and to fix her heart more surely where true peace can alone be found.

In the middle of April, after having been seven weeks in London, her father came to take her home, and very thankful she was to get back to the quiet country. A few days after, a letter came from William Savery, to whom she seems to have written asking his counsel. It was a long epistle, full of wise and faithful advice, and showing most loving interest in his young friend's welfare. A few sentences will give the substance of his letter, which may be read by others with as much advantage as it was by Elizabeth Gurney. "I know, my dear, thou hast, and wilt have, many temptations to combat with: thou wilt, doubtless, be frequently importuned to continue with thy gay acquaintance, in pursuit of that false glare of happiness, which the world, in too bewitching and deceitful colours, holds out to the unwary traveller, and which certainly ends in blinding the intellectual eye from discovering the pure source of soul-felt pleasure resulting from a humble heart, at peace with its God, its neighbour, and itself.

"Thee asks my advice, my dear friend, and without any premeditation when I sat down, I find I have been attempting to give it; but it is very evident thou art under the special care of an infinitely better Instructor, who has already uttered His soft and heavenly voice, to teach thee that the first step towards religion is true humility; because in that state only we can feel the need we have of an arm, stronger than human, to lean upon, to lead us out of and keep us from things which hinder our access to, and confidence in, that boundless source of purity, love, and mercy; who, amidst all the vicissitudes of time, is disposed to be our Shepherd, Guardian, and Friend, in whom we may trust and never be afraid; but this blessed confidence is not, cannot be enjoyed by the gay, the giddy, proud, or abandoned votaries of this world."

Up to this time she had adopted none of the distinctive peculiarities of the Society of Friends. Although from custom attending the meetings, she did not confine herself to the services there; for we read such entries as this, "I went to St. Peter's and heard a good sermon. The common people seemed very much occupied, and wrapt up in the service, which I was pleased to see; afterwards I went to the cathedral." She had already commenced efforts to be useful to others, visiting the sick, and teaching the children of her poorer neighbours, in Norwich, or at Bramerton, then a quiet, pleasant village, where the family usually resided in summer. "I have some thoughts," she says, "of increasing by degrees my plan for Sunday evening, and of having several poor children, at least, to read in the Testament and religious books for an hour. It might increase morality among the lower classes if the Scriptures were oftener and better read to them." Sunday school work she for herself discovered to be a profitable, as she found it to be a delightful task. All this time she was diligent in study, and in the intellectual culture of her own mind, as we find from her Journal.

"I had a good lesson of French this morning, and read much in Epictetus." Later on, we find her intent on the books of Dr. Isaac Watts, his *Logic* especially, which Dr. Johnson had commended strongly to all who sought the "improvement of the mind."

IV.

AT COLEBROOK DALE, AND ON A JOURNEY TO WALES.

In the summer of 1798, John Gurney took the whole of his seven daughters an excursion through parts of England and Wales. At Colebrook Dale, where they saw several relatives, members of the Society of Friends, Elizabeth Gurney received the deepest impressions. She was especially struck with the veteran philanthropist, Richard Reynolds, who having made a large fortune in his well-managed iron-works, spent his money and time in seeking the moral good of the working people. At Colebrook Dale also she spent some days with an elderly cousin, Priscilla Hannah Gurney, cousin to the Earlham Gurneys by both father and mother, her father being Joseph Gurney and her mother Christiana Barclay. Being left by her father alone for some days with this cousin, the influence of the visit was very powerful on her. "She was exactly the person to attract the young; she possessed singular beauty, and elegance of manner. She was of the old school; her costume partook of this, and her long retention of the black hood gave much character to her appearance. She had early renounced the world and its fascinations; left Bath, where her mother and sister Christiana Gurney resided; became eventually a minister among Friends; and found a congenial retreat for many years at Colebrook Dale."

The travelling party went on to make a tour in Wales and to attend the gathering of Friends at the Welsh half-yearly meeting. Most of the

Colebrook Dale Friends were present, and further converse with Priscilla Gurney induced her niece to resolve openly to conform to Quaker customs, though at what precise time she became professedly a Friend we are not told. As to the costume, she was very slow in adopting it—not till some time after returning to Norwich.

In this early Welsh journey a singular prediction was given in an address by an aged Friend, Deborah Darby, who said of her that "she would be a light to the blind, speech to the dumb, and feet to the lame." "Can it be? She seems as if she thought I was to be a minister of Christ. Can I ever be one?" asks Elizabeth Gurney in her Journal.

V.

THE LAST YEAR AT HOME.

The early months of 1799 were passed in Norwich, where she engaged in works which she believed to be right and useful. She visited the poor, doing what she could to relieve distress, yet cautious lest she should appear to do too much, telling her friends that in such charity she was only agent for her father, who approved of her thus helping others. She held what are now called "mothers' meetings," reading and talking to a little group of people about fifteen in number. Her "Sunday School" had also gradually increased, till there were sometimes seventy poor children receiving instruction from her. Cutting out and preparing clothes for the poor, and occasional visits to hospitals, and once to Bedlam to see a poor woman, were among the occupations of the winter months. She had not yet, however, made any decisive change in her social habits, for she occasionally accompanied her sisters to balls and other entertainments, yet finding less and less satisfaction in what she in calmer moments disapproved.

The doubtful, wavering condition of mind led her to think more seriously of openly avowing her religious principles.

In the autumn her father travelled to the north of England, taking with him his son Samuel and his daughters Priscilla and Elizabeth. He was going to visit an estate belonging to him; also to attend the general meeting at the Friends' School at Ackworth, after which they were going to Scotland. All this expedition Elizabeth much enjoyed. At Ackworth she took part in the examination of the scholars, and had pleasant conversation with the headmaster Doctor Binns, and with Friends assembled on the occasion. At York they saw the wonderful Minster; at Darlington, found themselves in a living colony of Friends; and Elizabeth was gratified by receiving a note and a book of grammar from the famous Lindley Murray, whom she had met and taken tea with at York. Durham, Newcastle, Alnwick Castle, and Edinburgh, were successively visited, and afforded abundant materials for entries in her Journal, and for agreeable recollections after returning home.

VI.

MARRIAGE, AND SETTLEMENT IN LONDON.

On August 19, 1800, Elizabeth Gurney was married, at the Friends' Meeting House, Norwich, to Joseph Fry, youngest son of William Storrs Fry, of London. He had been to Earlham, and made an offer of marriage, during the preceding year, but nothing had then been settled, Elizabeth Gurney being afraid that any change at that time might interfere with her spiritual welfare and her newly-formed plans of active usefulness. But after some correspondence, when the proposal was renewed, she felt it right to give her consent. It was the custom more generally prevailing than now for the junior partner to reside in the house of business, and in accordance with this, Joseph and Elizabeth Fry prepared to establish themselves in Mildred's Court in the City, a large, commodious and quiet house, since pulled down in consequence of alterations in London. The parents of her husband occupied a country-house at Plashet, Essex. The Fry family, like that of the Gurneys, had long been members of the Society of Friends; but unlike her own parents, they had adhered strictly to the tenets and the habits of Quakers. She thus came to be surrounded by a large circle of new connexions, different from her own early associates at Norwich.

During the fortnight occupied by the Yearly Meeting, Mildred's Court was an open house for the entertainment of Friends from all parts of the kingdom, who would come in to midday dinner, whether formally invited or not. On one occasion, when an American Friend, George Dilwyn, was a guest, she commenced regular family worship, with the approval of her husband, this now recognised duty not having been previously the practice in the house.

Occasionally she got rest in staying at Plashet, but her life was a busy one, and hardly favourable to spiritual advancement. At Plashet, on the 9th of seventh month (July) she wrote: "We live at home in a continual bustle; engagement follows engagement so rapidly, day after day, week after week, owing principally to the number of near connexions, that we appear to live for others rather than ourselves. Our plan of sleeping out so often I by no means like, and yet it appears impossible to prevent it; to spend one's life in visiting and being visited seems sad."

It is evident that the circumstances under which she began her married life were too fatiguing for her, and to these were added the usual domestic troubles at times with servants. All this told upon her, then approaching her first confinement, depressing not merely her bodily powers and natural energy, but in some degree her spiritual liveliness. But she must attend to present duty, and when her first child, a girl, was born, she was absorbed in the anxieties, pleasures and responsibilities of a mother.

From the feeble state of her health, she was some time in regaining strength enough to attend Meeting, or to resume her usual activity. She was confined to her room when she heard the great tumult of joy, at the thanksgiving and the illuminations, for restoration of Peace in 1801, on the 10th of October; and the noise of the mob in the streets disturbed her even in this quiet house. A fortnight later the parents went to Norfolk, taking with them their little treasure, a lovely infant, which gave great delight to the relatives there. The child was vaccinated by Dr. Simms on their return to London, and the doctor's advice was taken about the health of the mother, who then was in a state of much bodily weakness, with a troublesome cough. These trials caused interruption in the Journal for some weeks; but she and the child gradually got better; and at the Yearly Meeting of 1802, she was able to attend almost all the meetings, and to receive the customary crowd of visitors at her house; among them her much-loved uncle, Joseph Gurney, whose presence was of much service to her.

VII.

FAMILY CARES AND TRIALS.

In the autumn her husband took her a journey into the north of England, going by Warwick, Stratford-upon-Avon, Chester, Liverpool, and the Lakes, some of the excursions at which she went on horseback. She was even able to climb Skiddaw, so that her health had been much restored by the expedition. They were glad to get back to their comfortable home, mother and child both better for the trip. Soon after their return, her brother Samuel came to reside at Mildred's Court, to learn details of the banking business, and it was to both a great pleasure to be near one another. A second girl was born in March, 1803; and altogether she had in future years a very large family, eleven sons and daughters; regarding which it is sufficient to say that the succession of illnesses caused so much nervousness and debility, that we can only the more marvel at the indomitable spirit with which she afterwards undertook the labours of charity and beneficence which have made her name so famous. There were also, besides her personal illnesses, many events of trial and of bereavement, as must necessarily happen where there are numerous relatives. Writing at Earlham on the 20th of August, 1808, she says, "I have been married eight years yesterday. Various trials of faith and patience have been permitted me; my course has been very different from what I expected; and instead of being, as I had hoped, a useful instrument in the Church militant, here I am, a careworn wife and mother, outwardly nearly devoted to the things of this life. Though, at times, this difference in my destination has been trying to me, yet I believe those trials that I have had to go through have been very useful, and brought me to a feeling sense of what I am: and at the same time have taught me where power is, and in what we are to glory; not in ourselves, nor in anything we can be, or do; but we are only to desire that He may be glorified, either through us, or others, in our being something or nothing, as He may see best for us."

That same year in late autumn, her dear father-in-law Fry was at Mildred's Court, very ill; and he died there, being carefully and tenderly nursed by his daughter-in-law. She also, at risk to her own family, went to nurse her sister Hannah, in what turned out to be scarlet fever, about which she says, that "she did not know what malady it was when she went; and that she was the only sister then at liberty to wait on her." Through God's mercy, no harm came to her own family from being there, and no one else took the complaint. "This I consider," she says, "a great outward blessing. May I be enabled to give thanks, and to prove my thankfulness by more and more endeavouring to give up body, soul, and spirit, to the service of my beloved Master."

In February, 1809, she and her husband left Mildred's Court to occupy the house at Plashet; to her a pleasant change from the smoke and din of the great city. Here, her sixth child, a boy, was born in autumn of that year. Shortly afterwards she was summoned to Earlham, where she witnessed the death of her own father. It was a heavy blow to her, but she had the satisfaction of finding that his mind was at peace when he drew near his end. "He frequently expressed that he feared no evil, but believed that, through the mercy of God in Christ, he should be received in glory; his deep humility, and the tender and loving state he was in, were most valuable to those around him. He encouraged us, his children, to hold on our way; and sweetly expressed his belief that our love of good (in the degree we had it) had been a stimulus and help to him." At the meeting before the funeral she resolved to say nothing, but her uncle Joseph spoke words of comfort and encouragement; and then she could not refrain from falling on her knees, and exclaiming, "Great and marvellous are Thy works, Lord God Almighty; just and true are all Thy ways, Thou King of saints; be pleased to receive our thanksgiving." She could say no more, though intending to express thankfulness on her beloved father's account. The great tenderness of her uncle gratified her, "and my husband," she adds, "has been a true helpmate and sweet counsellor."

VIII.

WORK AT PLASHET.

As soon as they were settled at Plashet, Elizabeth Fry formed and carried out various plans for the poor. She established a girls' school for the parish of East Ham, of which Plashet is a hamlet. The clergyman and his wife gave their help, and a school of about seventy girls was soon busily at work. The bodily wants of the poor claimed her attention. A depot of calico and flannel was always ready, besides outer garments. There was a cupboard well stocked with medicines. In the winter, hundreds of the destitute poor had the benefit of a soup kitchen, the boiler of an outhouse being applied to this use. About half a mile off, on the high road between Stratford and Ilford, there was a colony of Irish, dirty and miserable, as such settlements in England usually are. Some she induced to send their children to school, and, with the consent of the priest, circulated the Bible among them. Once when the weather was extremely cold, and great distress prevailed, being at the time too delicate to walk, she went alone to Irish Row, in the carriage literally piled with flannel petticoats for the poor women, others of the party at Plashet walking to meet her and help in the distribution. Her children were trained as almoners very young, and she expected them to give an exact account of what they gave, and their reasons for giving. She was a very zealous and practical advocate for vaccination, having been taught by the celebrated Dr. Willan, one of the earliest and most successful followers of Dr. Jenner.

It was an annual custom for numbers of gipsies to pitch their tents in a green lane near Plashet, for a few days, on their way to Fairlop Fair. The sickness of a child causing the mother to apply for relief, led Elizabeth Fry to visit the camp; and ever after she was gladly welcomed by the poor wanderers, to whom she gave clothing and medicines, and friendly faithful counsel. To those who could read she gave Bibles or Testaments, and little books or pictures to the children. Thus she ever abounded in good works for the benefit of others. All this she did in intervals snatched from home duties, there being in the house a constant succession of company and employments to occupy her. For her children she prayed that they might grow in favour with their Heavenly Father, by walking in humility and in the fear of God.

Such was the routine of work and duty at Plashet for several years after she went to live there. She had interruption from various illnesses in her family, five of her children being ill at one time; at other times overbusied with domestic duties, as many as eighteen, in addition to the family, once sleeping at the house. At the time of the Yearly Meeting she had to entertain many visitors in London at Mildred's Court. There were also occasional visits to Norfolk, during one of which she took active part in founding the Norfolk and Norwich Bible Society. The meeting at which this was inaugurated in 1811 was a most successful one. Old Bishop Bathurst spoke with much decision and liberality, and he was supported by many of the clergy, and ministers of all denominations, the Mayor of Norwich presiding. About £700 was subscribed at the meeting. Mr. Joseph Hughes, one of the secretaries, who, with his venerable colleague Dr. Steinkopff, arranged the meeting, in an account written of it, speaks of "a devout address by a female minister, Elizabeth Fry, whose manner was impressive, and whose words were so appropriate, that none present can ever forget the incident, or even advert to it without emotions alike powerful and pleasing. The first emotion was surprise; the second, awe; the third, pious fervour." Such was the impression made by the hearty words spoken by Elizabeth Fry.

IX.

FIRST SIGHT OF NEWGATE PRISON.

It was in 1813 that the attention of Elizabeth Fry was first directed to the condition of female prisoners in Newgate. At the beginning of that year four members of the Society of Friends had visited some persons about to be executed. One of the visitors, William Forster, asked Mrs. Fry if nothing could be done to alleviate the sufferings of the women, then living in the most miserable condition. The state of the prison was at that time disgraceful to a civilised country, even after all John Howard's labours. There were about three hundred women, with many children, crowded in four small rooms, badly lighted, badly ventilated, and with no bedding or furniture. They slept on the floor, some of the boards of which were partially raised, to supply a sort of pillow for rest; and here, in rags and dirt, the poor creatures cooked, washed, and lived. Prisoners, tried and untried, misdemeanants and felons, young and old, were huddled together, without any attempt at classification, and without any employment, and with no other superintendence than was given by one man and his son, who had charge of them by night and by day. When strangers appeared amongst them, there was an outburst of clamorous begging, and any money given went at once to purchase drink from a regular tap in the prison. There was no discipline of any sort, and very little restraint over their communication with the outside world, beyond what was necessary for safe custody. Oaths and bad language assailed the ear, and every imaginable horror distressed the eye of a stranger admitted to this pandemonium. Although military sentinels were posted on the roof of the prison, such was the lawlessness prevailing, that even the governor dreaded having to go to the female prisoners' quarters.

Into this scene, accompanied only by Anna Buxton, did Elizabeth Fry enter. Nothing was at the first visit done but giving warm clothing to the most destitute; William Forster having told of the wretchedness caused by the severity of the cold that January of 1813. What was then witnessed of the sad and neglected condition of these women and children sank deeply into the heart of the visitors, and Mrs. Fry formed the resolution to devote herself, as soon as circumstances permitted, to the work of prison reform, and improvement of the condition of female prisoners.

The work was not wholly new to her. When not sixteen years of age, she was deeply interested in the House of Correction in Norwich, and by her repeated and earnest persuasion she induced her father to allow her to visit it. She never forgot her experience there, and she afterwards said that it laid the foundation of her future greater work.

Several years were yet to elapse before the time came for taking up seriously the cause of prisons. These years were crowded with events of various kinds, both in the great world and in the little world of her own family circle. These events caused delays which we must suppose were needed for preparing more perfectly the instrument to be used in the great work. Every interval of time, amidst these years of busy and disturbed life, was occupied in some active and necessary work. There were meetings at various places, Westminster, Norwich, and also at Plaistow, after the removal to Plashet brought the family within its sphere. At most of the meetings she took part, both in the worship and in visiting the poor or the sick. Then there were family cares, troubles, and bereavements. The loss of little Elizabeth, the seventh child, was a sore trial, a child of much promise, and with wisdom and goodness beyond her years, early called to a heavenly home.

Her tenth child was born on the 18th of April, 1816, for whom she thus prayed with thanksgiving—"Be Thou pleased, O Lord God Almighty, yet to look down upon us, and bless us; and if Thou seest meet, to bless our loved infant, to visit it by Thy grace and Thy love; that it may be Thine in time, and Thine to all eternity. We desire to thank Thee for the precious gift."

After a visit to Norfolk, in consequence of the death of the only surviving son of her uncle Joseph Gurney; and to North Runcton, where her elder daughters were residing; and having placed her sons at school, she came to London, to commence the great work to which she now felt she must devote her life.

X.

PRISON WORK.

Three years had passed since the first visit to Newgate in 1813. The determination then formed to devote her life to prison-work had been cherished ever since, though hindrances delayed the carrying out of her purpose. Nothing but the constraining love of Christ could have thus induced a woman of Elizabeth Fry's position and character, a woman delicate and in feeble health, to devote herself to labours so arduous and painful, sacrificing personal ease and domestic comfort, for the sake of rescuing from destruction those who were sunk in vice and in wretchedness. But she was following the example of Him who came to seek and to save the lost. Her labour was not in vain in the Lord, for she succeeded not only in greatly lessening the sum of human misery, but was enabled to bring many to the knowledge and the love of the Saviour.

In the years of preparation for her work, she made herself acquainted with what had been done by others. At the suggestion of her brother-in-law, the late Samuel Hoare, she accompanied him to Coldbath Fields House of Correction, the neglected state of which much shocked him. She had also visited different prisons with another brother-in-law, the late Sir Thomas Fowell Buxton, at that time occupied, with other philanthropists, in forming a Society for reformation of juvenile criminals. The interest was thus kept alive in her mind about the women in Newgate, whom she again went to see about the end of 1816. On this her second visit she asked permission to be left alone among the women for some hours. As they flocked round her, she spoke to those who were mothers, of the miserable state of their children, dirty and almost naked, pining for want of proper food, air, and exercise. She said she would like to get a school for the children, to which they gladly assented. Then, after talking kindly to many of the women, she read to them aloud the parable of the Lord of the vineyard, in the 20th chapter of Matthew, making a few simple comments about Christ coming, and being ready to save sinners even at the eleventh hour, so wonderful was His pity and mercy. A few of the listeners asked who Jesus Christ was, so ignorant they were; others feared that their time of salvation was passed.

About the school, she said she would do all she could to help them, and get others to assist; only without their own help she could not undertake anything. She told them to think and to talk over her plan for the school, and left it to them to select a teacher or governess from among themselves. On her next visit they had chosen as schoolmistress a young woman, Mary Connor, recently committed for stealing a watch. An unoccupied cell was given to her as the schoolroom by the governor of the prison. On the next day, Mrs. Fry with a friend, Mary Sanderson (afterwards the wife of Sylvanus Fox), went to open the school. It was intended for children and young women under twenty-five, for from the small size of the room they were obliged to refuse admission to many older women who earnestly sought to share in the instruction.

The poor schoolmistress, Mary Connor, proved well qualified for her duties. She taught with the utmost carefulness and patience, and Mrs. Fry had the satisfaction of seeing her become one of the first-fruits of her Christian labour in the prison. A free pardon was granted to her about fifteen months afterwards; but it proved an unavailing gift, for a cough, which had attacked her some time before, ended in consumption. She displayed, during her illness, much penitence and true faith, and she died with a good hope of pardon through her Saviour.

It was in the visits to the school, where some lady attended every day, that the dreadful misconduct of most of the women in the female side of the prison was witnessed, swearing, gaming, fighting, singing, dancing; scenes so bad that it was thought right never to admit young persons with them in going to the school. But the way in which Mrs. Fry had been received when she went there among them alone, made her sure that much could be done by love and kindness, in dependence on Divine help, and with the power of the Word of God applied by the Holy Spirit.

Eleven members of the Society of Friends, with one other lady, the wife of a clergyman, formed themselves into an Association for the Improvement of the Female Prisoners in Newgate. The object was stated to be "to provide for the clothing, instruction, and employment of the women; to introduce them to a knowledge of the Holy Scriptures; and to form in them, as much as possible, those habits of order, sobriety and industry, which may render them docile and peaceable while in prison, and respectable when they leave it."

The concurrence of the sheriffs, of the City magistrates, and the officials of the prison must be obtained, and they were too glad to grant full permission to the visitors; all of them at the same time expressing doubt as to the success of the undertaking, on account of the women not submitting to the restraints it would be necessary to impose. Mrs. Fry had foreseen this, and had drawn up rules to be observed. On a fixed date the sheriffs met some of the ladies' association at the prison; the women were assembled, and asked by Mrs. Fry if they were willing to abide by the rules. With a unanimous shout they assured her of their resolution to obey them strictly.

After the adoption of the rules, a visitor to the prison would scarcely have recognised the place or the people. A matron, partly paid by the Corporation and partly by the associated ladies, had the women, now first divided into classes, under her superintendence. A yards-woman acted as porter. The prisoners, who formerly spent their time wholly in idleness or in card-playing, were now busily at work. A visitor, who went to see the change of which he had heard, describes his being "ushered to the door of a ward, where at the head of a long table sat a lady belonging to the Society of Friends. She was reading aloud to about sixteen women prisoners, who were engaged in needle-work. They all rose on my entrance, curtsied respectfully, and then resumed their seats and employment. Instead of a scowl, leer, or ill-suppressed laugh, I observed upon their countenances an air of self-respect and gravity, a sort of consciousness of their improved character, and the altered position in which they are placed. I afterwards visited the other wards, which were the counterparts of the first."

In 1818 there was a House of Commons Committee, before which Mrs. Fry gave evidence. Her statement is so remarkable as to be worth recovering out of a long-forgotten Blue Book. In answer to questions, she told the Committee that "There are rules, which occasionally, but very seldom, are broken; order has been very generally observed. I think I may say we have full power amongst them, for one of them said it was more terrible to be brought up before me than before the judge, though I used nothing but kindness. I have never punished a woman during the whole time, or even proposed a punishment to them.

"With regard to our work, they have made nearly twenty thousand articles of wearing apparel, the generality of which, being supplied by the shops, pays very little. Excepting three out of this number of articles that were missing (which we really do not think owing to the women), we never lost a single thing. They knit from about 60 to 100 pairs of stockings and socks every month, and they spin a little. The earnings of their work, we think, average about eighteen-pence per week for each person. This is usually spent in assisting them to live, and helping to clothe them.

"Another very important point is the excellent effect we have found to result from religious education; we constantly read the Scriptures to them twice a day; many of them are taught, and some of them have been enabled to read a little themselves. It has had an astonishing effect. I never saw the Scriptures received in the same way, and to many of them they have been entirely new, both the great system of religion and of morality contained in them."

XI.

OTHER BENEFICENT WORKS.

The work so successfully accomplished in Newgate was the precursor of similar work undertaken in other prisons, not in London only, but all over the country. With prisons now so much better managed, and with multitudes of workers, single or associated, striving for the welfare of prisoners, the record of Mrs. Fry's early labours may have lost much of its interest. But it is well to state clearly the nature of her work, and the spirit in which it was undertaken. Nor was it only in the interior of the prisons that her labours were carried on. At that time the transportation of criminals to penal settlements was very largely resorted to, and the state of convict ships was as bad as that of the worst prisons in England. Mrs. Fry made arrangements for the classifying of female prisoners; for obtaining superintendents and matrons; for providing schools and work on board ship; and in many ways attending to the welfare of the poor convicts. She used to go down to almost every ship that left the Thames, and saw everything done that was possible for their comfort. In one case, that of the *Wellington* convict ship, hearing that patchwork was an easy and profitable work, she sent quickly to different Manchester houses in London, and got an abundance of coloured cotton pieces. When the ship touched at Rio Janeiro, the quilts made by the women were sold for a guinea each, which gave them money to obtain shelter on landing, till they could get into service or find respectable means of subsistence. The children were taught to knit, and sew, and read; the schoolmistress and monitors being themselves chosen from the convicts, with guarantee of reward if they continued steady.

A more public and national benefit was the assistance given by Mrs. Fry to those who sought revision of the penal code by Parliament. Sir Samuel Romilly, Sir James Mackintosh, the Earl of Lansdowne, Mr. Wilberforce, all acknowledged the help obtained in their parliamentary efforts to amend the administration of the criminal law, in the facts and the experience supplied by her from her long and successful efforts in prison work. The popularity acquired by her brought all manner of persons, the very highest in Church and in State, to seek to know her and to do her honour. Even the aged Queen Charlotte, who had never taken much interest in philanthropic work, and had paid undue attention to small matters of court formalism and etiquette, was melted into admiration of what this Quaker lady had done. On the occasion of a public ceremony at the Mansion House, the Queen asked Mrs. Fry to be present, and paid particular attention to her. The pencil of the artist has left a record of this scene, as well as of the meetings in Newgate, where she is addressing the prisoners. Some years later she was introduced to Queen Adelaide by the Duke of Sussex, and it was the beginning of profitable intercourse with one whom she esteemed on account of her true piety and unbounded charity. With the Duchess of Gloucester and others in exalted position she had frequent interviews; and also more than once visited the Duchess of Kent, and her daughter, then the Princess Victoria. She was always glad to meet persons of rank, hoping to be of use to them personally, and also to increase their interest in works of charity and of mercy. But she valued above all aristocratic or royal recognition the good opinion of earnest and devoted Christian workers. Of many gifts which she received, few were more prized by her than a copy of the venerated Hannah More's *Practical Piety*, received by her on a visit to Barley Wood, in which the author wrote the following inscription: "To Mrs. Fry, presented by Hannah More, as a token of veneration of her heroic zeal, Christian charity, and persevering kindness, to the most forlorn of human beings. They were naked and she clothed them; in prison and she visited them; ignorant and she taught them, for His sake, in His name, and by His word who went about doing good."

Repeated visits to Ireland, to Scotland, and to different parts of England, Leicester, Derby, Nottingham, Plymouth, and the Channel Islands, were made at different times in her latter years; forming Prison Associations and fulfilling various engagements. In 1825 she wrote: "My occupations are just now multitudinous. I am sensible of being at times pressed beyond my strength of body and mind. But the day is short, and I know not how to reject the work that comes to hand to do." To enumerate all the good works which she originated or supported, would require more space than a brief memoir could allow. Societies for visiting prisons, libraries for the Coastguard men, reformatory schools for juvenile offenders, were among the many institutions which she established. An excellent institution at Hackney, bearing the name of the Elizabeth Fry Refuge, for the reception of discharged female prisoners, will long perpetuate the memory of her useful work.

In the summer of 1829, the family removed to a small but convenient house in Upton Lane, adjoining the Ham House grounds, the residence of her brother Samuel Gurney. In this place she passed most of her later years, and from it she went out on her many expeditions in England or on the Continent.

XII.

VISITS TO THE CONTINENT.

It was not till 1838, the year after the accession of Queen Victoria, that Mrs. Fry paid her first visit to France. She saw most of the prisons of Paris, and she had most pleasant interviews with King Louis Philippe, the Queen, and the Duchess of Orleans. The Queen was much pleased with the "Text Book," prepared some years before, and said she would keep it in her pocket and use it daily. Rouen, Caen, Havre, as well as Paris, were visited. A second journey in France, in 1839, began at Boulogne, and thence by Abbeville to Paris. Here she again took interest in the prisons, obtaining from the Prefect of Police leave for Protestant ladies to visit the Protestant prisoners. Avignon, Lyons, Nismes, Marseilles were visited, and the Protestants of the south of France were much gratified by the meetings held at various places. With the brothers Courtois of Toulouse they had much agreeable intercourse. At Montauban they saw the chief "school of the prophets," where the Protestant pastors are educated, They also went to Switzerland, enjoying the scenery, and also the intercourse with the Duke de Broglie's family, then at the house of the Baroness de Staël. Above a hundred persons were invited to meet her, at the house of Colonel Trouchin, near the Lake of Geneva. Several places were visited, and they returned by Frankfort, Ostend, and Dover.

In February, 1839, she was called to pay a visit to the young Queen Victoria at Buckingham Palace. She went, accompanied by William Allen, Lord Normanby, the Home Secretary, presenting them. The Queen asked where they had been on the Continent. She also asked about the Chelsea Refuge for Lads, for which she had lately sent £50. This gave opportunity for Mrs. Fry thanking Her Majesty for her kindness, and the short interview ended by an assurance that it was their prayer that the blessing of God might rest on the Queen and her relatives.

In the autumn of that year she went to the Continent, with several companions, her brother Samuel Gurney managing the travelling. They saw Bruges, Ghent, Brussels, and the great prison of Vilvorde; Rotterdam, Amsterdam, Pyrmont, and Hameln, where there were about four hundred prisoners, all heavily chained. The prisons in Hanover at that time were in deplorable condition, about which, at an interview with the Queen, Mrs. Fry took occasion to speak.

From Hanover they went to Berlin, where a cordial welcome was received. The Princess William, sister of the late King, was in warm sympathy with Mrs. Fry's prison-work, and, after the death of Queen Louisa, was a patron and a supporter of every good word and work. After Frankfort, they went to Düsseldorf, and paid a most interesting visit to Pastor Fliedner, at his training institution for deaconess-nurses, at Kaiserswerth. Pastor Fliedner had witnessed the good results of Mrs. Fry's labours at Newgate, and he had established a society called the Rhenish Westphalian Prison Association for similar work in Germany. Everywhere authority was given to see whatever the travellers desired, so that this Continental journey was very prosperous and satisfactory. They got back to England in the autumn of 1840.

In 1841 she once more went with her brother Joseph, who was going to some of the northern countries of Europe. She knew that such a journey would be fatiguing to a frame much enfeebled by illness and a life of continuous exertion, but she still had an earnest desire to work for the good of others, if it seemed the will of her Lord and Master. "I had very decided encouragement," she says, "from Friends, particularly the most spiritual among them;" and so, all difficulties being removed, she started, with her brother and two young nieces.

The most interesting of all their North German experiences was visiting the Prussian Royal Family, then in Silesia, whither, on leaving Berlin, they had been invited to follow them. Mrs. Fry had always misgivings in regard to her intercourse with exalted personages, chiefly, she herself explained, lest in anything she said or did she might not "adorn the doctrine of God her Saviour." But she was soon put at ease as to this, on finding that she was coming to real Christians, as devoted as she was to the service of the Master, for such there have generally been among members of the House of Brandenburg. The King and Queen of Prussia were at the time residing at Ermansdorf, and most of the Royal Family were with them or in the neighbourhood. Addresses and conversations on matters connected with prisons or with religious liberty were prominent as usual, but the especial feature in the Silesian visit was the intercourse with the poor Tyrolese refugees from Zillerthal, expelled from their own country by the Austrian Government, and settled in Silesia by the permission of the late King of Prussia. These people had become converts from Romanism to the Reformed faith, by reading the Bible and religious books. After much suffering, they were commanded to quit their homes at short notice. The King of Prussia, on hearing of this cruel edict, was willing to receive them all, and gave them a new home in the domain of Ermansdorf, which they called Zillerthal, after their native village. The Countess Reden, an excellent Christian lady, was authorised to do everything for their comfort. She had cottages built in the true Tyrolese style, with balconies and all the picturesqueness of Swiss chalets. Schools were established, and every means taken to benefit the exiled families. The good Countess Reden arranged for Mrs. Fry meeting the Zillerthallers, who came in their national costume, and heard words of kind and earnest counsel from the English lady. A Moravian brother was brought a distance of forty miles to be interpreter.

XIII.

IN LONDON AND IN PARIS

Not long afterwards Mrs. Fry's greatly enfeebled health compelled her return to England. She landed at Dover on the 2nd of October. After a short stay at Ramsgate with her husband and some of her family, she was taken to Norfolk. There she received letters from the Countess Reden, giving most gratifying tidings of the impressions made by her visit, and of the practical reforms in prisons, effected by royal order since her visit to Prussia. The chaplain of the great prison at Jauer stated that above two hundred Bibles and Prayer-books had been purchased by the prisoners out of their small earnings.

In the winter of 1841, a succession of family events from time to time occupied her attention, her strength gradually improving, till at the beginning of 1842 she again took part in public proceedings. Sir John Pirie was Lord Mayor that year, and Lady Pirie had been a most valued helper of Mrs. Fry in the cause of prison reform. They were anxious to give her an opportunity, at the Mansion House, of bringing her influence to bear on persons of position, and Sir John invited Prince Albert to dine there, with the most prominent members of the Government.

It was in this year the King of Prussia made a state visit to England, and the marked attention he showed to Mrs. Fry was much noticed. He went to meet her at Newgate, and he also insisted on going to Upton to dinner, where Mrs. Fry presented to the King her husband, eight daughters and daughters-in-law, seven sons, and twenty-five grandchildren, with other relatives, Gurneys, Buxtons, and Pellys—an English family scene much enjoyed by the Prussian guest. Other visits are described in her Journals, to the Queen Dowager, the Duchess of Kent, the Duchess of Gloucester, and others of the Royal Family; having interesting conversations about "our dear young Queen, Prince Albert, and their little ones; about our foreign journey, the King of the Belgians, and other matters." She often used to say she preferred visiting prisons to visiting palaces, and going to the poor rather than the rich, yet she felt it her duty to "drop a word in season" in high places, and at the same time to be "kept humble, watchful, and faithful to her Lord."

After the fatigues of the Continental and London season, she was glad in the summer to occupy the house of her brother-in-law Mr. Hoare at Cromer, and when there she saw much of the residents at Northrepps Hall, The Cottage, and other places famed far and wide for their philanthropic associations.

She got home to Upton Lane, and spent the winter there. The most noticeable event mentioned is her meeting at dinner Lord Ashley, at her son's house. "He is a very interesting man; devoted to promoting the good of mankind, and suppressing evil—quite a Wilberforce, I think." Such was her opinion of the good Earl of Shaftesbury in his early days.

In the spring of 1843, feeling her health to be somewhat restored, she surprised her friends by announcing her wish to visit Paris again, to complete works of usefulness formerly initiated there. More than once she saw the widowed Duchess of Orleans at the Tuilleries, the only other person present being her stepmother the Grand Duchess of Mecklenburg, "an eminently devoted pious woman," by whom the Duchess of Orleans had been brought up from childhood. They spoke much about the children of the House of Orleans, and "the importance of their education being early founded in Christian faith;" a desire which may be re-echoed in another generation. Another important series of interviews was with M. Guizot, then the chief statesman of France. Altogether the last visit to Paris was a pleasant and useful expedition.

XIV.

LAST YEARS.

The end was now drawing nigh—the end of her busy, useful life. In June, 1843, Elizabeth Fry attended the Quarterly Meeting at Hertford, the last time she left home expressly on religious service. She felt it her duty, she said, "to encourage the weary, and to stir up to greater diligence the servants of the Lord, who uses weak and foolish instruments for His work," yet who is "made unto His people, wisdom, righteousness, sanctification, and redemption."

Symptoms of increasing feebleness led to her removal that autumn from her home at Upton Lane, to various places, Sandgate, Tunbridge Wells, and Bath, in hope of recovering her strength. But she knew that her time for active service was over. She frequently said to those about her, "I feel the foundation underneath me sure." Her concern was not about herself, but about those near and dear to her.

One of the last entries in her Journal is this: "I do earnestly entreat Thee, that to the very last I may never deny Thee, or in any way have my life or conversation inconsistent with my love to Thee and most earnest desire to live to Thy glory; for I have loved Thee, O Lord, and desired to serve Thee without reserve. Be entreated, that through Thy faithfulness, and the power of Thy own Spirit, I may serve Thee unto the end. Amen."

The year 1844 was one of much trial and affliction. Her husband's only sister died of consumption on July 2nd; a grandson of much promise was taken off at the age of twelve by the same disease towards the end of July; in August and September her second son and two of his young daughters were rapidly carried off by malignant scarlet fever. In the spring of the following year the death of her brother-in-law, Sir Thomas Fowell Buxton, excited her tenderest feelings. In fact, there was a succession of bereavements, which caused her to say in her Journal, "Sorrow upon Sorrow!" and after writing the long list of deaths, she closes the entry with these words "O gracious Lord! bless and sanctify to us all this afflicting trial, and cause it to work for our everlasting good; and be very near to the widow and the fatherless; and may we all be drawn nearer to Thee, and Thy kingdom of rest and peace, where there will be no more sin, sickness, death, and sorrow."

As to her own health, she rallied a little after returning home from Bath, but it was thought well to move from place to place for change of air, and for the pleasure of communion with loved friends. The beginning of 1845 saw her again in Norfolk, her husband and her daughter taking her to Earlham, where she enjoyed, for several weeks, the companionship of her brother, Joseph John Gurney, his wife, and other relatives. She went frequently to Meeting at Norwich, drawn in her wheeled chair, and thence ministering with wonderful life and power to those present.

The Annual Meeting of the British Ladies Society, an excellent organisation for visiting and caring for female convicts, although usually held at Westminster, was this year held in the Friends' meeting-house at Plaistow. After the meeting, which she had addressed several times in a sitting posture, she invited those present to come to her home, and it was felt that her affectionate words at parting were probably the last they would hear from her in this world.

As the year passed, it was thought that the air of the south coast might be useful, and the house at Ramsgate, Arklow House, which proved her last abode, was prepared for her. Her bed-chamber adjoined the drawing-room, with pleasant views of the sea, in which she delighted. While driving in the country, or being wheeled to the pier in a Bath-chair, she still strove to be useful, distributing Bibles and tracts, accompanied with a few words of kindly exhortation. Thus she was employed till the close of her days in work for the Master. She lingered, with gradual decay; and passed away, after a few days' illness which confined her to bed, on the morning of the 13th of October, 1845, in her 66th year. The last words she was heard to articulate, were "O dear Lord, help and keep Thy servant."

There was much sorrow when she had ended her useful life; and when she was taken to Barking for interment, a great number of people assembled, and a solemn meeting was held. But far beyond any local gathering, her example will continue to speak, through all the ages, and in many a land. There are many workers in our time in every branch of Christian usefulness, but the name and the work of Elizabeth Fry will be for ever remembered.

JAMES MACAULAY, M.D.

SELINA, COUNTESS OF HUNTINGDON

Lady Selina Shirley, afterwards Countess of Huntingdon, was born August 24, 1707. She died June 17, 1791. Hence her long and useful life extended over almost the whole of the eighteenth century. She witnessed the rise of the great evangelical revival, which, beginning with the Holy Club at Oxford, gradually spread over the United Kingdom and the English colonies in America. For half a century she was a central figure in that great religious movement which affected so deeply all classes of the community, consecrating her position, her means, her influence to the glory and the extension of His kingdom.

I.

EARLY YEARS.

Lady Selina Shirley was the second of the three daughters of Washington Shirley, who in 1717 succeeded to the Earldom of Ferrars, being the second to bear that title. She was born at Stanton Harold, a country seat near Ashby de la Zouch, in Leicestershire. At a very early age she gave evidence of intelligence above the average, of a retentive memory, and of a clear and strong understanding. She manifested when but on the threshold of womanhood that sound common sense and keen insight into character and the true bearing of affairs which distinguished her so pre-eminently in mature and late life. She was serious by temperament, and when at the age of nine years she happened to meet the funeral cortège of a child the same age as herself, she was attracted to the burial, and used afterwards to trace her first abiding sense of the eternal world to the profound impressions produced upon her mind by that service. In after life she frequently visited that grave. She was earnest in her study of the Bible, much given to meditation, and at times almost oppressed by her convictions of the certainty and duration of a future state. By her station and education she was compelled to go out into society, and to take her place in circles in which religion was as far as possible ignored. But her prayer was that she might not marry into a frivolous, pleasure-seeking family.

On June 3, 1728, she became the wife of Theophilus, the ninth Earl of Huntingdon, who resided at Donnington Park. This proved a happy union, and even if, in later life, her husband was not always able fully to share her beliefs and sympathise with her actions, he never threw any obstacles in her way.

II.

HER CONVERSION.

At Donnington Park the Countess began the kindly and charitable deeds for which she afterwards became so noted. Her religious feelings were strong, and she strove earnestly to discharge fully her responsibilities to both God and man. And yet, as she afterwards came clearly to see, she was ignorant of the true nature of the Gospel, and she was attempting, by strict adherence to prayer, meditation, right living, and charitable action, to justify herself in the sight of God. But, all unknown to her, the mighty religious awakening begun at Oxford in 1729, and publicly preached in 1738 by Whitefield and the Wesleys, was destined to be the cause of her spiritual awakening also. Lady Margaret Hastings and Lady Betty Hastings, the Earl of Huntingdon's sisters, had come at Oxford under the influence of the Methodist movement. While on a visit at Ledstone Hall, in Yorkshire, they received great blessing under the preaching of Benjamin Ingham, a well-known member of the Holy Club, whom in 1741 Lady Margaret married. They both received the truth as it is in Jesus, and were led by the influence of the Holy Spirit to labour and pray for the salvation of their relatives and friends. In talking with her sister-in-law one day, Lady Margaret affirmed "that since she had known and believed in the Lord Jesus Christ for life and salvation she had been as happy as an angel."

These words depicted an experience so different from her own that they exerted a very abiding influence upon Lady Huntingdon's thoughts.

She felt her need, she was conscious of sin, and yet the more she strove to attain salvation the further she seemed removed from it. "A dangerous illness having, soon after, brought her to the brink of the grave, the fear of death fell terribly upon her, and her conscience was greatly distressed. She now perceived that she had beguiled herself with prospects of a visionary nature; was entirely blinded to her own real character; had long placed her happiness in mere chimaeras, and grounded her vain hopes upon imaginary foundations. It was to no purpose that she reminded herself of the morality of her conduct; in vain did she recollect the many encomiums that had been passed upon her early piety and virtue. Her best righteousness now appeared to be but 'filthy rags,' which, so far from justifying her before God, increased her condemnation. When upon the point of perishing, in her own apprehension, the words of Lady Margaret returned strongly to her recollection, and she felt an earnest desire, renouncing every other hope, to cast herself wholly upon Christ for life and salvation. From her bed she lifted up her heart to her Saviour, with this important prayer, and immediately all her distress and fears were removed, and she was filled with peace and joy in believing . . . Her disorder from that moment took a favourable turn; she was restored to perfect health, and, what was better, to newness of life. She determined thenceforward to present herself to God, as a living sacrifice, holy and acceptable, which she was now convinced was her reasonable service . . . No sooner was her heart surrendered to God, and her alienated affections restored to their original claimant, than outward fruits appeared in her conversation: her renovation introduced new light into her understanding, and new desires into her heart and affections, and produced its effect upon her temper; not wholly to eradicate its constitutional peculiarity, but to sanctify and render it subservient to the glory of God and the good of souls."[1]

The Countess on recovering from her illness, hearing that John and Charles Wesley were preaching near by, sent them a message wishing

---

1 *The Life and Times of Selina, Countess of Huntingdon*, vol. 1. pp. 14, 15.

them God-speed and testifying to her own purpose to live entirely for the Saviour who had died for her. Her friends failing in their attempt to persuade her husband to exert his influence against what they considered fanaticism, enlisted the aid of Dr. Benson, Bishop of Gloucester, who had been Lord Huntingdon's teacher. But the bishop, as many another in later days, found that the Countess was fully equal to giving cogent reasons for her faith and practice. It was he who had ordained Whitefield, and to the latter the bishop ascribed the change in her opinion. So far from accepting the bishop's view, the Countess urged home upon him her opinion of *his* duty, enforcing her argument with such apt quotations from the Bible, the Articles, and the Homilies, that at length he left her presence openly regretting the fact that he had ever laid his hands upon Whitefield's head. "My Lord," was the last word of the Countess, "mark my words: when you are on your dying bed that will be one of the few ordinations you will reflect upon with complacence." It is pleasing to know that when on his death-bed in 1752, this prelate sent to Whitefield, and asked to be remembered in his prayers.

III.

HELP IN THE WORK OF WESLEY AXD WHITEFIELD.

Although in 1738 and 1739 Wesley and his followers frequented the Moravian meeting-house in Neville's Court, Fetter Lane, the first home of organised Methodism in London was the Foundry in Moorfields. Lady Huntingdon had identified herself with the Methodists, and thus was enabled to exert great influence upon a movement, small at first, but soon fraught with most potent consequences, the employment by Wesley of lay evangelistic agency. Wesley had already allowed some of his lay helpers to expound, but not to preach. Yet here, as in his strong desire to keep the Methodist movement within the borders of the Established Church, he was to find that his personal view, if enforced, would hinder the work which was so manifestly of God, and with his clear common sense he at once gave way. During 1739 Lady Huntingdon had frequently heard Thomas Maxfield pray, and, according to her biographer, it was at her suggestion that he began to expound the Scriptures. Wesley had been summoned from London, and no clergyman being available at that moment, he left Maxfield in charge, to pray with the members of the society and to give them such helpful advice as he could. In a letter to Wesley, written either at the close of 1739 or the beginning of 1740, Lady Huntingdon writes of Maxfield: "He is one of the greatest instances of God's peculiar favour that I know: he is raised from the stones to sit amongst the princes of His people. The first time I made him expound, expecting little from him, I sat over against him and thought what a power of God must be with him to make *me* give any attention to him. But before he had gone over one-fifth part, any one that had seen me would have thought I had been made of wood or stone; so quite immovable I both felt and looked. His power in prayer is quite extraordinary."

The border line between such expounding and preaching is very narrow, and it is hardly to be wondered at that Maxfield soon found that he was not only preaching, but doing so with the most true and certain warrant of fitness for the office—souls were being born again under his ministrations. On hearing such unexpected tidings, Wesley hurried back to London, and entering his house next door to the Foundry with clouded face, replied to his mother's question as to the cause, "Thomas Maxfield has turned preacher, I find." Great was his surprise to receive the rejoinder, "Take care what you do with respect to that young man, for he is as surely called of God to preach as you are." Such testimony from such a source could not fail to move John Wesley. He wisely heard for himself, and expressed his judgment in the words of Scripture—"It is the Lord: let Him do what seemeth Him good."

Thus Methodism passed through what might have been its first great crisis. Thus it equipped itself to keep pace with the ever-increasing claims of its work. The quick spiritual insight of Lady Huntingdon recognised both the need and the fitness of the hitherto unrecognised worker.

One of the first members of the noble band of itinerating preachers thus called into the active exercise of their spiritual gifts was David Taylor, a servant in Lord Huntingdon's household, who did much fruitful evangelistic work in the villages surrounding Donnington Park. It was this man who stood by John Wesley's side when the drunken curate of Epworth refused him admission to what had been his father's pulpit, and who announced to the congregation as they left the church that in the afternoon Wesley would preach in the graveyard. And there that same afternoon Wesley, standing upon his father's tombstone, preached to a congregation, the like of which Epworth had never seen before, the first of a series of sermons that afterwards became famous.

Having thus aided one of the brothers during a critical administrative stage, Lady Huntingdon shortly afterwards was of great service to the other in a crisis of spiritual experience. Soon after the organisation of the first Methodist Society, the "still" heresy developed among the Moravian members of the Fetter Lane Chapel. This was the view, "that believers had nothing to do with ordinances—were not subject to them—and ought to be *still*; that they ought to leave off the means of grace, and not go to church; not to communicate; not to search the Scriptures; not to use private prayer till they had living faith; and to be *still* till they had it."[1] Wesley used all his influence and all his persuasive power to counteract these opinions, but without avail. At length he decided to sever all connection with those who insisted upon acting in accordance with them, and removed Methodism to the Foundry. Charles Wesley at first went cordially with his brother, but at a later date he ceased attending the Foundry, and manifested signs of a desire to return to Fetter Lane. Lady Huntingdon, for whose views he entertained feelings of the deepest respect, remonstrated with him, and in conjunction with John Wesley's efforts kept him from a step that might have proved fatal to his further usefulness. In a letter written to John Wesley in October, 1741, Lady Huntingdon writes: "Since you left us the *still ones* are not without their attacks. I fear much more for your brother than for myself, as the conquest of the one would be nothing to the other . . . I comfort myself very much that you will approve a step with respect to them your brother and I have taken. No less than his declaring open war with them . . . Your brother is also to give his reasons for quite separating. I have great faith God will not let him fall; He will surely have mercy on him, and not on him only, for many would fall with him."

---

1 *Life and Times of Selina, Countess of Huntingdon*, vol. 1. p. 36.

IV.

FAMILY BEREAVEMENTS.

Lady Huntingdon at this period of her life was called upon to endure some very heavy domestic griefs. She had to mourn for two of her sons, George, aged thirteen, and Fernando, aged eleven, who died of smallpox. They were both buried in Westminster Abbey. On October 13, 1746, she lost her husband, who was carried off by an apoplectic seizure, in his fiftieth year. The Countess had only just passed her thirty-ninth birthday when this last great sorrow came upon her. She herself was at the same time tried by a long and severe illness. The effect of these repeated and heavy afflictions was to further develop her character, and to increase the devotion and self-sacrifice with which she gave herself to works of benevolence and to the extension of the Saviour's kingdom. On Lord Huntingdon's death, besides having entire control of her own means, she became sole trustee of the children and their fortune. In regard to the latter she proved herself a good steward; the former she devoted very largely to the evangelistic and charitable work in which she delighted.

Early in 1747 she wrote to Dr. Doddridge: "I hope you will comfort me by all the accounts you can gather of the flourishing and spreading of the glad tidings. Oh, how do I lament the weakness of my hands, the feebleness of my knees, and coolness of my heart! I want it on fire always, not for self-delight, but to spread the Gospel from pole to pole." And in other letters: "My heart wants nothing so much as to dispense *all—all* for the glory of Him whom my soul loveth." "I am nothing—Christ is all; I disclaim, as well as disdain, any righteousness but His. I not only rejoice that there is no wisdom for His people but that from above, but reject every pretension to any but what comes from Himself. I want no holiness He does not give me, and I could not accept a heaven He did not prepare me for; I can wish for no liberty but what He likes for me, and I am satisfied with every misery He does not redeem me from; that in all things I may feel that without Him I can do nothing . . . To preach Christ and His blessing upon repentance over the earth is the commission—the event must be with Him—all else is from man and of man. May the Lord give us all such love, to live and die to Him and for Him alone."

At a later period in life, May, 1763, she sustained another serious bereavement in the loss of her youngest daughter. Although only twenty-six years of age, she had long been a great comfort to her mother, who, writing after her death, called her "the desire of my eyes and the continual pleasure of my heart." Many were the letters of sympathy she received from Venn, Berridge, Romaine, Fletcher, and others; but it was a loss that could not be replaced. But it could and it did help to purify still more the loving and trusting heart which could see, even as Fletcher urged, in so sore a trial, "mercy rejoicing over judgment." One of the sayings of her daughter on that death-bed must often have come to the mother's mind in later days, "I am as happy as my heart can desire to be."

V.

WHITEFIELD AS LADY HUNTINGDON'S CHAPLAIN.

Prior to 1744, the date of Whitefield's first voyage to the American colonies, the Countess had made his acquaintance, and had often heard him preach. She, in common with multitudes of her contemporaries, had come under the extraordinary spell of his pulpit oratory. In 1748, after a four years' absence in North America, Whitefield returned to England, and at her request Howel Harris, the famous Welsh evangelist, brought the great preacher to Lady Huntingdon's house in Chelsea. In a reply to a letter sent the next day, conveying the request that he would come again, as "several of the nobility desired to hear him," Whitefield wrote, August 21, 1748: "How wonderfully does our Redeemer deal with souls! If they will hear the Gospel only under a ceiled roof, ministers shall be sent to them there. If only in a church or a field, they shall have it there. A word in the lesson, when I was last at your Ladyship's, struck me, 'Paul preached privately to those who were of reputation.' This must be the way, I presume, of dealing with the nobility who yet know not the Lord. Oh, that I may be enabled, When called to preach to any of them, so to preach as to win their souls to the blessed Jesus! I know that you will pray that it may be so."

Thus began the series of drawing-room services which were attended by so many of those who were high in rank, and at which some of the most famous incidents in Whitefield's career occurred. At these services the Word of God often found an entrance into worldly hearts, and once and again Whitefield tried to win for the Saviour such men as Chesterfield and Bolingbroke. Lady Huntingdon made him one of her chaplains, and in order to afford greater facilities for this special work, she removed from Chelsea to a house in Park Street, and for six weeks Whitefield carried on these special services, in addition to all his other work. When, for his own spiritual refreshment, he left London for an evangelistic tour to Bristol, Exeter, and Plymouth, this special work was continued by John and Charles Wesley, and several of their fellow-workers.

The young Earl of Huntingdon came of age in 1750, and the Countess gave up Donnington Park to him, removing her household to Ashby, living there with her other children and two of the Ladies Hastings. Towards the close of 1749 Whitefield desired, if possible, with the aid of Lady Huntingdon, to organise the vast numbers who had been greatly blessed by his evangelistic work, into a corporate body, like that which the clear, practical wisdom of John Wesley had created for the societies which looked up to him as leader. Whitefield had already seriously differed from Wesley on the tenets of Calvinism and much trouble was to ensue in after years from a renewal of the controversy between the two sections, Calvinistic and Arminian Methodism. Lady Huntingdon seems to have been attracted by Whitefield's wish and plan; though it was not at this time destined to bear fruit. But early in 1750 she exerted herself, and with success, to bring about a renewal of thoroughly friendly relations between the two great leaders. On January 19 and 26, 1750, Whitefield and Wesley took part in combined services; Wesley reading prayers and Whitefield preaching on the former, these respective functions being reversed on the latter date. Until Whitefield's death this harmony was never again broken.

At this period Whitefield paid several visits to Ashby. Here and in London he had fellowship with Dr. Doddridge, whose MS., "from Corinthians to Ephesians," of *The Family Expositor*, was nearly consumed by fire at Ashby; Hervey, the author of that well-known book of which so many have heard but so few have read, *Meditations among the Tombs*;

Madan, a lawyer who, going to hear John Wesley, in order that he might mimic him before his companions, listened to a sermon on the text, "Prepare to meet thy God," was converted by it, and upon his return, said in reply to the question, "Have you taken off the old Methodist?" "No, gentlemen, but he has taken me off!" and from that day devoted himself to the service of God; Moses Browne, afterwards Vicar of Olney, and many others.

"Good Lady Huntingdon," he wrote from Ashby, "goes on acting the part of 'a mother in Israel' more and more. For a day or two she has had five clergymen under her roof, which makes her Ladyship look like a good archbishop with his chaplains around him. Her house is a Bethel; to us in the ministry it looks like a college. We have the sacrament every morning, heavenly conversation all day, and preach at night: this is to live at Court indeed."

Lady Huntingdon's London house continued for very many years to be a centre of evangelistic effort on behalf of many of the highest rank and social status in the capital. In addition to Whitefield, John and Charles Wesley, Romaine, Madan, Venn, and others preached. Among those who were converted by these sermons were the wife and sister of Lord Chesterfield; the latter, Lady Gertrude Hotham, opening her house for the preaching of the Gospel. Lady Huntingdon was no recluse. Uncompromising as she was in every matter where religious principle was involved, she was always ready to avail herself of the true privileges of pleasure which her rank and position enabled her to enjoy. In this way she cultivated the acquaintance of many of the distinguished personages of her time. She was fond of music, and in early life had become acquainted with Handel. In the closing years of the great composer, the intimacy was renewed, and not long before his death she paid him a visit, of which she has left this account: "I have had a most pleasing interview with Handel, an interview which I shall not soon forget. He is now old, and at the close of his long career; yet he is not dismayed at the prospect before him. Blessed be God for the comforts and consolations which the Gospel affords in every situation and in every time of our need!

Mr. Madan has been with him often, and he seems much attached to him." With Giardini also, whose skill on the violin was at that time the theme of universal admiration, Lady Huntingdon was well acquainted. He often played at concerts of sacred music given at her house, and those of Lady Gertrude Hotham and Lady Chesterfield. At the request of the Countess he composed tunes for some of the hymns in frequent use at her chapels, thus giving Horace Walpole occasion to remark, "It will be a great acquisition to the Methodist sect to have their hymns set by Giardini." Tomaso Giordani, another Italian, composed at her request the old familiar tune "Cambridge," for the hymn in the Countess's book commencing, "Father, how wide Thy glory shines!"

VI.

LADY HUNTINGDON'S CHAPELS.

From the appointment of Whitefield as her chaplain, Lady Huntingdon took a commanding position in the development of that section of Methodism which looked rather to Whitefield than to Wesley as its leader, and which held Calvinistic views. Around the Countess gradually gathered such fellow-workers as Romaine, Venn, Toplady, Fletcher of Madeley, and many others equally with them aflame with love for the perishing souls of men. Religion having become largely a mere matter of outward form where it was not wholly ignored, great numbers of the clergy being both ignorant of the true nature of the Gospel and very unwilling that others should preach it, Lady Huntingdon was led to establish chapels in different parts of Great Britain. In some parts she rented buildings; in others she built chapels; and gradually a considerable number of places of worship, largely originated by her, and almost wholly sustained by her, came into being. She herself always wished these to remain connected with the Church of England. She endeavoured to keep their pulpits supplied with clergymen of her way of thinking, and for a time succeeded. But the growth of the work early led her to apply the free agency of lay preachers; and later in life the refusal of the Church of England, upheld by the Courts, to consider her action legal in considering them to belong to the Established Church, drove her in self-defence to constitute her chapels into a connexion with a legal standing and rights. The hostility on the part of many within the Established Church of the eighteenth century, to true New Testament ministry and practice, on the one hand expelled the Wesleyans from the National Church, and on the other compelled Lady Huntingdon to add one more to the dissenting bodies.

The most noted of the churches which thus came into being were those at Brighton, Bath, and Spa Fields. The first named stood upon the site in North Street, now occupied by a later, larger, and more ornate structure. Whitefield visited Brighton, first preaching there in the open air in 1759. This led to the formation of a Christian Society, and in 1761 Lady Huntingdon built a chapel, to defray the cost of which she sold her jewels, realising in this way the sum of nearly £700. The building was opened in 1761, Martin Madan conducting the first services, and being immediately succeeded by such notable preachers as Romaine, Berridge, Venn, and Fletcher.

Lady Huntingdon's connection with Bath began as early as 1739, and for the next twenty-five years she was frequently in that fashionable resort; but it was not until 1765 that she bought the land and established the famous Vineyards Chapel. On October 6, 1765, the chapel was dedicated, and Whitefield preached the first sermon. "Though a wet day," he wrote, "the place was very full, and assuredly the Great Shepherd and Bishop of souls consecrated and made it holy ground by His presence." Romaine and Fletcher often preached at Bath in the early months of the chapel's history, and the latter thus referred to his ministry: "This place is the seat of Satan's gaudy throne; the Lord hath, nevertheless, a few names here, who are not ashamed of Him, and of whom He is not ashamed, both among the poor and among the rich."

It was in this chapel that there was the noted "Nicodemus Corner," a seat carefully shrouded from the public gaze, where sometimes a nobleman and sometimes a bishop heard the goodness of the Gospel.

In this connection may be quoted the following anecdote, given in the Life of Mary Anne Schimmelpenninck, who visited Bath with her mother in 1788. She writes:—

"My mother grew better, she frequently took me with her to the Pump Room, and she sometimes told me anecdotes of those she had seen there when a child. On one occasion, when the room was thronged with company—and at that time the visitors of Bath were equally distinguished for rank and fashion—a simple, humble woman, dressed in the severest garb of the Society of Friends, walked into the midst of the assembly and began an address to them on the vanity and follies of the world, and the insufficiency of dogmatic without spiritual religion. The company seemed taken by surprise, and their attention was arrested for a few moments; as the speaker proceeded, and spoke more and more against the customs of the world, signs of disapprobation appeared. Amongst those present was one lady with a stern yet high-toned expression of countenance, her air was distinguished; she sat erect, and listened intently to the speaker. The impatience of the hearers soon became unrestrained. As the Quaker spoke of giving up the world and its pleasures, hisses, groans, beating of sticks, and cries of 'Down, down!' burst from every quarter. Then the lady I have described arose with dignity, and slowly passing through the crowd, where a passage was involuntarily opened to her, she went up to the speaker, and thanked her, in her own name and in that of all present, for the faithfulness with which she had borne testimony to the truth. The lady added, 'I am not of your persuasion, nor has it been my belief that our sex are generally deputed to be public teachers; but God who gives the rule can make the exception, and He has indeed put it in the hearts of all His children to honour and venerate fidelity to His commission. Again I gratefully thank you.' Side by side with the Quaker she walked to the door of the Pump Room, and then resumed her seat. This lady was the celebrated Countess of Huntingdon."[1]

---

1 *Autobiography of Mary Anne Schimmelpenninck*, vol. 1. pp. 89, 90.

VII.

THE COLLEGE AT TREVECCA AND CHESHUNT.

So rapidly did places of worship multiply under the Countess's fostering care, that very shortly after the opening of the Vineyards at Bath, the question of supplying preachers for their pulpits became so pressing that finally the scheme of founding a college for the training of suitable preachers took definite shape. Lady Huntingdon had already contributed liberally to Western College, Plymouth, Brecon College, and Dr. Doddridge's Academy at Northampton. She held much consultation with her most trusted advisers, Whitefield, Wesley, Venn, Romaine, and others. All were favourable except Berridge, who, although "the most dubious man in the world about his own judgment," yet wrote, "Will not Jesus choose, and teach, and send forth His ministering servants now, as He did the disciples aforetime; and glean them up when, and where, and how He pleaseth? The world says no, because they are strangers to a Divine commission and a Divine teaching. And what if these asses blunder about the Master's meaning for a time, and mistake it often, as they did formerly? No great harm will ensue, provided they are kept from paper and ink, or from a white wall and charcoal."

In 1768 Lady Huntingdon fixed upon an old mansion at Trevecca in Brecknockshire, as the home of the new experiment. Her relations with Welsh evangelistic work had long been close and helpful, and by means of Howel Harris, Trevecca had become familiar to her. Fletcher of Madeley was appointed President, although he was not to reside there permanently; and Joseph Easterbrook resident tutor. Students soon began to appear, the first on the roll being in all probability James Glazebrook, a collier in Fletcher's parish. To Fletcher the Countess had sent the circular describing what she wished the college to be, and asking him, in common with all her ministerial friends, whether he could recommend any suitable persons as students. He replied: "After having perused the articles and looked round about me, I designed to answer your Ladyship that out of this Galilee ariseth no prophet. With this resolution I went to bed, but in my sleep was much taken up with the thought and remembrance of one of my young colliers who told me some months ago that for four years he had been inwardly persuaded that he should be called to speak for God. I looked upon the unusual impression of my dream as a call to speak to the young man, and at waking designed to do so at the first opportunity. To my great surprise he came to Madeley that very morning, and I found upon inquiry that he had been as much drawn to come as I to speak to him."

The man who in this remarkable way secured the recommendation and interest of Fletcher was the first of what is now the long roll of good and useful men whom the college has sent forth into the evangelical ministry at home and into the great mission field of the world.

Trevecca House was formally opened and dedicated as a theological college on August 24, 1768, the anniversary of the birthday of the foundress. Whitefield preached the sermon, choosing as his text Exodus xx. 24, "In all places where I record My name, I will come unto thee and bless thee." The next Sunday he addressed a congregation of some thousands gathered in the courtyard of the college, from the words, "Other foundation can no man lay than that is laid, which is Jesus Christ."

From its foundation the college has combined both the literary and theological training. While estimating literary and theological learning at a very high value, the aim has always been first and foremost to train earnest spiritual evangelistic preachers. The college has been almost as much a home as a seminary. The students have always resided within its walls, enjoying intimate relationship with each other, and friendly intercourse with the principal. Lady Huntingdon made the college in a very real sense her home, and the institution has never lost the impress of her own fervent piety and the saintly benediction bestowed upon it by Fletcher.

From the very beginning the students combined regular preaching, either in the village near Trevecca, or in the pulpits of the Countess's chapels, with the prescribed courses of study. The college prospered at once, and even Berridge bestowed his characteristic blessing upon it. "I am glad to hear of the plentiful effusion from above on Talgarth. Jesus has now baptized your college, and thereby shown His approbation of the work. You may therefore rejoice, but rejoice with trembling. Faithful labourers may be expected from thence; but if it is Christ's college, a Judas will certainly be found among them."

Mr. Easterbrook's stay at Trevecca was brief. He left early in 1769, and was succeeded, on John Wesley's recommendation, by Joseph Benson, afterwards so eminent in the Methodist movement, and the biographer of Fletcher. But prior to his coming into residence the first anniversary was held, and the occasion was utilised for the holding of a series of very remarkable services. From August 20-23 crowds of people flocked to hear sermons twice daily in the courtyard by Shirley, Fletcher, Rowlands, Peter Williams, Howel Harris, and others. On August 24, 1769, John Wesley administered the sacrament to his fellow-ministers, the students, the Countess and her household. At ten o'clock "Mr. Fletcher preached an exceedingly lively sermon in the court; when he had finished William Williams preached in Welsh till about two o'clock. At two they all dined with Lady Huntingdon; and baskets of bread and meat were distributed among the people in the court, many of whom had come from a great distance. Public service commenced again at three o'clock, when Mr. Wesley preached in the court, then Mr. Fletcher; about five the congregation was dismissed." "Truly," wrote Lady Huntingdon, "our God was in the midst of us, and many felt Him eminently nigh. The gracious influence of the Spirit seemed to rest on every soul."

Although Fletcher did not reside at Trevecca, he frequently visited it during the first three years of its history. "Being convinced that to be filled with the Holy Ghost was a better qualification for the ministry of the Gospel than any classical learning (although that too be useful in its place), after speaking awhile in the schoolroom, he used frequently to say, 'As many of you as are athirst for this fulness of the Spirit, follow me into my room.' On this many of them have instantly followed him, and there continued for two or three hours, wrestling like Jacob for the blessing."

Lady Huntingdon spent much of her time at Trevecca, and for some years bore the entire cost of the college, expending upon it from £500 to £600 a year. The lease of the property at Trevecca expired within a few months of the Countess's death in 1791, and it having become imperative to find a new location, the college was in 1792 removed to Cheshunt in Hertfordshire, about twelve miles from London, where it has ever since continued to flourish.

During the century and a quarter of its existence Cheshunt College has rendered good service to the Church of Christ. Among the students educated at Trevecca were such men as John Clayton of the Weigh House Chapel, Roby of Manchester, and Matthew Wilks of the Tabernacle. The longer roll of those who entered after 1792 contains such names as Joseph Sortain of Brighton, and James Sherman of Surrey Chapel, in the ministry of the home churches; and is peculiarly rich in men who have done and are still doing noble service in the great mission field of the world. The flame of missionary enthusiasm has ever burnt brightly at Cheshunt. Among the many who have gone to their well-earned rest are men like Dr. Turner of Samoa, and James Gilmour of Mongolia. In the succession of able and devoted workers for the Church at home and for the heathen abroad, sent forth year by year, the good work begun at Trevecca is still living and growing.

VIII.

THE CALVINISTIC CONTROVERSY.

The leaders of the great revival of the eighteenth century were divided into two great groups, the one headed by John Wesley, the other by George Whitefield. The Calvinism of the latter at times seemed dangerously rigid to the former; while Whitefield sometimes spoke and acted as though he feared that in preaching free grace Wesley lost sight altogether of the Divine sovereignty. So sharply marked was the divergence of view that for a time it interfered with their co-operation. Mainly by Lady Huntingdon's influence, as we have seen, in 1750 unity was restored. For twenty years the two wings of the evangelical army laboured harmoniously; but in 1770 the doctrinal strife was renewed in a way and with a vehemence that separated the two sections; although in most cases it did not affect the mutual love and personal esteem in which the contending parties held each other.

At the annual conference of his ministers, held in August, 1770 (the year of Whitefield's death), John Wesley drew up his fateful minute on Calvinism. Intended solely for the guidance of his own preachers, Wesley apparently had not contemplated the use to which these statements might be put in controversy; if so, they would in all probability have been more carefully guarded. He also expected them to be considered *as a whole*, and could hardly have foreseen the use soon to be made of fragments torn from their context. However this may be, soon after their publication the sky was overcast, and Wesley found himself in the centre of an embittered theological controversy, in which, after he had in vain striven to maintain peace by explanation and concession, he vigorously maintained what he held to be the truth. He did this the more because the Calvinism of the eighteenth century found itself face to face with a dangerous Antinomianism. This was rife among the Moravians; some of Wesley's own preachers adopted it; John Nelson fought it to the death in Yorkshire; and it was in the face of this state of affairs that the minute was penned.

Lady Huntingdon from the first took great umbrage at the teaching of the minute. She apprehended "that the fundamental truths of the Gospel were struck at and considering Mr. Wesley's consequence in the religious world, as standing at the head of such numerous societies, thought it incumbent on them to show their abhorrence of such doctrines." She further declared "that whoever did not wholly disavow them should quit her college."

Wesley, on the other hand, thought the time had come when it was his duty to act the part of a faithful pastor towards the good Countess. "For several years I had been deeply convinced that I had not done my duty with regard to that valuable woman; that I had not told her what I was convinced no one else would dare to do, and what I knew she would hear from no other person, but *possibly* might hear from *me*. But being unwilling to give her pain I put it off from time to time. At length I dare not delay any longer lest death should call one of us hence; so I at once delivered my own soul by telling her all that was in my heart."

Lady Huntingdon on her part acted promptly and vigorously. Mr. Benson having defended the minute, was dismissed from Trevecca. Fletcher, by whom Benson's appointment had been arranged, visited the college in March, 1771, preached under great difficulties, and proffered his resignation, which Lady Huntingdon accepted at once.

All hope of a peaceful settlement was now at an end. Lady Huntingdon drew up a circular inviting the clergy of all denominations to assemble at the Wesleyan Conference at Bristol in August, 1771, and protest against the obnoxious minute. It is needful to quote some extracts from this circular in order that the position of the Countess may be fully perceived. "The minutes given by John Wesley we think ourselves obliged to disavow, believing such principles repugnant to Scripture and the whole plan of salvation under the new covenant. In union with all Protestant and Reformed Churches we hold *faith* alone in the Lord Jesus Christ for the sinner's justification, sanctification, righteousness, and complete redemption. And that He, the only wise God, our Saviour, is the First and Last, the Author and Finisher, the Beginning and the End of man's salvation: wholly by the sacrifice of Himself to complete and perfect all those who believe. And that under this covenant of free grace for man He does grant repentance, remission of sins, and meetness for glory, for the full and true salvation to eternal life; and that all called good works are alike the act of His free grace . . . We mean to enter into no controversy on the subject; but, separated from all party bigotry, and all personal prejudice to Mr. Wesley, the Conference, or his friends, do hereby most solemnly protest against the doctrine contained in these minutes."

The leader and champion on the part of Lady Huntingdon was the Honourable and Rev. Walter Shirley, grandson of the first Earl Ferrars, and her own first cousin. He was an able, fervent, eloquent man, who both in Ireland and England had given full proof of his ministry, and at first was left almost alone in the conflict. Wesley wrote to Lady Huntingdon on June 19, 1771, ending with these words, "You have one of the first places in my esteem and affection; and you once had some regard for me. But it cannot continue if it depends on my seeing with your eyes, or my being in no mistake. What if I were in as many errors as Mr. Law himself? If you were, I should love you still, provided your heart was still right with God. My dear friend, you seem not well yet to have learned the meaning of these words, which I desire to have ever written upon my heart, 'Whoever doeth the will of My Father which is in heaven, the same is My brother, and sister, and mother.'"

As the time for the conference drew on, it became apparent that the protestors had no standing place there. Only those who were actual members of the conference could attend. Hence, instead of the large number looked for, Shirley and seven others only appeared. The circular, which perhaps was needlessly strong in its statements, had been withdrawn the day before the conference met. Wesley allowed Shirley to appear at the third session of the conference, and after careful consideration a declaration was drawn up stating that as the minutes of 1770 "have been understood to favour justification by works," "we abhor the doctrine of justification by works;" "that we have no trust or confidence but in the alone merits of our Lord and Saviour Jesus Christ, for justification or salvation, either in life, death, or the day of judgment. And though no one is a real Christian believer (and consequently cannot be saved) who doth not good works when there is time and opportunity, yet our works have no part in meriting or purchasing our justification, from first to last, either in whole or part." Wesley and fifty-three of his ministers signed this, John Nelson and Thomas Olivers alone refusing.

Shirley, on the other hand, was constrained to sign a public avowal that "he was convinced that he had mistaken the meaning of the doctrinal points" of the minute. Fletcher meanwhile had written his five letters to Shirley, and the MS. was in Wesley's hands during the conference. Unfortunately he ordered it to be printed, and then left for Ireland. Fletcher, after learning the issue of the conference, would have liked to stay their publication, but in Wesley's absence this could not be done. Thus appeared the first portion of Fletcher's famous *Checks to Antinomianism*. Into the subsequent controversy, extending over several years, many writers were drawn, the chief being on Wesley's side, Fletcher and Olivers; and on Lady Huntingdon's, Shirley, Toplady, Berridge, Sir Richard and Rowland Hill. Many bitter words were written, and much said and done that would have been far better left unsaid and undone. But through it all even Toplady, Wesley's bitterest opponent, could say of Olivers, "I am glad I saw him, for he appears to be a person of stronger sense and better behaviour than I had imagined;" and Berridge welcomed Fletcher to Everton after a twenty years' absence, with tears in his eyes, crying, "My dear brother, how could we write against each other when we both aim at the same thing, the glory of God and the good of souls!"

IX.

SPA FIELDS CHAPEL.

In addition to the constant services held in her different London houses by her chaplains and others, Lady Huntingdon opened and supported several chapels in the capital. The first was leased in 1770 in Ewer Street. The next was in Princess Street, Westminster, and was opened in 1774. Then came Mulberry Gardens Chapel at Wapping, where George Burder sometimes and John Clayton very often preached. Towards the close of 1776 negotiations for the purchase of what was known as the Pantheon, a large building in Spa Fields, one of "the places where Satan had his seat," were commenced. Owing to the advice of Shirley and Toplady, the completion of the purchase was delayed; but at length the Countess wrote: "My heart seems strongly set upon having this temple of folly dedicated to Jehovah-Jesus, the great Head of His Church and people. I feel so deeply for the perishing thousands in that part of London that I am almost tempted to run every risk; and though at this moment I have not a penny to command, yet I am so firmly persuaded of the goodness of the Master whose I am and whom I desire to serve, that I shall not want gold or silver for the work." Nor did she. A company of gentlemen secured it, fitted it up as a chapel, and on July 5, 1777, John Ryland of Northampton preached the opening sermon.

Unforeseen and far-reaching consequences followed hard upon the opening of this place of worship. The Rev. W. Sellon, incumbent of St. James, Clerkenwell, the parish in which the new chapel stood, was a pluralist, holding no less than four ecclesiastical appointments, yielding him in all £1500 a year. Destitute himself of any knowledge of or sympathy for Gospel preaching, he resented this attempt to feed "the hungry sheep" of his parish. He invoked the law against Mr. Jones and Mr. Taylor, both clergymen of the Established Church, who were conducting the services at Spa Fields with conspicuous success. Sellon claimed the right of preaching in Spa Fields whenever he wished, and asserted his right to all the moneys derived from sittings and other sources. He obtained a verdict in the Consistorial Court inhibiting Jones and Taylor and closing the church. To meet this state of affairs, Lady Huntingdon acquired the building in her own right, changed the earlier name of Northampton Chapel into Spa Fields Chapel, and appointed Dr. Haweis, one of her chaplains, to preach. Sellon again applied to the Ecclesiastical Courts, and obtained an inhibition prohibiting any clergyman of the Established Church, whether Lady Huntingdon's chaplain or not, from preaching in Spa Fields.

Lady Huntingdon rose to the occasion. She was not the woman to allow an altogether unworthy opposition to defeat what she felt to be God's work. Since the law upheld Sellon, she in her turn invoked it. Under the Toleration Act she claimed and exercised her rights. "I am reduced," she wrote, "to turn the finest congregation, not only in England, but in any part of the world into a Dissenting meeting." Mr. Wills and Mr. Taylor, two clergymen who were prominent at this time among the Countess's helpers, both determined to secede from the Established Church; and thus once and for ever she disposed of Mr. Sellon's claims and prerogatives. Mr. Wills became the regular minister of the church. It was in this building that the first annual sermon of the London Missionary Society was preached by Dr. Haweis, and for over a hundred years Spa Fields Chapel was a centre of light and help and healing for that part of London.

This legal conflict had placed those numerous and able clergymen who had been in the habit of preaching in Lady Huntingdon's chapels in a very awkward position. They had to choose between two masters. Not unnaturally they remained in the Established Church. Hence from 1779 Romaine, Venn, Jones, and many others, though still in full sympathy with the Countess's work, ceased to preach in her chapels.

The students educated at Trevecca now rendered services of great value. In addition to their itinerating labours, they gradually filled the pulpits thus left vacant in the chapels. Hitherto the great majority of them had sought ordination in the Church of England, such having always been Lady Huntingdon's desire for them. This being no longer possible, the first public ordination of Trevecca students took place at Spa Fields March 9, 1783, when Mr. Wills and Mr. Taylor ordained six young men to the work of the ministry. It was on this occasion that the well-known Fifteen Articles, subscription to which became essential for entrance into the college, or into any of the pulpits under Lady Huntingdon's control, were first publicly read.

"Lady Huntingdon never intended her chapels or societies to be organised into a denomination—she never thought of providing for them an ecclesiastical constitution as such. As she intended and sustained them they were simply evangelising agencies. The spiritual necessities of her day induced her to become a builder of chapels for Evangelical preaching and worship. These she sustained and ruled as her own private property, devoted by her to the service of Christ, but disposable by her own uncontrolled will. No elements of ecclesiastical constitution or permanence are to be found in such an agency. Nor are there in the trusts declared after her death. The trustees of her chapels are invested with absolute powers of government, like her own."[1]

By her will dated January 11, 1790, Lady Huntingdon bequeathed "all her chapels, houses, furniture therein, and all the residue of her estates and effects to Thomas Haweis and Janetta Payne, his wife, Lady Ann Erskine, and John Lloyd." These persons were thus constituted trustees

---

1 Address by Dr. Allon in the *Centenary Celebration of Cheshunt College*, p. 33.

of all her property, to administer it all to the best of their ability, in harmony with what they knew to be her wishes. Many of the buildings associated with her name and ministers were local trusts, so that the power of the Connexion trustees never extended over more than a portion of the churches which her evangelistic zeal had founded or strengthened. It was almost inevitable that such an arrangement should be fatal to development, and so it has proved.

The latest sketch of Lady Huntingdon's life thus sets forth the present position of the Connexion: "The Fifteen Articles are the bond and doctrinal basis of administration in the Connexion; and in the words of the Countess, written when she left the Church of England, 'Our ministers must come recommended by that neutrality between Church and Dissent—secession.' Beyond this the Connexion has no act of uniformity. The worship, according to the varying needs of different localities, may be liturgical or non liturgical. Congregations are allowed much liberty in the form of their self-government."[1]

When Lady Huntingdon died there were only seven chapels in the legal possession of her representatives; but there were in all about one hundred in close union with and considered as together forming her Connexion. In the century succeeding her decease, while the number vested in the trustees of the Connexion increased from seven to thirty-three, the total number diminished to less than one half. Not a few of those included in the latter half became Congregational Churches, and remain in that fellowship up to this time. Some have been swept away by modern improvements, and never rebuilt elsewhere. The steady pressure of life and thought during the last half century has told rather against the development of churches which stand apart from the life and associations on the one hand of the Established Church, and on the other of Nonconformity. But the mere enumeration of the chief

---

1 *The Countess of Huntingdon and her Connexion*, edited by Rev. J.B. Figgis, M.A., p. 48.

chapels yet remaining, either in the central or in special local trusts, is interesting as an illustration of how the evangelising influence of Lady Huntingdon and her preachers extended to all corners of the kingdom. They are found at Bath, Bristol, Brighton, Canterbury, Cheltenham, Ely, Exeter, Hereford, Kidderminster, Malvern, Margate, Norwich, St. Ives, Cornwall, Rochdale, Swansea, Spa Fields, Tunbridge Wells, Worcester, and Yarmouth.

X.

CLOSING YEARS.

Until the close of her long life of eighty-four years, Lady Huntingdon retained much of that vigour of intellect which had marked the whole of her career. In spiritual life also she continued to develop year by year. In a letter written to an old ministerial friend on April 26, 1790, she says, "Here (in my heart) every wild and warm imagination, intoxicated by pride and self-love, must end; and submit, not only to learn of the poorest and most afflicted Man in our nature, but also to find in Him, and in Him alone, a suitable relief for all our misery; and, through the same medium, a free access to all divine and heavenly wisdom, whenever a sense of our own evil renders us sufficiently conscious of our wants. Thus faith, that faith which is the substance or subsistence of things hoped for, the evidence of things not seen, must carry the day; and by it walking in the light, as God is in the light, the blood of Jesus Christ cleanses us from all sin; while His heavenly and Divine Spirit, daily carrying us forward, leads us experimentally into those various states which He Himself has declared to be truly blessed."

The decay of her bodily powers was hastened by the breaking of a blood-vessel in November, 1790. During the ensuing illness at her house next door to Spa Fields Chapel she said to Lady Ann Erskine, who was continually with her, "I am well, all is well—well for ever; I see wherever I turn my eyes, whether I live or die, nothing but victory." From this attack she partially recovered, and for months she lingered in a weakened state, eager up to the last for the extension of her Master's kingdom. About a week before her death she was confined to her bed, and during this time she was greatly interested in a scheme for sending missionaries to the South Seas. Lady Ann Erskine and the other watchers, who were unremitting in their attentions, heard her praying day and night, and saying at one time, "I am reconciled in the arms of love and mercy;" and at another, "I long to be at home; oh, I long to be at home!" Only an hour before her death she asked, "Is Charles' letter come?" referring to a request that had been sent to the Rev. Thomas Charles of Bala, asking him to come and preach at Spa Fields. Almost the last words that fell from her lips were a testimony to the strength and clearness of her faith: "My work is done—I have nothing to do but to go to my Father." Soon after saying these words, on June 17, 1791, she "fell asleep in Jesus." She was buried in the family vault at Ashby de la Zouch.

Lady Huntingdon, whose long life thus triumphantly closed, was happy in many ways. She possessed rank and a competency and all the social advantages which such things involve. She was blessed with exceptional vigour of body, of mind, and of spirit. She was happy also in the time of her earthly life. Above all was she happy in the fact that she came so early and so completely under the power of saving faith in the Lord Jesus and under the renewing power of the Holy Spirit. From that time she threw herself into God's work; and by her zeal, ability, and consecration, quite as much as by her rank and wealth, became one of the spiritual landmarks of a wonderful century.

From a course which she believed to be right even John Wesley could not move her; and on one occasion she showed her power even to the Archbishop of Canterbury. About 1770 the prelate then holding that high office, and his wife, gave some balls and parties which scandalised even the gay votaries of fashion who attended them. Remonstrances which Lady Huntingdon addressed to the archbishop, Dr. Cornwallis, through relatives, being treated with ridicule and contempt, she appealed direct to George III. The King and Queen received her most graciously, conversed with her about her religious work for more than an hour, and a few days later surprised the Archbishop by a letter requesting the summary suppression of these "improprieties." The prelate was probably as much astonished as shortly afterwards a lady was, who, in the King's presence, said Lady Huntingdon must surely be insane since she had ventured to "preach to His Grace." "Pray, madam," said the King after he had assured her she was quite mistaken, "have you ever been in company with her?" "Never!" "Then never form your opinion of any one from the ill-natured remarks and censures of others."

Fitted to shine in courts, in an age notoriously pleasure-loving, profligate, and irreligious, she deliberately and whole-heartedly cast in her lot with the despised people of God, "accounting the reproach of Christ greater riches than the treasures of Egypt." She was tried by repeated bereavements, and she had to bear the heavy cross of a son who lived and died in hostility to the Christian faith. But these sorrows only deepened her trust in and her hold upon the Lord Jesus Christ. In 1747 she had written, "My heart wants nothing so much as to dispense *all—all*, for the glory of Him whom my soul loveth." In 1791, after forty-four long years of hard labour, steady faith, and self-sacrificing zeal, she passed to her eternal rest, with the simple trust that He whose glory she had so humbly and earnestly sought had glorified Himself in her. No nobler close could have been desired for such a life than that which God granted: "My work is done—I have nothing to do but to go to my Father."

RICHARD LOVETT, M.A.

RACHEL, LADY RUSSEL.

I.

It is not often that we find the names of person illustrious in the annals of this world also pre-eminent in the records of the kingdom of heaven. "Not many wise, not many noble are called;" but sometimes the wisest and noblest appear among the truest and best of Christians. Such were, in our English history, William, Lord Russell, patriot and martyr, and his wife Rachel, Lady Russell, whom all agree in regarding as at once a heroine and a saint.

With the cause of civil and religious liberty the name of Lord Russell will be for ever associated. He died, as he had lived, the friend of true religion and a firm adherent of the reformed faith. He said that he hoped his death would do more for the Christian good of his country than his life could do. He was beheaded on Saturday, July 21,1683. Upon the scaffold, just before his execution, he handed to the sheriffs a written declaration, in which, after denial of the false charges on which he had been condemned, he concludes with a prayer which shows that far higher than mere political feelings moved him: "Thou, O most merciful Father, hast forgiven all my transgressions, the sins of my youth, and all the errors of my past life, and Thou wilt not lay my secret sins and ignorance to my charge, but wilt graciously support me during the small time of life now before me, and assist me in my last moments, and not leave me then to be disordered by fear or any other temptations, but make the light of Thy countenance to shine upon me. Thou art my Sun and my Shield;

and as Thou supportest me by Thy grace, so I hope Thou wilt hereafter crown me with glory, and receive me into the fellowship of angels and saints in the blessed inheritance purchased for me by my most merciful Redeemer, who is at Thy right hand, I trust preparing a place for me, and is ready to receive me, into whose hands I commend my spirit!"

It is of Lady Russell, the wife and the worthy partner of this good man, that we are about to give a brief memoir in our gallery of *Excellent Women*.

II.

Rachel Wriothesley, born in 1636, was second daughter of Thomas Wriothesley, Earl of Southampton, by his first wife, Rachel de Ruvigny, of an ancient Huguenot family. Her mother died during her infancy. An elder sister, Lady Elizabeth, married Edward Noel, son of Viscount Campden, afterwards Earl of Gainsborough. Lord Southampton married twice after his first wife's death, but he had only one surviving daughter by his second marriage, who being heiress of Sir Francis Leigh, afterwards Earl of Winchester, the whole of the Southampton property was left to the children of his first marriage, who thus became considerable heiresses. Lady Rachel, when yet young, married Francis, Lord Vaughan, eldest son of the Earl of Carberry, but it was an alliance rather of acceptance than of choice on either side, and the early death of Lord Vaughan left her free to marry again. All we know is that she possessed the love and attachment of her husband and the respect of his family. They had one child who died in infancy.

In 1667, on the death of her father, she inherited the estates of Stratton, but she passed most of her time with her beloved sister, Lady Elizabeth Noel, at Tichfield, in Hampshire. There she became engaged to Mr. Russell, younger son of the Earl of Bedford. They were married in 1669, but she still retained the name of Vaughan till in 1678, on the death of his elder brother Francis, William succeeded to the courtesy title of Lord Russell, when she assumed that of Lady Russell.

Lord Southampton, her father, was a man of high character and great influence. During the civil troubles he took no very decided part until after the misfortunes of Charles I., when his loyalty overmastered all other feelings. In the first disputes between the king and the parliament he disapproved of the high-handed measures of the Court, and, disliking the government of Strafford and the principles of Archbishop Laud, he was considered to be one of the peers attached to the popular cause. But, like Lord Falkland, he could not heartily join the party opposed to the king, whom he accompanied to York and to Nottingham. He was at the fight at Edgehill, and thence went to Oxford, where he remained with the Court during the rest of the war. He was hopeless all along of the success of the royal cause, and was ever the strenuous and unwearying advocate of accommodation and peace. When the execution of the misguided king took place, he was one of the four faithful servants who obtained permission to pay the last sad duty to his remains. From that time he retired to his seat at Tichfield, taking no further part in public affairs. When Cromwell rose to supreme power he greatly wished to meet Lord Southampton, but the meeting was avoided by the earl, and he continued in retirement. His daughter was educated on strict Protestant lines, with every predilection for the doctrines which her mother's family, professing a faith persecuted in their own country, were likely to encourage. Southampton, though attached to the Church of England, was most tolerant towards Dissenters, so much so that Clarendon in his History, while describing him as "a man of exemplary virtue and piety, and very regular in his devotions," says, "He was not generally believed by the bishops to have an affection keen enough for the government of the Church, being willing and desirous that something more might be done to gratify the Presbyterians than they thought right." This spirit of her father was probably the source of the Christian charity as well as piety of Lady Rachel's life, appearing in her letters and animating her whole conduct. Or rather we may say, that both father and daughter were influenced by the old Huguenot principles and connection.

III.

The Marquis de Ruvigny, head of an old family in Picardy, had long been the leader of the Protestant cause in France; in fact, he was almost the minister plenipotentiary of the Huguenots at the Court of Louis XIV. As "Deputy-General of the Reformed Church," he well served the interests of that body, both in getting a patient hearing of their grievances, and obtaining knowledge of the designs of their enemies. He possessed the personal favour and the support of Cardinal Mazarin, and the king himself put confidence in Ruvigny. He was several times employed in services of a confidential kind to the English Government, but was given to understand that any military position or further advancement must be purchased by a change of his religion. To this he never could consent, being a man of sincere and enlightened piety, as well noted for his ability, courage, and conduct. On the recall of Colbert in 1674, he was minister plenipotentiary in England, and remained so for two or three years, when a more pliable tool was found in a M. Courtin. He still retained the good opinion of the French king and his advisers, for on the revocation of the Edict of Nantes he had permission to emigrate to England with his family, a permission granted to no other Protestant noble. His estates, however, were confiscated, as were those of all the *émigrés*. It was the sister of this Marquis, Rachel de Ruvigny, who became the wife of Lord Southampton. For the family of the Ruvignys Lady Russell always retained a warm affection.

IV.

During the fourteen years of her happy married life with William Russell, she was seldom parted from her husband. Their only moments of separation were during his visits of duty to his father at Woburn, and short absences on private or political business. The longest absence was when Lord Russell attended a meeting of parliament summoned by the king at Oxford. Her letters during this period are such as would be written by a loving wife and a tender mother—happy, cheerful messages of personal or domestic interest; yet even in these familiar epistles displaying a character of good sense and deep piety as well as womanly affection. "They are the most touching love-letters I have ever read," says the editor of the published selection from her correspondence. Two or three short bits out of many letters will suffice to show the spirit in which she then wrote. August 24, 1680. "Absent or present, my dearest life is equally obliging, and ever the earthly delight of my soul. It is my great care (or ought to be so) so to moderate my sense of happiness here, that when the appointed time comes of my leaving it, or its leaving me, I may not be unwilling to forsake the one, or be in some measure prepared and fit to bear the trial of the other. This very hot weather does incommode me, but otherwise I am very well, and both your girls. Your letter was cherished as it deserved, and so, I make no doubt, was hers, which she took very ill I should suspect she was directed in, as truly I thought she was, the fancy was so pretty. I have a letter about the buck, as usual, from St. Giles's [the seat of the Earl of Shaftesbury, in Dorsetshire]; but when you come up I suppose it will be time enough to give order. Coming so lately from St. Giles's, I am not solicitous for news for you, especially as Sir Harry Capel is to see your lordship to-morrow. The greatest discourse we have is (next to Bedloe's affidavit) Tongue's accusing of Lord Essex, Lord Shaftesbury, and Lord Wharton, for the contrivers of the plot, and setting his father and Oates to act their parts. This was told me by a black-coat who made me a visit yesterday, but I hear it by nobody else. My sister and Lady Inchiquin are coming, so that I must leave a better diversion for a worse, but my thoughts often return where all my delight is. I am, yours entirely, R RUSSELL."

In a letter sent to Oxford in March, 1681, she says: "The report of our nursery, I humbly praise God, is very good. Master [her son] improves really, I think, every day. Sure he is a goodly child; the more I see of others, the better he appears; I hope God will give him life and virtue. Misses and their mamma walked yesterday after dinner to see their cousin Alington. Miss Kate wished she might see the new-born son, so I gratified her little person. Unless I see cause to add a note, this is all this time,

"From yours only entirely, R. RUSSELL."

The postscript of this letter conveys a curious idea of the suspicion and insecurity of the times: "Look to your pockets. A printed paper says you will have fine papers put into them, and then witnesses to swear."

A later letter, October 20, 1681, written on Saturday night, begins: "The hopes I have, my dearest life, that this will be the concluding epistle, for this time, makes me undertake it with more cheerfulness than my others." And it thus closes: "I pray God direct all your consultations; and, my dearest dear, you guess my mind. A word to the wise. I never longed more earnestly to be with you, for whom I have a thousand kind and grateful thoughts. You know of whom I learned this expression. If I could have found one more fit to speak the passion of my soul, I should send it you with joy; but I submit with great content to imitate, but shall never attain to any equality, except that of sincerity; and I will ever be, by God's grace, what I ought and profess,

"Thy faithful, affectionate, and obedient wife,

"R. RUSSELL.

"I seal not this till Sunday morning, that you might know all is well then. Miss sends me word that she is so, and hopes to see papa quickly; so does one more."

V.

In October, 1680, Lord Russell moved in the House of Commons a resolution that they ought to take into consideration how to oppose Popery and prevent a Popish successor to the throne. A Bill was accordingly brought in for excluding the Duke of York from the crown, which passed the House of Commons, but was thrown out by the Lords, to whom it was carried up by Lord Russell, attended by nearly the whole of the Commons. About the same time Lords Shaftesbury, Russell, and Cavendish presented the Duke of York to the grand jury for Middlesex at Westminster Hall, as indictable, being a Popish recusant. In January, 1680-1, the Commons resolved that "until a Bill be passed for excluding the Duke of York, they could not vote any supply, without danger to His Majesty and extreme hazard to the Protestant religion."

Things had come to this crisis after years of arbitrary power, and the humiliation of England in its king being a pensioner of Louis XIV. As far back as 1669 a secret treaty was made with France, Charles engaging to declare war against Holland, France to pay the king £800,000 annually and make a division of the conquests, of which France would have the largest share. In 1670 Colbert mentions Charles's ratification of this treaty, having the king's seal and signature, and a letter from his own hand. This treaty was kept secret from his ministers, and a pretended treaty *(un traité simulé)* was to be promulgated, to which the Protestant members of the Cabinet were to be parties. Colbert further states that he was told in confidence by the Duke of York that the king was ready to declare himself a Catholic, and that he was determined to rule independently of any parliament. The object of Charles was mainly to obtain money from the French king, but the Duke of York had deeper and more dangerous plots to carry out. The marriage of the Princess Mary to the Prince of Orange in 1677 somewhat disturbed the understanding, but a renewal of the treaty in 1678 brought England again to lie at the mercy of the French king. The impeachment of Lord Danby, Lord Treasurer, for the part taken by him in these disgraceful transactions, showed that there were still many Englishmen prepared to act for the honour and freedom of their country. To Lord Russell most men looked as the leader of the patriotic party, and it was determined to get him out of the way as the chief opponent of the arbitrary power of the king and the Popish designs of his brother, who showed the most unrelenting hatred of Russell. It was resolved that he should be brought to trial for treason, as compassing the overthrow of the government of the king. He was arrested on January 26, 1683; after examination was committed to the Tower the same day, and afterwards removed to Newgate.

Lord Russell was found sitting in his study, neither seeking to conceal himself nor preparing for flight. As soon as he was in custody, he gave up all hopes of life, knowing how obnoxious he was to the Duke of York, and only thought of dying with honour and dignity. The Earl of Essex was at his country house when he heard of the arrest of his friend. He could have made his escape, and when pressed by his people to fly, he answered that "his own life was not worth saving if, by drawing suspicion on Lord Russell, it might bring his life into danger." He was taken to the Tower, where, it was announced, he killed himself on the morning of Lord Russell's trial. It is more probable, as was generally believed, that he was murdered, and the report of suicide was spread in order to strengthen the charges against Russell. Monmouth had disappeared, but, actuated by the same generous motive with Essex, he sent a message to Russell, on hearing of his arrest, that "he would surrender himself and share his fate, if his doing so could be of use to him." Russell answered in these words: "It will be of no advantage to me to have my friends die with me."

VI.

The trial of Lord Russell is one of the darkest events in the annals of our courts of law, while it is also one of the most important in the history of England. He was tried at the Old Bailey on the charge of conspiring the death of the King's Majesty, and of raising rebellion in the kingdom. Every point in the legal indictment was strained, and every artifice resorted to, in order to obtain a verdict of guilty. When it was objected that the jury were not freeholders, the objection was overruled, although in a recent trial, when made in the king's behalf, it had been admitted without any difficulty. The evidence of two or three false witnesses was received, and was made to weigh against a mass of testimony borne by the noblest and best men of the time. Nothing could be proved against him, except that he had been seen in the company of Monmouth, Shaftesbury, Algernon Sidney, and others known to be opposed to the measures of the Government. Lords Anglesey, Cavendish, and Clifford, the Duke of Somerset, Doctors Burnet, Tillotson, Cox, FitzWilliam, and many others testified to his mild and amiable character, his peaceable and virtuous life, and the improbability of his being guilty of the charges brought against him. His public services in defence of freedom and of the Protestant religion were the real causes of the resolution to get rid of him. Towards the close of the trial, one of his enemies, the notorious Jefferies, made a violent declamation, and turned the untimely end of Lord Essex in the Tower into a proof of Russell's being privy to the guilty conspiracy. This base insinuation evidently had effect on the jury, who brought in a verdict of guilty. The sentence was considered by all right-minded persons as a shameful injustice. Burnet afterwards spoke of him as "that great but innocent victim, sacrificed to the rage of a party, and condemned only for treasonable words said to have been spoken in his hearing."

Among the incidents of the trial, one of the most memorable was when the prisoner asked for somebody to write, to help his memory. "You may have a servant," said the Attorney-General, Sir Robert Sawyer. "Any of your servants," added the Lord Chief Justice Pemberton, "shall assist you in writing for you anything you please." "My wife is here, my Lord, to do it." "If my Lady please to give herself the trouble," was the civil reply of the Lord Chief Justice. So the noble wife sat by his side throughout the trial to assist and support her husband.

After the condemnation she drew up and carried to the king a petition for a short reprieve of a few weeks; but this was rejected, though the king saw at his feet the daughter of the Earl of Southampton, the best friend he ever had. His answer was, "Shall I grant that man a reprieve of six weeks, who, if it had been in his power, would not have granted me six hours? Besides," he said, "I must break with the Duke of York if I grant it." Seeking the king's life had never been made a charge, far less attempted to be proved, though something had been said about attacking the king's guards. But Russell denied with his last breath any design against the person of the king. All considerations were weak against the passion of revenge with which the king and the Duke of York were actuated. The Duke of York descended so low in his personal animosity that he urged that the execution should take place before Russell's own door in Bloomsbury Square, but the king would not consent to this. An order was signed for his being beheaded in Lincoln's Inn Fields, a week after the trial. It is said that at that time Southampton House, on the north side of Bloomsbury Square, was visible from the place where the scaffold was erected.

Lord Cavendish generously offered to manage his escape, and to stay in prison for him while he should go away in his clothes; but Russell would not entertain the proposal. It was then planned that Cavendish, with a party of horse, should attack the guard on the way to the scaffold, and rescue the innocent victim; but this, too, was overruled, as Russell refused to allow any lives being endangered to save his own. He prepared to receive the stroke with meekness, and with a dignity worthy of his name.

On the Tuesday before his execution, when his wife had left him, he expressed great joy in the magnanimity of spirit he saw in her, and said that parting with her was the worst part of his pain. On Thursday, when she left him to try to gain a respite till Monday, he said he wished she would cease from seeking his preservation, but he did not forbid her trying, thinking that these efforts, though unavailing, might bring some mitigation of her sorrows. On the evening before his death he suffered his young children to be brought by their mother for the final parting. In this trying time he maintained his constancy of temper, though his heart was full of tenderness. When they had gone he said that the bitterness of death was passed, and then spoke much of the noble spirit of her whom he had so loved, and who had been to him so great a blessing. He said, "What a misery it would have been to him if she had not that magnanimit of spirit, joined to her tenderness, as never to have desired him to do a base thing for the saving of his life. There was a signal providence of God in giving him such a wife, where there was birth, fortune, great understanding, true religion, and great kindness to him; but her carriage in his extremity was beyond all. He was glad she and his children were to lose nothing by his death; and it was a great comfort to him that he left his children in the hands of such a mother, and that she had promised to him to take care of herself for their sakes."

It should be stated that when they partook of the Communion together for the last time, she so controlled her feelings, for his sake, as not to shed a tear; although afterwards she wept so much that it was feared she would lose her sight.

The scene of the parting in prison is not only memorable in history, but has been a favourite theme in art, and one of the frescoes in the new Houses of Parliament commemorates it. Many poets have written about the death of Lord Russell, among them Canning, in a supposed letter to his friend Lord Cavendish, in which the noble character of his wife is celebrated as well as the virtues of her husband.

The execution took place not on Tower Hill, as usual with persons of high rank, but in Lincoln's Inn Fields, in order that the citizens of London might be humbled and terrified by the sight, as he was carried in a coach to the scaffold through the City. The effect was very different from what was intended. The death of this one man made many enemies to the king, and though the triumph of liberty and religion was delayed for a few years, the execution of Lord Russell did much to secure the overthrow of arbitrary power, and the defeat of Popery in England at no distant time. The trial took place July 13 and 14, and the execution on July 21, 1683.

VII.

Lord Russell died for the civil and religious liberties of his country. All men, even those who were far from agreeing with his political principles, agreed in regarding him as a man of probity and virtue, and the model of a patriot. He passed through this world with as great and general a reputation as any one of the age, and his memory will be held in everlasting remembrance.

> "Bring every sweetest flower, and let me strew
> The grave where Russell lies, whose tempered blood
> With calmest cheerfulness for thee resigned,
> Stained the sad annals of a giddy reign;
> Aiming at lawless power, though, meanly sunk
> In loose inglorious luxury."

So sang of him the poet of the Seasons, Thomson, in his famous apostrophe to Britannia as the land of liberty.

One of the first Acts of King William III. after the Revolution, was to reverse the attainder of Lord Russell. In the preamble of this Bill, which was the second that passed in his reign, after receiving the Royal assent, his execution was called a murder: and in November of the same year, 1689, the House of Commons appointed a committee "to inquire who were the advisers and promoters of the murder of Lord Russell." In the year 1694 his father was created Marquis of Tavistock and Duke of Bedford. The reasons for bestowing these honours were stated in the preamble of the patent in these terms: "And this, not the least, that he was the father of Lord Russell, the ornament of his age, whose great merits it was not enough to transmit by history to posterity, but they (the King and Queen) were willing to record them in their royal patent, to remain in the family as a monument consecrated to his consummate virtue, whose name could never be forgot, so long as men preserved any esteem for sanctity of manners, greatness of mind, and a love of their country, constant even to death. Therefore, to solace his excellent father for so great a loss, to celebrate the memory of so noble a son, and to excite his worthy grandson, the heir of such mighty hopes, more cheerfully to emulate and follow the example of his illustrious father, they entailed this high dignity upon the Earl and his posterity."

The first Duke of Bedford (fifth Earl) lived till September, 1700. He had six sons and three daughters, besides the martyred son. William, married to the daughter of the Earl of Southampton. They had one son, Wriothesley, who succeeded his grandfather as Duke of Bedford in 1700, and died of small-pox, in 1711, in the 31st year of his age. Of two daughters, the elder married William Lord Cavendish, afterwards Duke of Devonshire, and the second married John Manners, Lord Ross, afterwards Duke of Rutland. A third daughter died unmarried.

A striking anecdote is recorded of King James II. addressing himself in the time of his extremity, in 1688, to the aged Earl of Bedford, saying, "My Lord, you are an honest man, have great credit in the State, and can do me signal service." "Ah, sir," replied the Earl, "I am old and feeble, I can do you but little service; but I had a son once that could have assisted you, but he is no more." James was so struck with this reply, that he could not speak for some minutes, and it is to be hoped that he felt remorse for the death of Lord Russell.

When the attainder on Russell was removed by King William III., the same justice was done to his friend Algernon Sidney, who is united with him in the famous lines of Thomson's patriotic remembrance:

> "With him
> His friend the British Cassius, fearless lad,
> Of high determined spirit, roughly brave,
> By ancient learning to the enlightened love
> Of ancient freedom warmed."

Algernon Sidney, unlike Russell, was in theory not averse to Republicanism, but the accusations are false as to his being a sceptic or a deist, as his own dying apology attests. He says: "God will not suffer this land, where the Gospel has of late flourished more than in any part of the world, to become a slave of the world. He will not suffer it to be made a land of graven images; He will stir up witnesses of the truth, and in His own time spirit His people to stand up for His cause, and deliver them. I lived in this belief, and am now about to die in it. I know my Redeemer liveth; and as He hath in a great measure upheld me in the day of my calamity, I hope that He will still uphold me by His Spirit in this last moment, and giving me grace to glorify Him in my death, receive me into the glory prepared for those that fear Him, when my body shall be dissolved. Amen." These were the last words of Algernon Sidney. It is noteworthy that the Duke of Monmouth, in his Declaration against James II, among other things, accuses him of ordering the barbarous murder of the Earl of Essex in the Tower, and of several others, to conceal it; and he gave as a reason for his appeal to arms, in his unhappy rebellion, the unjust condemnation of Sidney and of Russell.

VIII.

It has been remarked that the incidents in the life of Lady Russell, apart from the one memorable public event of her husband's trial and death, are so few and her merits confined so much to the domain of private life and feminine duties, that her character, unlike that of most heroines, deserves to be held up more to the *example* than the *admiration* of her countrywomen. Few of her sex have been placed in such a conspicuous situation, but fewer, after behaving with unexampled fortitude and dignity, have shrunk from public notice, and in the sight of God only have led unobtrusive, quiet lives in the daily performance of domestic duties as a careful and conscientious mother and guardian of her children.

It is this that makes the record of her life so valuable for all time. If she, who had such an unusual and terrible affliction, was enabled, by the grace of God in the exercise of reason and religion, to show such complete submission to the Divine will, and such patient continuance in well-doing, her example is well fitted for the comfort and succour of all who in this transitory life are in trouble, sorrow, need, sickness, or any other adversity.

One of the earliest letters, written to a friend who sought to comfort her in her deep sorrow, reveals the noble spirit and wise resolution of a true Christian. She says: "Fresh occasions recalling to my memory the dear object of my affections must happen every day, I may say every hour of the longest life I can live. But I must seek such a victory over myself that immoderate passions may not break forth, and I must return into the world so far as to act that part incumbent upon me, in faithfulness to him to whom I owe as much as can be due to man. It may be that I may obtain grace to live a stricter life of holiness to my God, who will not always let me cry to Him in vain. On Him I will wait till He hath pity upon me, humbly imploring that by the mighty aid of His Holy Spirit He will touch my heart with greater love to Himself. Then I shall be what He would have me. But I am unworthy of such a spiritual blessing, who remain so unthankful a creature for those earthly ones I have enjoyed, because I have them no longer. Yet God, who knows our frames, will not expect that when we are weak we should be strong. This is much comfort under my deep dejections." And in a letter to Doctor Tillotson she said: "Submission and prayer are all we know that we can do towards our own relief in our distresses. The scene will soon alter to that peaceful and eternal home in prospect."

It is interesting to know that one who helped to bring her to this state of mind was the Rev. John Howe, a man noted for wisdom as well as piety, who had been chaplain to Oliver Cromwell and to his son Richard Cromwell. Although too long to insert in full, some sentences selected from the letter are worthy of quotation.

"The cause of your sorrow, madam, is exceeding great. The causes of your joy are inexpressibly greater. You have infinitely more left than you have lost. Doth it need to be disputed whether God is better and greater than man? Or more to be valued, loved, and delighted in? And whether an eternal relation be more considerable than a temporary one? Was it not your constant sense, in your best outward state, 'Whom have I in heaven but Thee, O God, and whom can I desire on earth, in comparison of Thee?' (Psalm lxxiii. 25). Herein the state of your ladyship's case is still the same, if you cannot with greater clearness and with less hesitation pronounce these latter words. The principal causes of your joy are immutable, such as no supervening thing can alter. You have lost a most pleasant, delectable earthly relation. Doth the blessed God hereby cease to be the best and most excellent good? Is His nature changed? His everlasting covenant reversed or annulled, which is ordered in all things, and sure, and is to be all your salvation and all your desire, whether He make your house on earth to grow or not to grow? (2 Samuel xxiii. 5).

"Let, I beseech you, your mind be more exercised in contemplating the glories of that state into which your blessed consort is translated, which will mingle pleasure and sweetness with the bitterness of your afflicting loss, by giving you a daily intellectual participation through the exercise of faith and hope in his enjoyments. He cannot descend to share with you in your sorrows; but you may thus every day ascend and partake with him in his joys."

After much devout reasoning of this kind, the good and wise preacher makes a practical appeal: "Nor should such thoughts excite over-hasty, impatient desire of following presently to heaven, but to the endeavour of serving God more cheerfully on earth for your appointed time, which I earnestly desire your ladyship to apply yourself to, as you would not displease God, who is our only hope; nor be cruel to yourself, nor dishonour the religion of Christians, as if they had no other consolations than the earth can give, and earthly power can take from them. Your ladyship, if any one, would be loth to do anything unworthy of your family and parentage. Your highest alliance is to that Father and family above, whose dignity and honour are, I doubt not, of highest account with you."

Mr. Howe wrote to Lady Russell without revealing his name, but she laid to heart the excellent counsel he gave. The style of the letter, and some special phrases in it, discovered who was the author, and Lady Russell, as we learn from Dr. Calamy, Howe's biographer, wrote to him a letter of warm thanks, and told him he must not expect to remain concealed[1]. She promised to endeavour to follow the excellent advice he had given. She often afterwards corresponded with him, and the friendship lasted during Howe's life.

---

1 Cf. *John Howe*, Biographical Series, No. 94 (R.T.S.).

IX.

In the great public affairs of the time she could not but feel interest, and her letters abound in references to the most striking events as they occur. Her sister, Lady Elizabeth Noel, was in Paris at the time of the Revocation of the Edict of Nantes, and describes the terrible scenes of which she heard or witnessed. Hundreds of thousands were driven into exile, their property seized by their persecutors; those who remained being exposed to the cruelty of the dragonnades. Then there were the excitements at home, following the Monmouth rebellion and the bloody assizes where Judge Jefferies obtained his notoriety. The trial of the seven bishops; the overthrow of the Stuart cause; the glorious revolution of 1688 and the accession of King William and Mary; the war in Ireland, where the de Ruvignys served under William and the Mareschal Schomberg; the reign of Queen Anne and the Hanoverian succession under George I.; all these historical events are referred to in Lady Russell's correspondence which she carried on with the most notable persons of the time. A letter of hers to King William about the King's favourable designs for the Duke of Rutland and his family was found in his pocket when he died. Several letters are addressed to Queen Mary. The great Duke of Marlborough told her that if ever there appeared a chance of Popery getting again the upper hand, he would retire from public affairs. Even the proud Sarah, Duchess of Marlborough, regarded Lady Russell with marked deference and respect. In reference to the accession of King William she wrote, "Regard for the public welfare carried me to advise the princess to acquiesce in giving William the crown. However, as I was fearful about everything the princess did while she was thought to be advised by me, I could not satisfy my own mind till I had consulted with several persons of wisdom and integrity, and particularly with the Lady Russell of Southampton House, and Dr. Tillotson, afterwards Archbishop of Canterbury. I found them all unanimous in the opinion of the expediency of the settlement proposed, as things were then situated."

Her friends and her country shared with her own family the heart and the correspondence of Lady Russell. Her children she lived to see well provided for in honourable and influential positions. Her second daughter was married to the son of her husband's dearest friend, Lord Cavendish, and she became the Duchess of Devonshire. The eldest daughter was unmarried, but the third became the Duchess of Rutland. Her only son, afterwards Duke of Bedford, was in high favour in the reign of William and Mary, and acted as High Constable of England at the coronation of Queen Anne. His education and training was carefully directed by his mother. One of her letters is to his grandfather, then Earl of Bedford, interceding with him for one of the errors of her son's early life. He had been tempted, as many young Englishmen still are, to gamble when on his travels, but his debt taught him a lesson which saved him from ever after getting into trouble in this way. Lady Russell, while pleading for his forgiveness, undertook to be answerable for the whole loss which had been incurred. It is a sensible and motherly letter.

To give adequate idea of the whole correspondence would occupy much space, and we can only briefly refer to a few of the letters at different periods of her long life of widowhood. To Burnet, the Bishop of Salisbury, she writes, in 1690: "When anything below is the object of our love, at one time or other it will be a matter of our sorrow. But a little time will put me again into my settled state of mourning; for a mourner I must be all my days on earth, and there is no need I should be other. My glass runs low: the world does not want me nor do I want it: my business is at home and within a narrow compass. I must not deny, as there was something so glorious in the object of my biggest sorrow, I believe that in some measure kept me from being overwhelmed."

At one time Lady Russell was in danger of losing her sight, but being couched for cataract, she recovered sufficiently to continue her correspondence.

In the early years of her great loss, while at first overwhelmed in spirit, she yet resolves, in submission to the will of God, to bear her calamities with patience and courage. "My yet disordered thoughts," she writes to Dr. Fitzwilliam, "can offer me no other than such words as express the deepest sorrows, and confused as my yet amazed mind is. You, that knew us both, and how we lived, must allow I have just cause to bewail my loss. Who can but shrink at such a blow, till, by the mighty aid of His Holy Spirit, we will let the gift of God, which He hath put into our hearts, interpose. That reason which sets a measure to our souls in prosperity, will then suggest many things which we have seen and heard to moderate us in such sad circumstances as mine." "Can I regret his quitting a lesser good for a bigger? Oh! if I did steadfastly believe, I could not be dejected; for I will not injure myself to say I offer to my mind any infirm consolation to supply this loss. No, I most willingly forsake this world, this vexatious troublesome world, in which I have no other business but to rid my soul from sin; secure by faith and a good conscience my eternal interests with patience and courage bear my eminent misfortunes; and ever after be above the smiles and frowns of it. And when I have done the remnant of the work appointed me on earth, then joyfully wait for the heavenly perfection, in God's good time, when by His infinite mercy I may be accounted worthy to enter into the same place of rest and repose where he is gone, for whom only I grieve."

Many letters in similar strain are preserved, to Dr. Burnet, Dr. Patrick and other pious friends who like Dr. Fitzwilliam had sent messages of sympathy and consolation. She often refers to the refreshment and satisfaction she had in "endeavouring to do that part towards her children, which their most dear and tender father would not have omitted. These labours, if successful, though early made unfortunate, may conduce to their happiness for the time to come and hereafter." Attendance to these children, through childhood till they were settled in life, she ever reckoned, "her first and chief business," but she gradually undertook various matters of business for relatives and friends, many of whom had recourse to one so wise, unselfish, and sympathetic.

As an example of the interest she took in passing affairs, part of a letter to Dr. Fitzwilliam, in 1689, may be quoted. After replying to some inquiries about the Cambridgeshire clergy, which she could not learn from Lord Bedford, "the parliament houses being so exacting of time," she says: "You hear all the new honours, I suppose: not many new creations, but all are stepping higher; as Lord Winchester is Duke of Bolton; Lord Montague an Earl, still Montague; Falconbridge, who married Mary, daughter of Oliver Cromwell, an Earl called the same; Mordaunt, Earl of Monmouth (afterwards Earl of Peterborough); Churchill an Earl (afterwards Duke of Mailborough); Lumley (Scarborough) made a Viscount, Bentinck is an Earl (afterwards Duke of Portland); Sidney, a Viscount (afterward Earl of Romney). Those that saw this and the last coronation tell me this was much finer and in better order; and if the number of the ladies were fewer, yet their attendance was with more application near the Queen all the time, and with more cheerful faces by a great deal. By what is heard from Scotland, they mean to take the example from England. The last reports from Ireland say, that King James was moving with his army towards the north. And yesterday Lord Burlington said, Coleraine, a great town, was besieged by 6000 men, but that Lord Blaney had sallied out, and so behaved himself that they had raised the siege. D'Avaux who was the French ambassador in Holland, would not speak in council till all the Protestants were put out. So they were, and, as they say afterwards, discharged altogether . . .

"Lord Devonshire is to be installed at Windsor on St. George's day. My young folks have a longing desire to see the ceremony, and they cannot do it without a night's lodging at Windsor. If I can have that accommodation of your house I will think it a great favour, and will go with them, and look to your house while everybody is gone to the show. I doubt the post can't bring me a return time enough so I am put in hopes this may come to you by a coach; if it does, I do not question your order to your housekeeper to let us in. In confidence of it, I think to send to her, that I believe I shall come and ask your beds for the night."

X.

The following letter to her son (afterwards second Duke of Bedford), written from Stratton in July, 1706, is throughout so wise and good, that we give it without any curtailment. She was then past seventy years of age, and no words could be more fitly pondered by the young, than these from an aged and tried and experienced Christian woman.

"When I take my pen to write this, I am, by the goodness and mercy of God, in a moderate and easy state of health—a blessing I have thankfully felt through the course of a long life, which (with a much greater help), the contemplation of a more durable state, has maintained and upheld me through varieties of providences and conditions of life. But all the delights and sorrows of this mixed state must end; and I feel the decays that attend old age creep so fast on me, that, although I may yet get over some more years however, I ought to make it my frequent meditation, that the day is near, when this earthly tabernacle shall be dissolved, and my immortal spirit be received into that place of purity, where no unclean thing can enter; there to sing eternal praises to the great Creator of all things. With the Psalmist, I believe, 'at His right hand there are pleasures for evermore:' and what is good and of eternal duration, must be joyful above what we can conceive; as what is evil and of like duration, must be despairingly miserable.

"And now, my dear child, I pray, I beseech you, I conjure you, my loved son, consider what there is of felicity in this world, that can compensate the hazard of losing an everlasting easy being; and then deliberately weigh, whether or no the delights and gratifications of a vicious or idle course of life are such, that a wise or thoughtful man would choose or submit to. Again, fancy its enjoyments at the height imagination can propose or suggest (which yet rarely or never happens, or if it does, as a vapour soon vanishes); but let us grant it could, and last to fourscore years, is this more than the quickest thought to eternity? Oh, my child! fix on that word, eternity! Old Hobbes, with all his fancied strength of reason, could never endure to rest or stay upon that thought, but ran from it to some miserable amusement. I remember to have read of some man, who reading in the Bible something that checked him, he threw it on the ground; the book fell open, and his eyes fixed on the word eternity, which so struck upon his mind, that he, from a bad liver, became a most holy man. Certainly, nothing besides the belief of reward and punishment can make a man truly happy in his life, at his death, and after death. Keep innocency, and take heed to the thing that is right; for that shall bring a man peace at the last—peace in the evening of each day, peace in the day of death, and peace after death.

"For my own part, I apprehend, I should not much care (if free from pain) what my portion in this world was,—if a life to continue, perhaps one year or twenty, or eighty; but then, to be dust, not to know or be known any more,—this is a thought that has something of horror in it to me, and always had; and would make me careless, if it were to be long or short; but to live, to die, to live again, has a joy in it; and how inexpressible is that joy, if we secure an humble hope to live ever happily; and this we may do, if we take care to live agreeably to our rational faculties, which also best secures health, strength, and peace of mind, the greatest blessings on earth.

"Believe the word of God, the Holy Scriptures. What most hinders faith, I am persuaded, is ignorance of God's true nature. Look up to the firmament, and down to the deep, how can any doubt a divine power? And if there is, what can be impossible to infinite power? Then, why an infidel in the world? In His Gospel the terrors of God's majesty are laid aside, and He speaks in the still and soft voice of His Son incarnate, the fountain and spring whence flow gladness. The idolatrous heathen perform their worship with trouble and terror; but a Christian, and a good liver, with a merry heart and lightsome spirit: for, examine and consider well, where is the hardship of a virtuous life? (when we have moderated our irregular habits and passions, and subdued them to the obedience of reason and religion). We are free to all the innocent gratifications and delights of life; and we may lawfully, nay, further I say, we ought to rejoice in this beautiful world, and all the conveniences and provisions, even for pleasure, we find in it; and which, in much goodness, is afforded us to sweeten and allay the labours and troubles incident to this mortal state, nay, inseparable, I believe, by disappointments, cross accidents, bad health, unkind returns for good deeds, mistakes even among friends, and what is most touching, death of friends.

"But in the worst of these calamities, the thought of a happy eternity does not alone support, but also revive the spirit of a man; and he goeth forth to his labour with inward comfort, till the evening of his day (that is, his life on earth), and, with the Psalmist, cries out, 'I will consider the heavens even the work of Thy fingers, the moon and the stars which Thou hast ordained. What is man, that Thou art mindful of him? or the son of man, that Thou shouldest so regard him?' (Psalm viii.) 'Thou madest him lower than the angels, to crown him with glory.' Here is matter of praise and gladness. 'The fool,' as the Psalmist expresses it, 'hath said in his heart, There is no God.' Or, let us consider the man, who is content to own an invisible power, yet tries to believe, that when man has done living on this earth he lives no more: but I would ask, if any of these unhappy creatures are fully persuaded, or that there does not remain in those men at times (as in sickness or sober thoughtfulness) some suspicion or doubt, that it may be other than they try to think. And although they may, to shun such a thought, or be rid of such a contemplation, run away from it to some unprofitable diversion, or, perhaps, suffer themselves to be rallied out of such a thought, so destructive to the way they walk in; yet, to be sure, that man does not feel the peace and tranquillity he does who believes a future state, and is a good man.

"For, although this good man, when his mind may be clouded with some calamity very grievous to him, or the disorder of vapours to a melancholy temper, I say, if he is tempted to some suspicion, that it is possible it may be other than he believes (pray observe) such a surmise or thought, nay, the belief, cannot drive him to any horror: he fears no evil, because he is a good man, and with his life all sorrow ends too: therefore, it is not to be denied, he is the wisest man who lives by the Scripture rule, and endeavours to keep God's laws. His mind is in peace and tranquillity; he walks sure who keeps innocence, and takes heed to the thing that is right. He is secure, God is his friend, that Infinite Being; and He has said, 'Come unto Me, ye that are heavy laden, My yoke is easy.' But guilt is, certainly, a heavy load; it sinks and damps the spirits. 'A wounded spirit who can bear!' And the evil subtle spirit waits (I am persuaded) to drive the sinner to despair; but godliness makes a cheerful heart. Let not past errors discourage; who lives and sins not? God will judge the obstinate, profane, unrelenting sinner, but is full of compassion to the work of His own hand, if they will cease from doing evil and learn to do well, pray for grace to repent, and endeavour with that measure which will be given, if sincerely asked for; for at what time soever a sinner repents (but observe, this is no licence to sin, because at any time we may repent), for that day we may not live to see; and so like the fool in the parable, our lamps be untrimmed when we are called upon. Remember, that to forsake vice is the beginning of virtue; and virtue certainly is most conducive to content of mind and a cheerful spirit. He (the virtuous man) rejoiceth with a friend in the good things he enjoys; fears not the reproaches of any; no evil spirit can approach to hurt him here, or accuse him in the great day of the Lord, when every soul shall be judged according as they have done good or evil. Oh, blessed state! fit for life, fit for death! In this good state I wish and pray for all mankind; but most particularly, and with all the ardour I am capable of, to those I have brought into the world, and those dear to them. Thus are my fervent and frequent prayers directed,—that you may die the death of the righteous, and to this end, that Almighty God would endue you all with spiritual wisdom, to discern what is pleasing in His sight."

XI.

On May 28, 1716, she wrote to her kinsman, the Earl of Galway the second son of the old Marquis de Ruvigny. The elder son was killed at the battle of the Boyne; King William created the brother Earl of Galway. To him the aged lady thus wrote: "'Tis our duty to pray for and trust in the merciful providence of God; then it shall be well in the end, in this world or a better. I beseech God to give the consolation of His Holy Spirit to enable you to struggle with bodily pains; your resignation I have no doubt of, yet Nature will shrink, when the weight is heavy, and presses hard, which will not be imputed, because it is natural.

"I also pray to God to fortify your spirit under every trial, till eternity swallows all our troubles, all our sorrows, all our disappointments, and all our pains in this life. The longest, how short to eternity! All these ought to be my own care to improve my weak self, as the fortitude of your mind, experiences, and knowledge does to you. And I pray for such a portion of them in mercy to me, as may secure an endless glorifying, to so feeble, so ignorant, so mean a creature as myself, that I cannot be too little in my own sight.

"If there be a regency, the intended journey to Chatsworth must be laid aside, as I must now lay aside my pen for want of the day. I am certain of this being a truth, that I am,

"Faithfully and affectionately yours,
"R. RUSSELL."

Later letters to Lord Galway are couched in the same way, the last one thus ending—

> "God, for the good you do mankind, grant you some easy years to do good upon earth before you change for a happy eternity. So does desire and pray Lord Galway's truly affectionate cousin, and faithfully such to gratify to the utmost of her ability, R. RUSSELL."

The dear old lady speaks in this letter of "evening creeping upon her," but she lingered to an extreme old age, dying on September 29, 1723, in her 87th year. She lived to see the Protestant rule firmly secured by the Hanoverian succession. In public affairs she continued to take interest, but always in subservience to the higher cause of moral and spiritual advancement. In one of her last letters she says of the son of the king, "I have inquired from Doctor Sloane how the Prince is to-day. He says, 'In a way to do well.' I trust, in the mercy of God, all our divisions shall be so with time."

One of her latest letters is dated September 4, 1716, addressed to her second daughter, the Duchess of Devonshire: "It is to no use to murmur that you could not be satisfied with taking the journey; the rather also because I believe I should have done the same. It is so fine a season I trust your return to Derbyshire will be easy; your mind would not have been such had you not done as you did. I shall be easy with a line or two from Lady Mary [her eldest daughter, who died unmarried in 1719] how you got to Chatsworth. At your first coming you will have a great deal to do, and so for the short time you can stay. I see no cause to fear, but that all will be, as we are, quiet; it is the temper of most to fear, or seem to do so." (She referred to the public tranquillity, of which the rebellion of the year before had left doubts.) "The season is exceedingly fine, not much burnt up; but the farmers, for talk's sake, ever wishing for what they have not; but it is good walking, and that is my best diversion. I cannot easily add any words to make this more a diversion to you, than that I thank God I have as much health as my years can have; and memory as yet enough to take a pleasure when I hear of what I love most, and desire all good may be their portion; which will afford content, while any thought whatever of good or ill remains in the head or heart of

"Your ever-affectionate mother, R. RUSSELL."

The spirit in which she bore the first overwhelming passion of grief may be best seen in the letters written by her to Doctor Fitzwilliam, who had been chaplain at Woburn, and who afterwards returned them to Mr. Solwood, the librarian there, by whom they were published. In 1819 another volume of letters was published, from the originals in the possession of the Duke of Devonshire. These range from her early married life down to her extreme old age; and contained greater variety of reference to the passing events of her time than are found in the Woburn letters, which are chiefly occupied with personal feelings and experiences. From them may be obtained as perfect a portraiture of Lady Russell as can be desired.

"Her letters," says Bishop Burnet, "are written with an elegant simplicity, with truth and nature, which can flow only from the heart. The tenderness and constancy of her affection for her murdered lord presents an image to melt the soul." Horace Walpole says, "I have now before me a volume of letters of the widow of the beheaded Lord Russell, which are full of the most moving and impressive eloquence." In fact it would be difficult to find a combination of so much good sense, tender affection, womanly fortitude, and deep piety in any collection of letters. It is observable also that in the whole course of these letters there is not to be found a trace of resentment or of reflection upon any person who had caused her husband's death. When James II. was no more king, but a fugitive in a foreign land, she utters no word of triumph over him, nor says that he was justly punished for his cruel crimes. Even the inhuman Jefferies, whose violence helped to get her husband condemned, is passed over in silence, and no reference is made to his disgrace, and his shameful end. She had attained to such moderation of spirit that no trace of anger appears against the unworthy instruments that had brought overwhelming grief upon her. In nothing more than this is the excellence of her Christian character conspicuous.

JAMES MACAULAY, M.A., M.D.

FRANCES RIDLEY HAVERGAL

I.

HER EARLY LIFE.

"Oh, 'Thine for ever!' What a blessed thing
   To be for ever His who died for me!
My Saviour, all my life Thy praise I'll sing,
   Nor cease my song throughout eternity."

Such were the words penned by Frances Ridley Havergal on an important day in her history; and they seem to be a fit expression of the purpose of one, the strains of whose songs shall reverberate through all ages.

Frances Ridley Havergal was born at Astley in Worcestershire on December 14, 1836. She was the youngest daughter of William Henry Havergal, who was rector of Astley. Her second Christian name she got from her godfather, Rev. W.H. Ridley, and rejoiced in the fact that he was descended from the godly martyr, Bishop Ridley.

Her eldest sister Miriam gives a glowing description of Frances:[1]

---

[1] The quotations, when not otherwise acknowledged, are made, and the chief of the facts taken, by kind permission of Messrs. Nisbet & Sons, from *Memorials of Frances Ridley Havergal*.

"My recollection of Frances begins with the first day of her life; a pretty little babe even then, and by the time she reached two years of age, with her fair complexion, light curling hair, and bright expression, a prettier child was seldom seen. At that age she spoke with perfect distinctness, and with greater fluency and variety of language than is usual in so young a child. She comprehended and enjoyed any little stories that were told her. I remember her animated look of attention when the Rev. J. East told her about a little Mary who loved the Lord Jesus. We were all taught to read early and to repeat by our dear mother, but as I had now left school I undertook the charming little pupil, teaching her reading, spelling, and a rhyme (generally one of Jane Taylor's), for half an hour every morning, and in the afternoon twenty or thirty stitches of patchwork, with a very short text to repeat next morning at breakfast. When three years old she could read easy books, and her brother Frank remembers how often she was found hiding under a table with some engrossing story. At four years old, Frances could read the Bible and any ordinary book correctly, and had learned to write in round hand; French and music were gradually added; but great care was always taken not to tire her or excite the precocity of her mind, and she never had a regular governess."

In the year 1859 she began to write an autobiography, commencing with her recollections of herself and her surroundings when she was four years old. She thus writes: "Up to the time that I was six years old I have no remembrance of any religious ideas whatever. Even when taken once to see the corpse of a little boy of my own age (four years) lying in a coffin strewn with flowers, in dear papa's parish of Astley, I did not think about it as otherwise than a very sad and very curious thing that that little child should lie so still and cold . . . But from six to eight I recall a different state of things. The beginning of it was a sermon preached one Sunday morning at Hallow Church by Mr. (now Archdeacon) Phillpots. Of this I even now retain a distinct impression. It was to me a very terrible one, dwelling much on hell and judgment, and what a fearful thing it is to fall into the hands of the living God. No one ever knew it, but this sermon haunted me, and day and night it crossed me. I began to pray a good deal, though only night and morning, with a sort of fidget and impatience, almost angry at feeling so unhappy, and wanting and expecting a new heart and have everything put straight and be made happy, all at once."

All this time she could not bear being "talked to," or prayed with, though she kept up a custom of going by herself every Sunday afternoon to a quiet room, and after reading a chapter in the New Testament would kneel down and pray; after that she "usually felt soothed and less naughty."

She appears even as a child to have appreciated very keenly the beauties of nature, and in the spring of 1845 she was most anxious to be made "a Christian before the summer comes" so that she might enjoy God's works as she believed a Christian alone could do.

Another soothing influence upon her spirited nature was the presence of any one whom she felt to be more than commonly holy, "not among those nearest and dearest to me at home," she confesses: "how perversely I overlooked them!—but any very pious clergyman or other manifest and shining Christian." "All this while," she continues, "I don't think any one could have given the remotest guess at what passed in my mind, or have given me credit for a single serious thought. I knew I was 'a naughty child,'—never entertained any doubts on the subject; in fact I almost enjoyed my naughtiness in a savage desperate kind of way because I utterly despaired of getting any better, except by being 'made a Christian,' which as months passed on, leaving me rather worse than better, was a less and less hoped-for, though more and more longed-for change."

When she was nearly nine years old, Mr. Havergal was appointed to the rectory of St. Nicholas, Worcester, and thither the family removed. Soon after their arrival, a sermon by the curate upon the text, "Fear not, little flock," aroused her from the feeling of self-satisfaction into which she had drifted. Having a favourable opportunity, she unburdened her heart one evening when alone with the curate, but he did not help the young seeker after peace. He said the excitement of moving and coming into new scenes was the cause most likely of her feeling worse, and that would soon go off; then she was to try and be a good girl and pray. So after that her lips were utterly sealed to all but God for another few years or rather more.

In 1848 her mother became seriously ill, and feeling that she was soon to leave her little girl, she said to her one evening: "Fanny dear, pray to God to prepare you for all that He is preparing for you." The sad event which the mother thus anticipated Frances could not or would not understand.

But what God had prepared for her she did in some measure realise when, a few weeks later, outside the house a funeral procession passed from the rectory to the churchyard, and inside a little girl flung herself on her bed with the lonely cry of a motherless heart, "Oh, mamma, mamma, mamma!" Her bright and apparently thoughtless manner led to the idea that she was heartless, but all the while she was heavy and sad for her loss, and weary because she had not yet received pardon of her sins.

Thus she went on, longing and trying to find peace, until she was fourteen years of age.

II.

RECEIVING "LIFE."

On August 15, 1850, Frances went to school at Belmont. The night before she left, her sister Ellen spoke to her of God's love, and she gave to her the first indication of her real feelings in the words, "I can't love God yet, Nellie!" But it was not to be so for long, however. During the first half-year at school a "revival," as she calls it, took place among the school girls, and she began to be more in earnest about her soul. One night she got into conversation with a Christian companion, and bursting into tears told her in French that she wished to love Jesus but could not. Her companion begged her to go to Jesus and tell Him this. Of this advice she says, "The words of wise and even eminent men have since then fallen on my ear, but few have brought the dewy refreshment to my soul which the simple loving words of my little Heaven-taught schoolfellow did." But peace had not yet come into her soul.

At length, in February, 1851, Frances made a confidante of Miss Cook, who in July, 1851, became her stepmother, and confessed that she desired pardon of her sins above everything else. She thus writes in her autobiography: "'Then, Fanny,' said Miss Cook, 'I think, *I am sure*, it will not be very long before your desire is granted, your hope fulfilled." After a few more words, she said, "Why cannot you trust yourself to your Saviour at once? Supposing that now, at this moment, Christ were to come in the clouds of heaven, and take up His redeemed, could you not trust Him? Would not His call, His promise be enough for you?

Could you not commit your soul to Him, to your Saviour, Jesus?' Then came a flash of hope across me which made me feel literally breathless. I remember how my heart beat. 'I *could* surely,' was my response; and I left her suddenly and ran away upstairs to think it out. I flung myself on my knees in my room, and strove to realise the sudden hope. I was very happy at last. I could commit my soul to Jesus. I did not and need not fear His coming. I could trust Him with my all for eternity. It was so utterly new to have any bright thoughts about religion that I could hardly believe it could be so, that I really had gained such a step. Then and there I committed my soul to the Saviour—I do not mean to say without *any* trembling or fear, but I did—and earth and heaven seemed bright from that moment—*I did trust the Lord Jesus.*"

In August, 1851, she went to school at Powick Court, near Worcester; but, owing to severe erysipelas in her face and head, she soon had to leave, and was ordered by the doctor to discontinue all study. She spent some time in Wales, and learnt Welsh very quickly. In November, 1852, she went with her parents to Germany, and attended school, standing alone as a follower of the Saviour among one hundred and ten girls. She progressed very rapidly in her studies. Though as a rule no girl was numbered in order of merit unless she had learnt everything (and she, through lack of time, had not done so), yet at the end of the term on the prize-giving day, when the names were called out, she heard with unspeakable pleasure the words, "Frances Havergal, *numero eins!*" (number one). The "Engländerin's" papers and conduct were so good that the masters agreed in council assembled to break through the rule for once and give her the place she deserved.

Her German master at Obercassel, Pastor Schulze-Berge, thus wrote of her: "She showed from the first such application, such rare talent, such depth of comprehension, that I can only speak of her progress as extraordinary. She acquired such a knowledge of our most celebrated authors in a short time as even German ladies attain only after much longer study."

She returned to England with her parents in December, 1853. On July 17, 1854, she was confirmed in Worcester Cathedral. In her case this public profession was a very real act. When asked by the bishop the solemn question to which all have audibly to answer, "I do," the reply of her heart was, "Lord, I cannot without Thee; but oh, with Thy almighty help, I do." In the cathedral she composed the lines with which this sketch begins. She always kept very solemnly the anniversary of this day.

She continued her German, French and English studies, and wrote many small pieces of poetry, the proceeds of which she gave to the Church Missionary Society. In the summer of 1856 she studied Hebrew very diligently; her knowledge and remembrance of the words of Scripture were very remarkable; she learnt the whole of the Gospels, Epistles, Revelation, the Psalms, and Isaiah, and later she added the Minor Prophets to the list.

While she thus grew in knowledge she grew also in grace. In August, 1859, she wrote: "I have lost that weary bondage of doubt and almost despair which chained me for so many years. I have the same sins and temptation as before, and I do not strive against them more than before, and it is often just as hard work. But whereas I could not see why I *should* be saved, I now cannot see why I should not be saved if Christ died for all. On that word I take my stand, and *rest* there. I still wait for the hour when I believe He will reveal Himself to me more directly; but it is the quiet waiting of present *trust*, not the restless waiting of anxiety and danger." That hour, in God's good time, did come.

In 1860 Canon Havergal resigned the rectory of St. Nicholas, Worcester, and Frances had to give up a class of unruly lads which she had taught with much success, one of the class becoming a minister of the Church of England, and another a Scripture-reader. The family removed to the country parish of Shareshill.

In 1861 Frances K. Havergal made her home at Oakhampton, the residence of her sister, and undertook the instruction of her two nieces. Her aim in teaching them was to fit them for eternity, but she did not fail to throw herself into their amusements and recreations, which she took up with her accustomed earnestness.

In the winter of 1865-66 F.R. Havergal visited her friends in Germany, and spent some time with her parents at Bonn. In 1806 her nieces went to school, and Frances left Oakhampton to reside at home.

Once again she confesses the presence of clouds on the horizon of her faith. "In reading, when one's heart leaps at some precious promise made to the children of God, a cold check comes, 'Am *I* one of them? what is my title?' Answer: 'Ye are all the children of God by faith in Jesus Christ.' Have I faith? Once introduce that *I*, and you get bewildered between faith and feeling. When I go on and grapple with the difficulty, it comes to this. As far as I know, I have come to Jesus, not once but many times. I have knelt and literally prostrated myself before Him, and told Him all, I have no other hope but what His *written* word *says* He did and said, that I know it is true, that the salvation it tells of is just *what* I want, and *all* I want, and that my heart goes out to it, and that I do accept it; that I do not fully grasp it, but I *cling* to it; that I want to be His only and entirely, now and for ever."

On September 23, 1867, she joined the Young Women's Christian Association, and found great benefit from her membership. She showed her practical interest in the Church Missionary and Irish Societies by wishing to give lessons in singing and German, the proceeds of which these societies were to have.

On April 19, 1870, she was called upon to part with her beloved father, after a short illness. In one of her poems she speaks of his

> "Valiant cry, a witness strong and clear,
> A trumpet with no dull uncertain sound."

Soon after his death she prepared for the press *Havergal's Psalmody*, which was afterwards largely used in the compiling of the Rev C. B. Snepp's hymn-book, called *Songs of Grace and Glory*, for which, she herself wrote several hymns. In June, 1871, she accompanied her friend Elizabeth Clay on a visit to Switzerland; there she thoroughly enjoyed the Alpine climbing, and revelled in the grand scenery of Mont Blanc and other snow mountains. On a subsequent visit Mont Blanc was ascended as far as the Grand Mulets. Here her delight in the exhilarating exercise of glissading landed her in a danger which, but for the presence of mind of Mr. Snepp, must have ended fatally to herself and one of the guides.

III.

LIFE MORE ABUNDANTLY.

We have now reached a time when Frances Ridley Havergal made a marked advance in spiritual life. It was the close of 1873. She received one day by post a little book entitled *All for Jesus*. She thus wrote about it to the clergyman who sent it to her: "*All for Jesus* has touched me very much . . . I know I love Jesus, and there are times when I feel such intensity of love to Him that I have no words to describe it. I rejoice too in Him as my 'Master' and 'Sovereign;' but I want to come nearer still, to have the full realisation of John xiv. 21—['He that hath My commandments, and keepeth them, he it is that loveth Me; and he that loveth Me shall be loved of My Father, and I will love him, and manifest Myself to him']—and to know the power of His resurrection,' even if it be with 'the fellowship of His sufferings;' and all this, not exactly for my own joy alone, but for others."

In reply to a letter from the clergyman, she wrote:[1] "I know I am not standing where I was two or three years ago. I think I first came to Jesus when I was only fourteen years of age, and I have been 'on the Lord's side' ever since. But of late, life has been a totally different thing to me, unspeakably brighter; Jesus so infinitely more precious: His service so infinitely sweeter and freer." But with this happiness she felt that there was a fuller consecration to God's service, to which she had not yet been able to yield herself. In a further communication her correspondent

---

1 *Such a Blessing*, p. 13.

reminded her of the truth that Jesus is able to keep us from falling, and abiding in Him, His blood cleanseth, *i.e.* goes on cleansing from all sin. "For conscious sin there is instant confession and instant forgiveness."

These words, though so simple, were made by the Holy Spirit a great comfort and help to her spiritual life. She replied,[1] "I see it all, and I *have* the blessing. But I cannot write about it yet, not even to you. I want first to test my gold and to count my new treasure. In two or three weeks (b.v.) I will write and tell you all about it."

The promised letter was duly sent, and in it she says,[2] "Your words, 'His blood *goes on* cleansing from unconscious sin,' and 'for conscious sin there is instant confession and instant forgiveness,' seem to include every need, and to settle all doubts and fears. Only one wants the holiness to be deep, inner *reality*: and so, I pray to be kept from unconscious, as well as from conscious sin. I do not want only to *think* I am not sinning. It is so sweet to look up to Jesus, in the joy of His keeping, and to tell Him how one longs, not merely not to grieve Him any more, but to please, really and truly *please* Him, all the days of my life. I had no idea there was such a blessing linked with being led into this truth." In a further letter she writes, "I never hated sin as I do now; and though I honestly thought I had given myself without reserve to Christ in full consecration, yet I see that there was an unconscious reserve of many little things."

The practical effect of this fuller insight into the blessings to be had by those who yield themselves up to Jesus Christ in simple faith, "was evident," remarks her sister, "in her daily true-hearted, whole-hearted service for her King, and also in the increased joyousness of the unswerving obedience of her home life, the surest test of all. To the reality of this I do most willingly and fully testify."

In 1874 F.R. Havergal went again to Switzerland. The first month of the visit was spent in quietly enjoying the scenery, and becoming

---

1 *Ibid.*, p. 15.
2 *Ibid.*, p. 20.

braced up by the invigorating air. During the second month she began working at various literary projects, the chief being the writing of her poem "Thoughts of God." The composition of this was often, however, interrupted by little acts of ministry, cheerfully undertaken on behalf of the spiritual needs of the Swiss around her.

She returned from Switzerland in good health, and resumed her active work at home. At one time it was helping a young friend into light and peace; at another, it was making an appointment to break her journey at Willesden Station, to talk with some one in trouble. For "it will be worth ANY fatigue if I can comfort her," was her unselfish remark. Amid so much activity, little could she have anticipated what was so soon to befall her.

IV.

TRIED IN THE FURNACE OF PAIN.

The journey was broken as arranged, though Frances R. Havergal was by that time very ill. Through some mistake she waited an hour and a half before the friend came, and then took her with her some miles so that they might not lose the longed-for interview. When home was reached, she was seized with shivering, fever set in and was pronounced to be typhoid fever. In the middle of November, 1874, it was thought her end was near. But prayer, continued and earnest, was made that her valuable life might be spared, and God graciously heard and answered, and brought her back from the gates of death. When asked afterwards if she had any fear of dying, her answer was, "Oh no, not a shadow." "Then was it delightful to think you were going home, dear Fan?" "No, it was not the idea of going home, but that *He* was coming for me and that I should *see my King*. I never thought of death as going through the dark valley, or down to the river; it often seemed to me a going up to the golden gates and lying there in the brightness, just waiting for the gate to open for me . . . I never before was, so to speak, face to face with death. It was like a look into heaven, and yet when my Father sent me back again, I felt it was His will, and so I could not be disappointed."

In January, 1875, she was removed to Winterdyne, where she heard of the sudden death of her brother Henry. After a few days a relapse set in, and her stepmother was sent for. After the fever had passed away she suffered very severe pain. She remarked to her sister once, "Oh, Marie, if I might but have five minutes' ease from pain! I don't want ever to moan when gentle sister Ellen comes in. How I am troubling you all!"

Health gradually returned to her, and with it she recommenced her active work for the Master.

V.

COMING FORTH AS GOLD.

The Refiner's work in F.R. Havergal was very evident. Of this year's illness and slow convalesence she speaks: "It has been the most precious year of my life to me. It is worth any suffering to prove for oneself the truth of 'when thou passest through the waters I will be with thee,' and worth being turned back (as it seemed) from the very golden gates if one may but 'tell of all His faithfulness.' It is so real."

"For two or three weeks [during my illness]," she writes again, "I was too prostrate for any consecutive prayer, or for even a text to be given me; and this was the time for realising what 'silent in love' meant (Zeph. iii. 17). And then it seemed doubly sweet when I was again able to 'hold converse' with Him. He seemed too so often to send answers from His own word with wonderful power. One evening (after a relapse) I longed so much to be able to pray, but found I was too weak for the least effort of thought, and I only looked up and said, 'Lord Jesus, I am *so* tired!' and then He brought to my mind 'rest in the Lord' with its lovely marginal reading, 'be silent in the Lord;' and so I just was silent to Him, and He seemed to overflow me with perfect peace, in the sense of His own perfect love."

When she was at length well enough to resume her literary work again, she busied herself in preparing an Appendix with music to *Songs of Grace and Glory*. She had completed it and sent it to the printers, and was hoping to be able to commence a book which she had contemplated writing, when she had the disappointing news that a fire at the printers' had destroyed the stereotype plates and paper as well as the MS.; and as she had kept no copy of the tunes, all her work had to be done over again. This "turned lesson," as she regarded it, was accepted with beautiful patience.

After a visit to Newport, Monmouth, followed by one to Ashley Moor, she spent some time in Switzerland. Here her quiet work went on among tourists and invalids, as well as Swiss. It was on this visit to Switzerland that she began the friendship with Baroness Helga V. Cramm, whose painted cards blend so beautifully with her words.

Towards the end of August, symptoms of her illness recurred, and she had not strength to return to England until October. It was on her journey back that the idea of her book *My King* came to her. It was, says her sister, at Oxford station on the way to Winterdyne. "I thought Frances was dozing when she exclaimed, with that herald flash in her eye, 'Marie! I see it all; I can write a little book, *My King*;' and rapidly went through divisions for thirty-one chapters."

The writer of this short biography may here refer to a never-to-be-forgotten hour that he spent with Frances R. Havergal. He had sent her some lines suggested by this little book, of which she most kindly expressed her approval, and naturally the book *My King* formed the subject of conversation, and she expressed her gratitude that she had been led to write this and other of her books in chapters for each day in the month; "for," said she, "they are read through in many cases twelve times a year instead of being perused once and thrown aside."

The year 1877 was passed uneventfully in paying various visits to relatives. But though uneventfully spent, not by any means idly or unprofitably, for her time was fully occupied with literary work.

A little later on we get a glimpse of this busy worker in another sphere. She had gone to Mildmay Park for rest.

"68, Mildmay Park, October, 1877.

"I was going away on Saturday, but caught cold at the quarterly meeting of the Association of Female Workers, . . . so I resigned myself to an extra week here; and verily, they *do* know how to nurse, *and* what's more (!) how to keep you quiet. Also, they do know how to pray! I have learned a little, I hope, on *that* subject this last week. What I hear and see here is quite a new light on intercessory prayer. I thought I knew something of its power and reality, but I see I did not know much.

"Mrs. Pennefather took me (before my cold) to Clapton House. I only wish every girl I care for was there; such a beautiful Christian school. I got any amount of bright looks (as it seems they knew my books), and I wanted exceedingly to go among them. Hearing the Principal say she would be prevented taking their Bible class, I ventured the proposal to take it. Afterwards, I had about a dozen all to myself in the drawing-room for a talk with any that wanted special help. They were told to get chairs. 'Oh!' I said, '*don't* sit all in a row a long way off; come up close and cosy; we can talk ever so much better then, can't we?' You should have seen how charmed they were, and clustered niece-fashion all round me. We did have such a sweet hour; it was rather after the 'question-drawer' manner; but all their little questions and difficulties seemed summed up by one of them, 'we do *so* want to come closer to Jesus.'"

As a help to her reading of the Bible, Frances R. Havergal joined the "Christian Progress Scripture Reading Union," conducted by her friend Rev. Ernest Boys, for whose magazine she acted, on one occasion, as editor during his absence. An amusing letter details her difficulties as editor, and she came out of them having formed this conclusion, "Never, except as an act of sheer mercy and pity, will I be an editor." This Reading Union was a great help to her own spiritual life, and also to her dealing with others, as the following sentences in a letter to the writer bears witness. "Not long ago I got five of my elder sister's servants to join, all Christians, but easy-going ones, and the result astonished me! It led to quite a revival of their spiritual life, and to reading together and speaking together, and to others; and I have since had a most beautiful letter from them full of gratitude for the *great* blessing which God had given them through joining. *Anything* to get people to read His Word! I find it continual help in corresponding with or meeting those who have joined, and any to whom God has let me be spiritually helpful are invariably delighted at the idea of reading with me. It is training many young Christians into *regular* reading."

On May 26, 1878, F. R. Havergal's stepmother passed away. This event broke up their Leamington home, and Frances and her sister spent some time in the quiet of the Mumbles near Swansea. They then went to stay at a farmhouse in Herefordshire, where, among other forms of work for the Master, she, ever thoughtful of others, interpreted on her fingers to the man of the house, who was quite deaf, the sermons she heard. It was here that she wrote her poem entitled *Zenith*.

The breaking up of the Leamington home she thought afforded a good opportunity of practically carrying out her dedication of her silver and gold to God's service. She had hoped to devote *herself* to missionary work, but her health prevented this being realised, so she sent off all her ornaments, including a valuable jewel-case, to the Church Missionary House in London, to be disposed of for missionary work. "I retain," she says, "only a brooch or two for daily wear, which are memorials of my dear parents; also a locket with the only portrait I have of my niece in heaven, my Evelyn; and her 'two rings' mentioned in *Under the Surface*. But these I redeem, so that the whole value goes to the Church Missionary Society. I had no idea I had such a jeweller's shop, nearly fifty articles are being packed off. I don't think I need tell you I never packed a box with such pleasure."

Towards the end of the year she joined her sister at the Mumbles. Here she could be quiet in her "workshop," the walls of which were adorned with pictures she had arranged herself. On her bookshelf stood her few choice books; the last she read were, *The Earth's Formation on Dynamical Principles*, by A.J. Ritchie, *Goodwin's Works*, *The Life and Letters of Rev. W.*

Pennefather, The Upward Gaze by her friend Agnes Giberne, and books by Rev. G. Everard. On her table was her American typewriter; her desk and table-drawers were all methodically arranged. It was at her study table that she read her Bible at seven o'clock in summer and eight in winter, her Hebrew Bible, Greek Testament and Lexicon being at hand. "Sometimes on bitter cold mornings," says her sister, "I begged that she would read with her feet comfortably to the fire, and received the reply, 'But then, Marie, I can't rule my lines neatly; just see what a find I have got! If one only searches, there are such extraordinary things in the Bible.'"

On Christmas-day, 1878, her last Christmas upon earth, she awoke in severe pain, and was ill for some days; but during the time she compiled a set of Christmas and New Year mottoes, which she called *Christmas Sunshine* and *Love and Light for the New Year*. She was ordered rest and felt she needed it. One remark as to her unceasing work is very touching:—"I do hope the angels will have orders to let me alone a bit when I first get to heaven." She was learning to use as her daily petition the prayer her mother taught her, "O Lord, prepare me for all Thou art preparing for me;" and this He was doing. By weakness and sickness and by unwearying trust and unwearied labour was she being prepared for that better rest above.

VI.

THE MINISTRY OF SONG

We may turn aside for a short time before we consider the last eventful weeks of Frances Ridley Havergal's sojourn upon earth, to deal with a subject that has been but lightly touched upon, namely, her ministry of song.

She had inherited from her gifted father a great talent for music. She was a remarkably skilful performer upon the pianoforte. So retentive was her memory that she could play without notes a large portion of the works of Handel, Beethoven and Mendelssohn.

Her musical compositions were of a very high order. When she was thirty years of age she went, while at Cologne, to show some of her compositions to Ferdinand Hiller. After looking through them and learning that she had had no instruction in harmony, he expressed his surprise and delivered his verdict, the worst part first.

He said her melodies bore the stamp of talent, not of genius. "But as to your harmonies," he said to her, "I must say I am astonished. It is something singular to find such a grasp of the subject, such power of harmonisation except where there has been long and thorough study and instruction; here I can give almost unlimited praise." She told him her question was, had she talent enough to make it worth while to devote herself to music as a serious thing, as a life-work? He answered, "Sincerely and unhesitatingly I can say that you *have*."

How spontaneous was her musical and poetical genius will be seen from the account of the genesis of her well-known missionary hymn and tune, "Tell it out among the heathen." She was unable to go to church at Winterdyne one snowy morning in 1873. She asked for her Prayer-book while still in bed, as she always liked to follow the services for the day. On Mr. Shaw, her brother-in-law, returning from church, he heard the piano sounding. "Why, Frances," he said, "I thought you were upstairs." "Yes, but I had my Prayer-book, and in the Psalm for to-day I read, 'Tell it out among the heathen that the Lord is King.' I thought what a splendid first line; and then the words and music came rushing on to me. There, it's all written out." She had written it out, the words and music and harmonies complete. And her sister remarks: "Only those who heard her could imagine the brisk ringing tone with which she sang this tune."

In her "Consecration Hymn" occurs the couplet—

"Take my voice and let me sing Always only for my King."

And to her these were no mere words of a song. She tried to consecrate all her singing to God's service. It was a real ministry. She strove always to sing the very words of the Bible, as she observed that persons could not with decency object to them, though they might have done so to her own words.

During a sojourn in Switzerland she was anxious to reach the people she saw wending their way to early mass. On learning that she would sing to them, many promised to come to her pension. She says, "First I sang to them, and then got the girls to join in the hymn which they had [previously] copied out. Then I read some passages . . . A few went away when I read . . . You will wonder what I sang! Well, I had been singing snatches of hymns to myself and especially 'Only for Thee,' and found this gave immense gratification in our little pension; so I thought God could as well give me French as English if He would, and I set to and wrote 'Seulement pour Toi!' (as they had liked the tune so much). Only it is quite a different hymn, making prominent the other side, He and He *only* is and does all for us." This hymn thus written was of good service on another occasion. On the way from Chamounix to Great St. Bernard Hospice, some of the passengers in the diligence sang French songs remarkably well. Her sister says: "We listened and commended, and then asked if they would join us in a new tune, 'Seulement pour Toi!' Finding the driver took up the chorus in bass, Frances went outside that he might see the words, and most heartily was it sung by all!"

The following Sunday was spent at the hospice; and once again was her musical talent used in proclaiming the Master's message. Her brilliant touch upon the piano attracted the attention of the "fathers" in the monastery, and they begged her to sing after dinner. She asked her sister to join in prayer that the King's message might be given, and that it might search some hearts. As there were different nationalities present, she very simply but gracefully said she was going to sing from the Holy Scriptures, repeating the words in German and Italian, and then sang Handel's "Comfort ye," "He shall feed His flock," and afterwards, "Rest in the Lord." An Italian professor of music, with many others, thanked her, and were expressing their admiration to her sister, when Frances bade them "good night," remarking to her sister, "You see, Marie, I gave my message, and so it is better to come away."

An instance illustrating the singing powers and also the friendliness of this sweet singer is recorded by Rev. S.B. James, D.D., in his *Frances Ridley Havergal, a Lecture Sermon*.[1] "After a garden-party in Somersetshire where she had almost exhausted herself, she happened to overhear her hostess's regret that the servants had not been present. 'Oh, if it is work for the Master,' she exclaimed, 'of course I can do it.' And though she had been just stung by a bee upon the hand, and was suffering intense pain, she threw off hat and gloves, took her seat eagerly at the piano, and . . . impressed a whole retinue of servants with the beautiful piece

---

1 Quoted in *The Sisters*. Charles Bullock, B.D., p. 100.

from the *Messiah*, 'Come unto Me, all ye that labour and are heavy laden, and I will give you rest.' And when it was all done she stood up and said, 'Now I am going to tell you what *you* must do when you have yourselves accepted the invitation,' and she sang out before that humble spell-bound audience, 'Tell it out among the heathen that the Lord is King.' . . . One person at least was turned to righteousness on that musical afternoon."

The ministry of song of F.R. Havergal will chiefly be remembered, however, by the goodly heritage of poetry which she has left to the Church of Christ, and in which she being dead yet speaketh. Here it is that her great influence is still felt. She had the happy gift of expressing the deep breathings of the consecrated soul in whole-hearted loyalty to the blessed Master. She strove to regard the Lord Jesus as a real living and personal Friend. She longed to be entirely yielded up to His service, and she put the thoughts of her heart, which had been warmed by the indwelling Spirit, in real and genuine expressions of love to and praise of her Master.

She began writing verses when she was only seven years of age.

In 1860 her poetry was so much appreciated that she received applications from the editors of various religions magazines to supply poetical contributions. In 1803 she received her first cheque of £10 17s. 6d. This she sent to her father: £10 for anything he liked to employ it on, 10s. for the Scripture Readers' collection, and 7s. 6d. for any similar emergency.

Her hymn "I gave my life for thee" first appeared in *Good Words*. It was written in Germany in 1858. She had come in weary and sat down opposite a picture with this motto. At once the lines flashed upon her and she wrote them in pencil on a scrap of paper. Reading them over, they did not satisfy her. She tossed them into the fire, but they fell out untouched. Showing them some months after to her father, he encouraged her to preserve them, and wrote the tune "Baca" especially for them.

The origin of the well-known hymn, 'Take my Life,' she thus describes—"I went for a little visit of five days. There were ten persons in the house, some unconverted and long prayed for, some converted, but not rejoicing Christians. He gave me the prayer, 'Lord, give me *all* in this house.' And He just *did*! Before I left the house, every one had got a blessing. The last night of my visit I was too happy to sleep, and passed most of the night in praise and renewal of my own consecration, and these little couplets formed themselves, and chimed in my heart one after another, till they finished with *'Ever*, ONLY, ALL, for Thee.'"

Some six months before she died she wrote thus about this hymn, "I had a great time early this morning, renewing the never-regretted consecration. I seemed led to run over the 'Take my Life,' and could bless Him verse by verse for having led me on to much more definite consecration than even when I wrote it—voice, gold, intellect, etc. But the eleventh couplet—"

'Take my love—my Lord, I pour
At Thy feet its treasure store'—

"that has been unconsciously *not filled up*. Somehow, I felt mystified and out of my depth here; it was a simple and definite thing to be *done*, to settle the voice, or silver and gold; but 'love?' I have to love others, and I do; and I've not a small treasure of it; and even loving *in Him* does not quite meet the inner difficulty . . . I shall just go forward and expect Him to fill it up, and let my life from this day answer really to that couplet. The worst part to me is that I don't in practice prove my love to Him, by delight in much and long communion with Him; hands and head seem so full of other things' (which yet are His given work), that 'heart' seems not 'free to serve' in fresh and vivid love."

In writing her hymns, F.R. Havergal looked up to God to give her the ideas and words, and they were often produced very rapidly. Mr. Snepp of Perry Bar left her leaning against a wall while he went in to visit the boys' school, and on his return ten minutes afterwards she handed him the well-known hymn "Golden harps are sounding," pencilled upon an old envelope.

A remarkable fact is recorded in connection with another hymn entitled, "Reality, Reality, Lord Jesus Christ, Thou art to me." She was much struck with the expression used by a working man in a prayer-meeting—"Father, we know the reality of Jesus Christ." This thought took hold of her and found expression in this hymn on a stormy night at Whitby, after she had seen the life-boat put forth to a wreck, hence the expressions, "Pilot," "Lifeboat," and "Haven." The very night she wrote the hymn, a young Christian four hundred miles away was pleading at a prayer-meeting, "Lord Jesus, let Thy dear servant write for us what Thou art, Thou living, bright Reality, and let her do it *this very night.*" "While they are yet speaking, I will hear."

Space does not permit any detailed account of her poetry. Her's were specially songs of the inner life. She revealed in her poetic works her own inner experience, and a perusal of them will give indications of her own growth in holiness.

A reader is impressed not only with the ease and brightness of her style, but with her firm grasp of things unseen. Her poetry was not just stringing together words, but it was the very expression of her heart. She thus writes on this point in *The Ministry of Song*:

"Poetry is not a trifle,
    Lightly thought and lightly made;
Not a fair and scentless flower,
Gaily cultured for an hour,
    Then as gaily left to fade.

'Tis not stringing rhymes together,
    In a pleasant true accord;
Not the music of the metre,
Not the happy fancies sweeter
    Than a flower-bell honey-stored.

'Tis the essence of existence,
    Rarely rising to the light;
And the songs that echo longest,
Deepest, fullest, truest, strongest,
    With your life-blood you must write."

So did the sweet singer herself write from her own experience.

Her hymns, which are very numerous, no less than seventy being in common use, have been the means not only of arresting the undecided and helping the saint, but of consoling the suffering and the doubting. So many of her poems were the expressions of a bright faith and simple trust shining out through storm and cloud, that others, storm-tossed and beclouded, catch the rays and are cheered thereby.

Although many of the poems are in a plaintive minor tone there are occasional bursts of more cheerful strain, as in the lines on "A Merrie Christmas," which appeared in the *Sunday at Home*.

"A Merrie Christmas to you!
    For we serve the Lord with mirth.
And we carol forth glad tidings
    Of our holy Saviour's birth.

So we keep the olden greeting,
    With its meaning deep and true,
And wish a Merrie Christmas
    And a Happy New Year to you.

Oh, yes! 'a Merrie Christmas,'
    With blithest song and smile,
Bright with the thought of Him who dwelt
    On earth a little while,

>   That we might dwell for ever
>   Where never falls a tear:
>   So 'a Merrie Christmas' to you,
>   And a Happy, Happy Year!"

The beautiful and aptly chosen titles alone in many cases are most suggestive and refreshing. Yes, Frances R. Havergal's power of giving expression to holy aspiration and Christian loyalty and heartfelt praise will live as long as English Hymnology lives.

VII.

"SEEING THE KING."

We come now to describe the closing months of this devoted life. Her sister recalls that the New Year's greeting given to her on January 1, 1879. was, "'He crowneth the year with His goodness,' and He crowneth me 'with loving-kindness and tender mercies.' You, dear Marie, are one of my mercies; and I do hope He will let me do something for you up in heaven."

The following subjects of prayer for 1878-79, found in her Bible, will not only illustrate her method of petition, but will be helpful to other Christians longing to excel in supplication.

"I have greatly enjoyed the regular praying of the Lord's Prayer, and take a petition each morning in the week. Intercession for others I generally make at evening. I take the fruits of the Holy Spirit in the same way and find this helpful."

GENERAL.

MORNING.
For the Holy Spirit.
Perfect trust all day.
Watchfulness.
To be kept from sin.
That I may please Him.

Guidance, growth and grace.
That I may do His will.
That He may use my mind, lips, pen, *all*.
Blessing and guidance in each engagement and interview of the day.

EVENING.

For forgiveness and cleansing.
Mistakes overruled.
Blessing on all said, written and done.
For conformity to His will and Christ's likeness.
That His will may be done *in* me.
For a *holy* night. Confession.
For every one for whom I have been specially asked to pray.

SPECIAL SUBJECTS.

SUNDAY.

That I may make the most of Sabbath hours and gain much from the Word.

Deliverance from wandering thoughts. *Pure* praise. Blessing on services and choir.

Hallowed be Thy name.

Intercessions. (Initials of many clergymen, of her brother, her godchildren, and "our servants.")

MONDAY—"For joy and peace."

That the life of Jesus may be manifest in me.

Thy kingdom come

Intercession for Church Missionary Society and Irish Society. (Initials of her eldest sister, *all* her family, and "Oakhampton servants.")

TUESDAY—"For longsuffering"

That my unconscious influence may be all for Him.
Thy will be done.
Intercession for Mildmay (and initials of her brother Henry's children and many Leamington friends).

'WEDNESDAY—"Gentleness."
For spirit of prayer and shadowless communion.
Give us this day our daily bread.
Intercession for the universities and public schools, for many friends, for M.V.G.H., and E.C.

THURSDAY—"Goodness."
For much fruit to His praise. Soul-winning. Spirit of praise.
Forgive us our trespasses.
Local work. Swansea and Mrs. Morgan. For my sister Ellen, all at Winterdyne, "and the servants."

FRIDAY—"Faith."
Wisdom to be shown more of His will and commands.
Lead us not into temptation.
For my brother and all at Upton Bishop.

SATURDAY—"Meekness and Temperance."
That the Word of Christ may dwell in me richly, open treasure of Thy Word to me, fill my seed-basket.
Deliver us from evil.
For the Church of England and the Queen. (Initials of many friends.)

A plan of work for 1879—"If the Lord will"—was sketched out, but it was not the Lord's will that it should he accomplished, and many subjects were not even attempted.

On her return from London in the early part of the year, her friends noticed the peculiar gladness of her service. She said one morning to her sister, "Marie, it is really very remarkable how everything I do seems to prosper and nourish. There is my 'Bruey Branch' growing and increasing, and now the temperance work, and so many letters tell me that God is blessing my little books."

The "Bruey Branch" here mentioned was an effort to get children to interest themselves in the Irish Society, and met with signal success. It had been started two years previously with eight collectors—now hundreds of collecting cards had gone out.

Of her temperance work she writes a little later: "May, 1879. I haven't taken up teetotal work, but teetotal work has taken up me! Morgan and Scott made me accept a big handsome pledge-book in February, and somehow the thing has fairly *caught fire* here. One led to another, and yesterday boys were coming all day to sign. I had twenty-five recruits yesterday alone, and a whole squad more are coming this evening! and we are going in for getting EVERY boy in the whole village! and now 'Please, miss, mayn't girls sign?' So I've got to open a girls' branch as well! So work grows!" Again, "Really a wonderful little temperance work here; all the rising generation have joined the pledge except about twelve, and now the men want to speak to me and I am to meet them to-night at the corner of the village (open air, having no place else) with my pledge-book. I have got 118 pledged, and each with prayer over it and personal talk about better things." On May 21 she met these men, carrying with her her Bible and temperance book. While standing, heavy clouds came up, and she was obliged to return home, wet and chilly, though some men were still waiting to speak to her. The next day (Thursday) she managed to get to church and received the Lord's Supper. She was very tired with the service, and rode home on a donkey. As she passed through the village, quite a procession of her boys followed her. She urged her donkey boy to "leave the devil's side and get on the safe side; that Jesus Christ was the winning side; that He loved him, and was calling him, and wouldn't he choose Him for his Captain?" Arrived at home, she ran in for her temperance book, and the boy signed it on the saddle. That evening she spoke to several persons with intense earnestness and pleading.

The next day she was to have attended a temperance meeting and have presented 150 cards to those who had signed her book; but the chilliness increased, and the doctor forbade her to go out. Unable to be present herself, she sent two messages by her sister: one to those who had signed—"Behold, God Himself is . . . our Captain;"[1] to those who had not signed—"Come thou with us and we will do thee good."[2]—While the meeting was going on she was busy at home stitching strong paper tract-bags for sailors at sea, till she felt ill and had to be assisted to her room.

On May 26 she was able to correct the proof of *Morning Stars*, on the text, "I am the bright and morning Star;" and then, as her sister says, the pen so long used in the service of her King was laid down. The last passage she looked at in her Bible was the *Christian Progress* chapter for May 28.[3] She asked that it might be read to her, and dwelt on "Be thou faithful unto death, and I will give thee a crown of life." On the 29th fever and internal inflammation rapidly came on, and she exhibited all the symptoms of peritonitis. She suffered very severe pain; but though the outward man was perishing, the inward man was being renewed. On May 30, speaking of justification by faith, she said, "Not for our own works or deservings; oh, what vanity it seems now to rest on our own obedience for salvation, any merit of our own takes away the glory of the atoning blood. 'Unto Him that loved us, and washed us from our sins in His own blood'—*that's it*." When asked if she had any fear, she replied, "Why should I? Jesus said, 'It is finished;' and what was His precious blood shed for? *I trust that*."

On Whit-Sunday she was better, and able to converse a little with her brother and sister. On the following day at early dawn she made the remark, "'Spite of the breakers, Marie, I am so happy. God's promises

---

[1] 2 Chron. xiii. 12.
[2] Num. x. 29.
[3] Rev. ii. 1-10.

are so true. Not a fear." At 8 A.M. it was thought she was departing. The Lord's Supper was administered at her request, and when it was over she whispered to her brother, "Frank dear, it is not the performance of the rite, *no safety in that*; but it is obedience to His command, and as a *remembrance* of His dying love." When the doctor told her she would soon be going home, she exclaimed. "Beautiful! too good to be true! . . . Oh! it is the Lord Jesus that is so dear to me, I can't tell how precious! how much He has been to me!" Afterwards she asked for "How sweet the name of Jesus sounds!"

To the vicar of Swansea, who visited her, she said, "Oh! I want all of you to speak *bright, bright* words about Jesus, oh, do, *do*! It is all perfect peace. I am only waiting for Jesus to take me in."

Her sufferings were very acute, and when told how patient she had been that even the doctors noticed it, she replied, "Oh! I am so glad you tell me this. I did want to glorify Him every step of the way, and especially in this suffering. I hope none of you will have five minutes of this pain."

On Tuesday, June 3, she was evidently worse. Among the words she uttered were these: "I am lost in amazement! There hath not failed one word of all His promise!" Mentioning the names of many dear ones, she said, "I want *all* to come to me in heaven; oh! don't, *don't* disappoint me; tell them, 'Trust Jesus.'" When one of her sisters repeated the words of the hymn, "Jesus, I will trust Thee," she sang the verse right through to her tune "Hermas." Violent sickness ensued, and when it was over she folded her hands on her heart, saying, "There, now it is all over! Blessed rest!"

Her sister thus describes the glorious sunset of her life on June 3, 1879, at the age of 42: "And now she looked up steadfastly as if she saw the Lord; and surely nothing less heavenly could have reflected such a glorious radiance upon her face. For ten minutes we watched that almost visible meeting with her King, and her countenance was so glad, as if she were already talking to Him. Then she tried to sing, but after one sweet high note—'HE—,' her voice failed, and as her brother commended her soul into her Redeemer's hand, she passed away. Our precious sister was gone, satisfied, glorified, within the palace of her King." And so she fell asleep, and her eyes saw the King in His beauty—that King of whom she sung so sweetly and wrote so loyally. On June 9 they laid her body to rest in the quiet churchyard of Astley Church in Worcestershire.

And thus within sight of the room which saw her birth, her body lies "until the day dawn."

VIII.

"UNDER THE SURFACE."

Upon the surface you saw a bright, accomplished lady. She had marked ability as a linguist. She acquired a great deal of German as a child by carefully attending while present at the German lessons given to her sisters. She learnt enough Greek and Hebrew to read her Hebrew Bible and to enjoy her Greek Testament, and often brings out in her letters the fact that she had been studying it. As we have seen, she was an accomplished musician, and she was untiring in her literary productions. Her books of poems comprise *Life-Chords*, consisting of "Under His shadow,"—"Her last poems"—"Loyal Responses," and "Her earlier poems;" *Life Mosaic*, comprising "The Ministry of Song," and "Under the Surface;" *Swiss Letters and Alpine Poems*, written during several tours in Switzerland.

Her chief prose works *Kept for the Master's Use, The Royal Invitation, My King, Royal Commandments, Royal Bounty, Starlight through Shadows, Morning Stars, Morning Bells, Little Pillows*, and *Bruey, a little Worker for Christ*.

Upon the surface, too, you saw a woman of sound-common sense. This was evidenced both in her writings, and her daily life. For example, she writes thus one day: "I felt as if I rather wanted a little intellectual bracing, as if something of contact with intellect were necessary to prevent my getting into a weak and wishy-washy kind of thought and language. I like intellects to rub against and have no present access to books which would do it, so I bethought myself of seeing what Shakespeare would do for me and I think my motive was really that I might polish my own instruments for the Master's use."

Again, as regards dress her sensible comment was, "If the King's daughter is to be 'all glorious within,' she must not be outwardly a fright! I must dress both as a lady and a Christian. The question of cost I see very strongly, and do not consider myself at liberty to spend on dress that which might be spared for God's work; but it costs no more to have a thing well and prettily made."

Yes, *on* the surface you saw an accomplished lady, and on the surface you saw also beaming out the fact that *under* the surface she was a whole-hearted Christian. This was the most marked feature in her character. No one could be in her company five minutes without recognising Whose she was and Whom she served. A clergyman, who knew perhaps more of her inner life than any one else, in a letter to the writer, says, "The two most prominent characteristics of the last five and a half years of her life seemed to me to be her unreserved consecration and her absolute confidence in the Lord and His Word." The preceding chapters will have shown the reader how true an estimate this is. The business of her life was to glorify God and enjoy Him for ever. Of delicate health, she might have spent a large portion of her time in fretful complainings; but she looked to her Heavenly Father to consecrate even her sicknesses to His service.

Her standard of Christian life was a very high one. She thus writes of a friend: "I write to you as one who is really wanting to follow Jesus altogether, really wanting to live and speak *exactly* according to His commands and His beautiful example; and where this is the standard, what seems a little thing or nothing at all to others, is sure to be sin, because it is disobeying His dear Word and not 'following, *fully*.'" Her intimate knowledge of Scripture, her sound common-sense kept her from falling into many of the errors into which some who have aimed high in holy things have fallen.

In a letter to her sister on this subject, she thus expresses herself: "As to 'perfectionism' or 'sinlessness,' I have all along, and over and over again, said I never did and do not hold either. 'Sinlessness' belongs *only* to Christ now, and to our glorified state in heaven. I believe it to be not merely an impossibility on earth but an actual contradiction of our very being, which cannot be 'sinless' till the resurrection change has passed upon us. But being kept from falling, kept from sins, is quite another thing, and the Bible seems to teem with commands and promises about it. First, however, I would distinctly state, that it is *only* as and while a soul is under the full power of the blood of Christ that it can be cleansed from all sin; that one moment's withdrawal from that power, and it is again actively, because really, sinning; . . . one instant of standing alone is certain fall."

While magnifying the Saviour's power to save, she had a just estimate of her own condition; only about two years before her death she thus expresses herself: "I can say for myself that I feel I have deserved the very suffering of hell for my transgression of the first great commandment of the law ('Thou shalt love the Lord thy God,' etc.), and for my sin of unbelief." While she aimed high, she knew full well that she had not attained, neither was already perfect.

"As to sanctification, that it is the work of the Holy Spirit, and progressive, is the very thing I see and rejoice in. He has brought me into the 'highway of holiness' up which I trust every day to progress, continually pressing forward, led by the Spirit of God."

The simplicity of her trust in God and His Word comes out strikingly in her writings. She seems to have grasped the fact that Jesus Christ was "a living bright reality," pledged to uphold and help and comfort all who go to Him as little children. Another marked feature in her life was her deep sympathy with others in their trouble and anxieties. And this spirit of unselfishness enabled her in her prose writings and her hymns to inspire something of her simple trust into those who read them with receptive minds.

To see under the surface of Frances Ridley Havergal's character, look into her works, and you find the humble servant of Jesus Christ revealed. She "walked with God," and by the attraction of a life bright with the beauty of holiness revealing itself in her writings, she has exercised and still exercises a great power upon Christians by lifting them up to a higher walk with God. And many singers will doubtless join hereafter in the song of "Moses and the Lamb" whose souls were on earth attuned to heavenly music through the pleading words or holy example of Frances Ridley Havergal.

John P. Hobson, M.A.

HANNAH MORE.

I.

EARLY II

Amongst the staunchest supporters of Presbyterianism in the days of Charles II. were the Mores of Harleston, Norfolk. Glorying in the risk incurred of proscription and imprisonment, they turned their dwelling into a conventicle. Here the faithful gathered stealthily at midnight to hear the Gospel preached, whilst one of the house, with drawn sword, stood at the threshold prepared to defend with his life both minister and congregation. From this sturdy stock sprang Jacob, the father of Hannah More. He married a sensible, high-principled farmer's daughter. A family of five girls was born to them, the fourth being Hannah, whose birth occurred on the 2nd of February, 1745.

Hannah displayed remarkable precocity. Before she was four she could repeat the Catechism, much to the astonishment of the parish minister; whilst startling questions about matters far beyond her age were put to those around her. At eight her thirst for knowledge increased. Sitting on her father's knee she listened eagerly to his recital of the brave deeds of Greeks and Romans and the wise sayings of Plutarch. Sometimes her father repeated orations of classic heroes, first in the original tongue, and then in English. The interest thus excited led the child to crave for a knowledge of Latin. Her father, although averse to girls exceeding the limits of the three "R's" and a few accomplishments, yielded at length to his promising daughter's desire. This early introduction to the classics paved the way to a diligent study of Latin in later years and of the best Latin models, which greatly helped in the formation of her literary style. She also gained a little knowledge of mathematics; but Euclid had to retire in favour of the less intricate study of French. The proficiency which she afterwards acquired in this language she owed to the assiduous tuition of her eldest sister, Mary.

Before the age of twelve she began to scribble short essays and poems. Her systematic education commenced on her becoming a pupil of her sisters' boarding-school at Bristol. Here she made rapid progress, often giving convincing proof of intellectual gifts, and before long becoming qualified to assist in tuition.

In her sixteenth year she was one of Sheridan's most delighted auditors during his delivery of a course of lectures on Eloquence. She expressed her admiration in a chaplet of verses which, finding their way into the orator's hands, so impressed him with the fair promise they contained, that he secured an introduction to the author. Thus originated one of Hannah's numerous warm friendships of after life.

Ferguson, the astronomer, was another of Hannah's early acquaintances. From him she gained a knowledge of science; whilst he, prompted by his high estimate of her abilities, took counsel with her respecting the style of his literary productions.

Her intellectual tastes were encouraged and directed, to a large extent, by a somewhat notable Bristol man, of the name of Peach. Although a draper by trade, his cultivated mind and excellent literary judgment were of distinct service to his young friend. He was entrusted by Hume with the revision of the proof-sheets of the famous History of England.

A humorous story is related of the interest which Hannah's conversation created in the minds of her elders. When laid aside by illness she was attended by a noted physician, Dr. Woodward, who one day became so absorbed in his patient's intellectual discourse that he forgot to make the usual inquiries about her health. "Bless me!" he exclaimed, as he went downstairs, "I forgot to ask the girl how she was!" He returned to the bedside, and rather awkwardly put the formal question to the amused invalid, "How are you to-day, my poor child?"

Hannah's training in the highest principles of morality and in religion, begun by her devoted parents, received the careful attention of her eldest sister as long as she remained under her care; when out of her teens, she commenced the study of theology under the guidance of Dr. Stonhouse, a clergyman of Bristol.

At the age of seventeen, finding that the young people in her circle were in the habit of learning passages from plays which frequently savoured of unhealthy sentiment, she conceived the idea of providing a harmless substitute, and thereupon wrote a pastoral drama, *The Search after Happiness*. A little later she produced another drama, *The Inflexible Captive*, founded on Metastasio's opera of *Regulus*.

Encouraged in various ways by numerous friends, on whose judgment she could safely rely, she appears to have taken pains to qualify herself for a literary career. She studied Latin, Italian, and Spanish, translated from the best compositions, wrote pieces in imitation of celebrated authors, and thus tried to cultivate her mind, and to form the groundwork of a good and pleasing style.

Such literary prospects, however, seemed likely to be exchanged for those of a rural domestic life; for at the age of twenty-two she received and accepted an offer of marriage from a country gentleman of wealth and high character. The wedding-day was fixed, but was postponed more than once, owing to the bridegroom's indecision. At length he lost his chance; for the bride, yielding to the advice of friends, declined to be trifled with any longer, and broke off the engagement. To make some amends for his treatment, and to compensate for her resignation, at the prospect of marriage, of her interest in the school which she and her sister were conducting at Bristol, he settled upon her an annuity, and at his death bequeathed her a thousand pounds. The settlement was made without her knowledge; and it was not without the utmost difficulty that her friends prevailed in persuading her to agree to the arrangement. From this time forward she seems to have set her face against matrimony, for she firmly declined other offers.

A few years afterwards, on arriving at the age of twenty-eight, a long-cherished wish was realised. Since childhood she had longed to visit London. As a child her favourite amusement was to make a carriage of a chair, and invite her sisters to ride with her to London "to see bishops and booksellers." Through girlhood to womanhood the desire gathered strength. In 1773 she set off with two of her sisters to pay her first visit to the Metropolis.

II.

IN "VANITY FAIR."

In order to estimate the complex influences surrounding Hannah More in London, and to appreciate the manner in which she stood the ordeal of passing through "Vanity Fair," it is necessary to bear in mind the social, moral, and religious aspects of the people about the middle of the eighteenth century.

What are now considered flagrant vices were either unnoticed or tacitly sanctioned. Of social refinement, as we now understand the term, there was comparatively little. Coarse jokes, swearing, and profanity were almost as common in "polite society" as in the back streets now. The literature of the day, excepting the writings of Addison, Johnson, Steele, and a few others, ministered to the low tastes prevalent amongst both the upper and the lower classes. Religion had well nigh lost all vitality. With the majority of people it had become the subject either of jest, sceptical hostility, or the utmost indifference.

One of Archbishop Seeker's charges contained the following startling statement:—"In this we cannot be mistaken, that an open and professed disregard of religion is become, through a variety of unhappy causes, the distinguishing character of the present age . . . Indeed, it hath already brought in such dissoluteness and contempt of principle in the higher part of the world, and such profligate intemperance and fearlessness of committing crimes in the lower part, as must, if this torrent of impiety stop not, become absolutely fatal . . . Christianity is now ridiculed and railed at with very little reserve; and the teachers of it without any at all."[1]

The great lawyer, Blackstone, says he went from church to church to hear noted London preachers, and it was impossible for him to tell from their discourses whether these luminaries were followers of Confucius, Mahomet, or Christ. George III. felt compelled to address a letter of expostulation to Archbishop Cornwallis for giving balls and routs at Lambeth Palace on Saturday nights, so that they ran into Sunday morning.[2] The Church had given hardly a thought to either the religious or secular education of the masses. Gross ignorance pervaded the ranks of the poor all over England. Although the English Bible was in the people's hands, it was almost a dead letter.

But the voice of awakening had been heard in the land. George Whitfield, John Wesley, and a few other brave men, whose hearts were roused by the Spirit of God, went up and down the country proclaiming the glad tidings of the cross, which for so long had been as an idle tale to the English people.

The wave of religious awakening had touched the highest circles of London society; and when Hannah More received her flattering welcome from fashion, wit, and genius in 1773, the spirit of indifference and neglect had given way in a slight degree to a spirit of inquiry and anxious concern. There was, however, no perceptible change as yet in the utter worldliness of the times, or in the low standard of morals.

It was a perilous thing for a young woman like Hannah More, with her enthusiasm, talents, and general attractiveness, to be suddenly launched in the turbid though fascinating current of London society. But the admirable training in strict moral principles with which she had been privileged furnished weapons of defence against the more specious temptations which presented themselves; whilst her quick discernment

---

1 Charge to clergy, 1738. See vol. v. of *Works*, Dublin, 1775.
2 This letter may be found in *The Life and Times of Lady Huntingdon*.

easily penetrated the thin shell of external polish covering worthlessness of character. It was also fortunate for her that at the outset of her London experience she became acquainted with such a sterling man as Dr. Johnson.

A few days after her arrival she was introduced to David Garrick and his wife. The famous actor had seen a letter of hers to a mutual friend, extolling one of his theatrical performances. He forthwith secured an interview, which resulted in favourable impressions on both sides, of amiability and intellectual powers. A very cordial friendship ensued.

Garrick's social circle was now thrown open to Miss More. At his house she first met Mrs. Elizabeth Montague, the authoress of an *Essay on the Writings and Genius of Shakespeare*, a work which brought around the writer the best literary men of the time.

Miss More's introduction to Dr. Johnson took place at the house of Sir Joshua Reynolds. This event, though much desired, was not without dread, lest the great man should happen to be in one of his querulous moods. All fear vanished on her seeing the Doctor approach with a smile on his rugged countenance, and Sir Joshua's macaw perched on his hand. Her surprise may be imagined when he greeted her with a verse from a Morning Hymn of her own composition.

The following extracts are from letters written by one of Hannah's vivacious sisters. "Since I last wrote, Hannah has been introduced by Miss Reynolds to Baretti and to Edmund Burke (the 'Sublime and Beautiful' Edmund Burke!). From a large party of literary persons assembled at Sir Joshua's she received the most encouraging compliments; and the spirit with which she returned them was acknowledged by all present, as Miss Reynolds informed poor us. Miss R. repeats her little poem by heart, with which also the great Johnson is much pleased." "We have paid another visit to Miss Reynolds. She had sent to engage Dr. Percy (Percy's collection,—now you know him), who is quite a sprightly modern, instead of a rusty antique, as I expected. He was no sooner gone, than the most amiable and obliging of women (Miss Reynolds) ordered the coach to take us to Dr. Johnson's *very own house*; yes, Abyssinia's Johnson! Dictionary Johnson! Rambler's, Idler's, and Irene's Johnson! Can you picture to yourself the palpitation of our hearts as we approached his mansion? The conversation turned upon a new work of his (the Tour to the Hebrides), and his old friend Richardson . . . Miss Reynolds told the doctor of all our rapturous exclamations on the road. He shook his scientific head at Hannah, and said, 'She was a *silly thing*.' When our visit was ended, he called for his hat, as it rained, to attend us down a very long entry to our coach, and not Rasselas could have acquitted himself more *en cavalier*. We are engaged with him at Sir Joshua's, Wednesday evening. What do you think of us?"

A second visit to London took place in the following year, and a third—prolonged to six months—in 1776. From this period down to about 1789 Miss More usually spent some time every year amongst her London friends, but chiefly with Mrs. Garrick, either at the Adelphi or at her country residence at Hampton.

Her "Life," written by Mr. Roberts and others, is rich with letters, which of themselves form a striking autobiography, revealing the writer's prominent phases of character, her steadfast adhesion to high principles, her progress in the path of literary fame, her wearying of fashionable society, and the gradual consecration of all her powers to the service of God. Besides these personal matters, we get glimpses of the notable people with whom she was brought into contact, and of the moral and religious condition of the higher classes. These letters conform to Hannah More's own idea of what epistolary effusions between friends should be. "What I want in a letter," she once wrote, "is the picture of my friend's mind, and the common course of his life. I want to know what he is saying and doing; I want him to turn out the inside of his heart to me, without disguise, without appearing better than he is." We can therefore obtain a more lifelike portraiture by making extracts from her correspondence than by attempting the task in any other way.

Describing her feelings in associating with persons of rank and wit, she says:—"I had yesterday the pleasure of dining in Hill Street, Berkeley Square, at a certain Mrs. Montague's, a name not totally obscure. The party consisted of herself, Mrs. Carter, Dr. Johnson, Solander, and Matty, Mrs. Boscawen, Miss Reynolds, and Sir Joshua (the idol of every company); some other persons of high rank and less wit, and your humble servant,— a party that would not have disgraced the table of Laelius or of Atticus. I felt myself a worm for the consequence which was given me, by mixing me with such a society; but as I told Mrs. Boscawen, and with great truth, I had an opportunity of making an experiment of my heart, by which I learnt that I was not envious, for I certainly did not repine at being the meanest person in company . . . Dr. Johnson asked me how I liked the new tragedy of Braganza. I was afraid to speak before them all, as I knew a diversity of opinion prevailed among the company: however, as I thought it less evil to dissent from the opinion of a fellow-creature than to tell a falsity, I ventured to give my sentiments, and was satisfied with Johnson's answering, 'You are right, madam.'"

Her conscience was uneasy from visiting the opera, and also from attending Sunday parties, which were greatly in vogue.

She thus wrote on this subject:—

"London, 1775.
"'Bear me, some god, oh, quickly bear me hence,
To wholesome solitude, the nurse of—'

"'Sense' I was going to add, in the words of Pope, till I recollected that *pence* had a more appropriate meaning, and was as good a rhyme. This apostrophe broke from me on coming from the opera, the first I ever *did*, the last I trust I ever *shall* go to. For what purpose has the Lord of the universe made His creature man with a comprehensive mind? Why make him a little lower than the angels? Why give him the faculty of thinking, the powers of wit and memory; and, to crown all, an immortal and never-dying spirit? Why all this wondrous waste, this prodigality of bounty, if the mere animal senses of sight and hearing (by which he is not distinguished from the brutes that perish) would have answered the end as well? and yet I find the same people are seen at the opera every night—an amusement written in a language the greater part of them do not understand, and performed by such a set of beings! . . . Conscience had done its office before; nay was busy at the time; and if it did not dash the cup of pleasure to the ground, infused at least a tincture of wormwood into it. I *did* think of the alarming call, 'What doest thou here, Elijah?' and I thought of it to-night at the opera."

The attractions of wealth and fame had not blinded her to the need of seeking satisfaction from a higher source. "For my own part, the more I see of the 'honoured, famed, and great,' the more I see of the littleness, the unsatisfactoriness of all created good; and that no earthly pleasure can fill up the wants of the immortal principle within."

She was much troubled by the extravagances of fashion in dress and adornments; and, although conforming to some extent to prevailing modes in order to avoid singularity, which she abhorred, she always dressed neatly and decorously, and never, through the whole of her life, wore an article of jewellery simply for ornament.

The following extract from a letter written by one of Hannah's sisters shows the cordial relationships with Dr. Johnson, and his interest in the five sisters. "Tuesday evening we drank tea at Sir Joshua's with Dr. Johnson. Hannah is certainly a great favourite. She was placed next him, and they had the entire conversation to themselves. They were both in remarkably high spirits; it was certainly her lucky night! I never heard her say so many good things. The old genius was extremely jocular, and the young one very pleasant. You would have imagined you had been at some comedy had you heard our peals of laughter. They, indeed, tried which could 'pepper the highest,' and it is not clear to me that the lexicographer was really the highest reasoner."

III.

CHARACTERISTICS, FRIENDSHIPS, AND EARLY LITERARY WORK.

Hannah More's flattering reception in London society, and the lively impression which she so quickly created, will give rise to some astonishment in the minds of many readers. She had not yet won reputation as an authoress; she did not possess the influence of wealth or of noble family; she was not remarkable for physical beauty; and she had none of the brazen ingenuity of patronage-hunters, by which admission is secured into the houses of distinguished people. She came to London a stranger, a plain schoolmistress from Bristol, and yet in a marvellously short time she was one of the best known characters in the ranks of the wise and great.

The causes of her rapid rise to distinction are not far to seek. Her wonderful talent for conversation at once proved an attraction to both men and women. But she was not merely a fluent talker, never at a loss for a word, a phrase or a metaphor; had this been her crowning recommendation, Dr. Johnson's long-standing friendship would never have been gained. Her talk was always sensible—the outcome of a well-furnished, retentive mind. Her judgment was sound, her discrimination delicate, and her grasp of fundamental truths consistently firm. She did not accommodate her opinions to meet the exigencies of different coteries, nor was she addicted to compromise. She was equally at ease in discussing the merits of *Rasselas* with Dr. Johnson, the curiosities of art with Lord Orford, Roman history with Gibbon, and the state of the Church with Bishop Porteus. Not that she pretended equality of learning with such men, but she had just sufficient knowledge of various subjects to provoke a conversation, and enough cleverness to sustain it by "drawing out" the scholar who might be seated at her side. But this was not all. Her conversation sparkled with wit and repartee. "The mind laughed," says her friend Zachary Macaulay, "not the muscles; the countenance sparkled, but it was with an ethereal flame: everything was oxygen gas and intellectual champagne: and the eye, which her sisters called 'diamond,' and which the painters complained they could not put upon canvas, often gave signal by its coruscation, as the same sort of eye did in her friend Mr. Wilberforce, that something was forthcoming which in a less amiable and religiously disciplined mind might have been very pretty satire, but which glanced off innoxiously in the shape of epigrammatic playfulness."

Her genial disposition and good temper disarmed difference of opinion of anything harsh or unpleasant, and formed another credential for the prominence she attained in society. The absence of all artificiality in sentiment and manners, when contrasted with the straining after effect acquired by fashionably-bred ladies, also added to her attractions in the eyes of thoughtful men.

But whilst to these causes may be attributed her rapid rise into favour, it was undoubtedly owing to her unswerving and unassuming piety that she retained for so long the respect, confidence, and affection of varied orders of mind in London society.

At first she appears to have done little to enforce religious teaching amongst her acquaintances. Her moral and religious principles were known by the firm stand she took against common incentives to dissipation and irreligion—such as card-playing and Sunday entertainments—against the introduction of questionable topics, unseemly language, and vacuous frivolity into conversation. Her religious influence, thus far, was almost a silent or negative one; but it had its effect on others, and laid the foundation of that direct searching and far-reaching influence, which, under the Divine blessing, she wielded in later years.

Her interest in young people was notably illustrated by her efforts to foster the intellectual tastes of Lord Macaulay when a lad. She supplied him with standard books, which formed the nucleus of an excellent library, and advised him in his studies. To the child of six she thus writes:—"Though you are a little boy now, you will one day, if it please God, be a man; but long before you are a man I hope you will be a scholar[1]."

When Hannah More began to produce books her reputation rose to literary fame. In 1775 she wrote a romantic poem, entitled *Sir Eldred of the Bower*, with which was published another poem, written earlier, *The Bleeding Rock*. In the first the element of religion was not forgotten; and both works met with a flattering reception. Though, as we have seen, a woman of high Christian tone, with what we should consider strange inconsistency, she both wrote plays, which were acted, and attended the theatre herself.

In 1777 her tragedy, *Percy*, was brought out at Covent Garden Theatre. One of the results of this venture was a shower of invitations to the author of the play from a new circle of titled and distinguished people. The play was afterwards translated into German, and performed at Vienna with notable success.

On the death of Garrick in 1779, Hannah More broke off attendance at the theatre. Garrick's widow sought relief and solace in Hannah's company, and for many years a close friendship was kept up between the two ladies, although there could be but little intercourse on religious matters, Mrs. Garrick being a Roman Catholic. Before the actor's death Miss More had completed another play, *The Fatal Falsehood*, which was afterwards performed, and which elicited almost as much applause as *Percy*.

Miss More's experience of fashionable life had now lasted about six years. As her fame increased, her taste for society declined. The constant round of

---

1 See *Life and Letters of Lord Macaulay*, by George Otto Trevelyan, M.P., vol. 1. pp. 35, 36

dinner-parties, conversation-parties, and assemblies of intellect and wealth, though at first full of attraction to one of her disposition, had begun to lose its charm. Her depth of character and her recognition of the claims of religion demanded a more satisfactory mode of spending her time and utilising her talents. For the next five years we find her often the guest of Mrs. Garrick, but gradually detaching herself from fashionable circles, studying theology, history, and science, writing poems, and engaged in other literary work.

Her chief literary work during this period consisted of *Sacred Dramas—Moses in the Bulrushes, David and Goliath, Belshazzar,* and *Daniel.* She was prompted to this undertaking by a desire to provide, not plays for the stage, but a substitute for some of the pernicious literature of the day which fell into the hands of young people, and also to afford instruction in the common facts of Scripture, The gross ignorance of the Bible amongst fashionable people astonished her one day, when Sir Joshua Reynolds told her that on showing his picture of Samuel to some great patrons they asked him who Samuel was? The work answered the purpose for which it was intended, and passed through nineteen editions, receiving high commendation from Bishop Lowth and others. Her poem *Sensibility* was also included in this successful volume.

A poem, *The Bas Bleu, or Conversation,* written in a lively and facetious strain, owed its origin to the mistakes of a foreigner who gave the literal designation of the *Bas-Bleu* to a party of friends who had been humorously called the "Blue Stockings."

At the King's request a manuscript copy of the poem was sent to him; and Dr. Johnson went so far in his praise of the effusion as to say that there was no name in poetry that might not be glad to own it. A little later Miss More wrote *Florio*, a poem describing the occupation of a young man of fashion, and his final escape from a life of pleasure to one of usefulness.

By the death of Dr. Johnson in 1784, Miss More lost the best friend she ever had in London. She had been with the Doctor at his last communion at St. Clement's Church, and saw too plainly his altered condition. Bound to each other by strong intellectual and stronger religious sympathies, the separation caused a void in Miss More's life which was never afterwards filled. Theirs was a friendship born at first sight. For more than ten years it grew and flourished, with mutual benefit and happiness to the stern moralist and his promising *protégé*. Whilst the rugged common-sense and sound literary judgments of the Doctor imparted increasing accuracy and insight to his friend's views of the world and of literature, it was the sparkle, freshness, and wit of Miss More's conversation, and her light-heartedness of character, that often dispelled the clouds of depression from the mental horizon of her sage and trusty adviser, and smoothed the rough edges of his outspoken opinions. In religion, it was probably the Doctor's uncompromising fidelity to first principles, and to a fearless practice of truth, that helped to fortify his "dear child," as he called Miss More, in maintaining her integrity amidst the bewildering voices and garish scenes of Vanity Fair.

IV.

COWSLIP GREEN.

About the time of Dr. Johnson's death, in 1784, Hannah More became the possessor of a rural spot, called Cowslip Green, some ten miles from Bristol. Here she built herself a cottage, intending to make it her place of retirement for a large portion of each year. In the cultivation of her garden she found leisure for reflection as well as an opportunity to pursue a favourite occupation.

The inroads which death had made in her circle of intimate friends, a growing dissatisfaction with the enjoyments of London life, and especially a keener sense of her responsibility, as a professed Christian, than she had hitherto experienced, led to a close self-examination, and to a scrutiny of the real motives of her life.

The result of this testing process showed itself in various ways. During occasional visits to London and attendance at parties she lost no opportunity of enforcing the truths of religion. Her silent witnessing was now exchanged for active exertion. The manners and practices of people who were amongst her most effusive admirers sometimes met with her indignant rebuke. Ladies of title, society beauties, and leaders of fashion, who were unapproachable by other religious influences, she urged in private to consider their spiritual interests. The method she adopted was not, usually, to start religious topics, but "to extract from common subjects some useful and awful truth, and to counteract the mischief of a popular sentiment by one drawn from religion." Perhaps a message which John Wesley once sent to her through a sister may have weighed considerably in deterring her from an entire severance from the fashionable world. "Tell her to live in the world; *there* is the sphere of her usefulness; they will not let *us* come nigh them."

Not content with personal and private reproof, advice, and entreaty, she now devoted her pen to the denunciation of folly and vice in high places. In her work, *Thoughts on the Importance of the Manners of the Great to General Society*, whilst protesting against prevalent irreligious practices and habits of dissipation, which even good people sanctioned, she sought to arouse a sensitive regard for mutual responsibility as set forth in the New Testament.

In 1788 the slave trade formed a burning question in Parliament. Miss More, intensely aroused by the descriptions presented of the horrible traffic, found vent for her feelings in a poem on the subject. About the same time a close friendship began with Wilberforce, which lasted to the end of life.

A yet more important friendship commenced at this period—one that was destined to work a powerful influence on Miss More's life. The Rev. John Newton, one of the leaders amongst the evangelical clergy, held the incumbency of St. Mary Woolnoth. Attendance on his ministry led to a correspondence and a deep friendship. John Newton was precisely the kind of man whom Hannah More needed to assist her in spiritual progress, and to direct her steps into paths of settled peace. Her letters to Mr. Newton, stating her difficulties and seeking counsel, breathe the spirit of the humble and sincere scholar of Christ. Her willingness to obey the Master whom she professed to serve, and her earnest desire to be brought into closer relations with God, although checked, had never been stifled by the claims of intellect or by the attractions of the world. From this time the work of the Holy Spirit in deepening her love for the Saviour became more and more prominent. Turning for a time from Christian work amongst the rich, Miss More now devoted her efforts to the improvement of the moral and religious condition of the poor.

About ten miles from Cowslip Green was the picturesque village of Cheddar, the population of which was sunk in ignorance and depravity. The incumbent lived at Oxford, and the curate at Wells, twelve miles off. There was but one service a week, and no pastoral visitation whatever. There were thirteen parishes in the neighbourhood without even a resident curate. Drunkenness and utter inefficiency prevailed to a terrible extent amongst the clergy in this district; whilst education was a question that never troubled either the clergy or the people.

At Cheddar Hannah and her sister Patty opened a school; and in a short time nearly 300 children attended regularly. The sisters had to combat strong prejudices amongst the farmers. By dint of much persuasion and flattery the opposing forces were at length won over, even to hearty concurrence.

Masters and mistresses were procured for teaching reading, seeing, knitting, and spinning, and giving religious instruction on Sundays. A second school was shortly opened in an adjoining parish, the vicarage-house, which had remained uninhabited for a hundred years, having been put into repair for the purpose.

During 1790 Miss More published a volume entitled, *An Estimate of the Religion of the Fashionable World*. The book was quickly bought up, and within two years reached a fifth edition. The prevailing indifference to vital religion, the corruptions of society, the decline of domestic piety, and the absence of religion from the education of the upper classes were the themes treated by the writer with unsparing candour and convincing force.

Encouraged by her success at Cheddar, Miss More, with her sister Patty, went further afield, and selected two mining villages on the top of the Mendip Hills as the next scene of her labours. The difficulties here were even greater than those at Cheddar. The neighbourhood was so bad, we are told, that no constable would venture to execute his office there. Friends warned the Misses More that their lives would be in danger if they persisted in their project. The people imagined that the sisters had come to make money by kidnapping their children for slaves.

Undaunted by obstacles and perils, the workers persevered, until in no less than ten parishes schools were commenced, which, before long, were attended by 1200 children. In every parish the acquiescence of the incumbent was first obtained before proceeding to open a school. At the evening meetings, to which adults were invited, a simple sermon was read by one of the sisters, and also a printed prayer and a psalm. Few mistresses could be found who had not owed their religious impressions to Wesleyan influence; and thus Hannah More was subsequently, though mistakenly, thought to be a Methodist. Although influenced by the Methodist revival, she always considered and professed herself to be a member of the Episcopal Church.

Whilst immersed in her village work, she was earnestly solicited to write a popular tract that might help to counteract the baneful influence of Jacobin and infidel publications, and infamous ballads, which were now scattered broadcast over England. She declined the task, doubtful of her efficiency to produce a pamphlet equal to the occasion. On second thoughts, however, she tried her powers in secret, and issued anonymously a lively dialogue called *Village Politics*, by "Will Chip." The success was phenomenal. Friends ignorant of the authorship sent her copies by every post within three or four days of publication, begging her to distribute the pamphlet as widely as possible. In a short time copies were to be found in all parts of the kingdom. Hundreds of thousands were circulated in London. Such was the enthusiasm that private persons printed large editions at their own expense, whilst the Government sent off quantities to Scotland and Ireland. At last the secret came out; and the author was deluged with congratulations and thanks. Some persons of sound judgment declared that *Village Politic* had essentially contributed, under Providence, to prevent a revolution, whilst others went so far as to allege that Miss More had "wielded at will the fierce democratie of England, and stemmed the tide of misguided opinion."

A little later Miss More wrote another pamphlet, by way of reply to the atheistical speech of Dupont to the National Convention, and devoted the profits, amounting to £240, towards the relief of the French emigrant clergy.

In 1794, or early in 1795, she commenced the issue of tracts. This was a form of literary work not much used in those days. The founders of the Religious Tract Society, realising the value of this kind of work, but considering that Miss More's tracts needed supplementing with some which should in every case contain the simple communication of the Gospel, began in 1799 to undertake the dissemination of religious knowledge. Sunday schools, through the energy of Mr. Raikes, were rising in various parts of the country; the poorer classes were learning to read; and nothing in the shape of cheap literature was provided to meet their new craving, except mischievous broadsheets and worthless doggerel. Hannah More set to work to supply something healthy to amuse, instruct, and edify the new order of readers. She produced regularly every month for three years, three tracts—simple, pithy, vivacious, consisting of stories, ballads, homilies, and prayers. She was sometimes assisted by one of her sisters and two or three friends; but the burden of the work, including heavy correspondence with local committees in almost every district of England, fell upon her shoulders. In order to issue the brochures at a cheap rate and to undersell pernicious publications, she found it necessary to raise a subscription. Her appeal met with a liberal response; and very shortly the lively tracts, with a rough woodcut on the title-page, came by thousands from the printer's hands. In the first year no less than two millions were sold. Amongst the tracts were *The Shepherd of Salisbury Plain, Black Giles the Poacher, History of Mr. Fantom, The Two Shoemakers, History of Tom White the Postilion, The Strait Gate and the Broad Way;* and amongst the ballads *Turning the Carpet, King Dionysius and Squire Damocles, The Honest Miller of Gloucestershire, The Gin-Shop, or A Peep into a Prison.*

It would be difficult to over-estimate both the direct and secondary value of the Cheap Repository Tracts. Their beneficial influence must have been incalculable; and for this reason they should be placed amongst the greatest and best work of Hannah More's useful life.

By 1798 Miss More had withdrawn almost entirely from London society, contenting herself with a yearly visit of two months, which she divided between Mrs. Garrick, Bishop Porteus, Lord Teignmouth, and one or two others. Her schools occupied the best part of her time; but frequent attacks of illness often interfered with her duties.

In 1799 her active pen was at work again. Her third ethical publication, *Strictures on Female Education*, came out, forming yet another counterblast to the corrupt systems in vogue amongst the wealthy classes.

It would have been marvellous had Miss More escaped persecution in her work amongst rural populations. Combating prejudices, introducing unheard-of innovations, adopting plans which rumour stated were deeply tainted with Methodism (and therefore bad, according to clerical and general opinion in those days), she had to encounter at last a pitiless storm of hostility. This violent and prolonged attack, whilst it showed to what infamous lengths the tongues of slander, envy, and bigotry could go in attempting to destroy a noble woman's reputation, tested to the utmost Hannah More's fine qualities of Christian forbearance and courage.

V.

BARLEY WOOD, CLOSING YEAES AND DEATH.

In 1802 Miss More removed from Cowslip Green to a house which she had built at Barley Wood, about a mile distant. Soon afterwards her sisters, having disposed of their house at Bath, came to live with her. For the next twenty years, or more, friends from all parts sought her society, and strangers of all ages and of all ranks came for advice, sympathy, and help. Her immense correspondence occupied a very large portion of her time. There was scarcely a person at all prominent in the religious world who was not brought into association with her.

Miss More's prolonged life did not close until 1833, when she had arrived at her eighty-ninth year. The thirty-one years that remained to her after quitting Cowslip Green was as full of work and usefulness as the previous part of her life. It will be impossible within the space now left to do more than indicate the chief events of this period, which was not remarkable for any fresh departure either in educational or religious work. Miss More had already marked out for herself two distinct and definite lines of usefulness—the education of the poor, and the improvement of morals and religion amongst the rich. By her active exertion and by her busy pen she continued to pursue these two lines of work down to the year of her death. It must be remembered that she was a martyr during these latter years to long attacks of illness, one of which almost completely prostrated her for two years; and when upwards of seventy she was unable to leave the house for more than seven years. At this period she stated that she had never been free from pain for long together since she was ten years old. Such physical hindrances render her persistent activity and the great work she accomplished all the more remarkable. When not entirely incapacitated she still worked with her pen, attended to business connected with her schools, and received visitors in the sick room. It used to be said amongst her friends that when she was laid aside they always expected a new book from her.

In 1805 she published *Hints towards forming the Character of a Young Princess*. It was undertaken, at the request of a bishop, with reference to the education of the Princess Charlotte.

In 1809 her religious novel, *Coelebs in Search of a Wife*, issued anonymously, roused universal attention. In twelve months as many editions came out; and during the author's lifetime thirty editions of a thousand copies each were printed in America. This was followed shortly by *Practical Piety*, which soon ran to the tenth edition, and which brought the author to the end of her life numerous gratifying testimonies of its results. As a sequel to this work, *Christian Morals* was published in 1812, and was also widely circulated. Three years later, when the author had entered her seventieth year, she wrote an *Essay on the Character and Writings of St. Paul*, in two volumes, which, notwithstanding absorbing political events, was received with the same eagerness which greeted her former works. *Moral Sketches of Prevailing Opinions and Manners, Foreign and Domestic*, was published in 1819, being chiefly directed against the rage for copying French customs and manners. At the age of eighty-two she collected from her later works her *Thoughts on Prayer* and re-issued them in a little volume, with a short preface. This was her last literary effort. She said to a friend that the only remarkable thing which belonged to her as an author was that she had written eleven volumes after the age of sixty.

Between 1813 and 1818 her four sisters died. The last to go was Martha, Hannah's trusty helpmeet and lieutenant in all her benevolent schemes, and her tender consoler in many a season of sickness. Soon after this event Miss More's long illness of seven years occurred. Unable to give proper supervision to her servants, she was victimised in household matters in various ways. Extravagance and misconduct at length gave rise to scandal; and at the representation of friends Miss More reluctantly decided to break up her establishment, and remove to another and smaller residence at Clifton. It was with a sad heart that she left her charming dwelling; and as she glanced back into the beautiful garden, with its shady bowers, she exclaimed, "I am driven, like Eve, out of Paradise; but not, like Eve, by angels."

She lived five and a half years at Clifton, tranquilly waiting for the end, and attending, as far as failing strength would permit, to the distribution of her charities, the work of her schools and the entertainment of friends.

Almost to the last she retained unimpaired the use of her faculties. The intellectual vivacity of early days often reappeared. During one of her illnesses some one remarked, in allusion to the struggle of the remnant of sin in a person recently awakened to the truth, "The old man dies hard!" "The old woman dies hard!" exclaimed the invalid. At eighty-three she said, "I have too many petty cares at that age when the grasshopper is a burden. I have *many* grasshoppers, and seem to have less time and more labour than ever."

Her last days were spent almost entirely in prayer, invoking blessings on those around her and on the village work which lay so near her heart. She said to a friend during her last illness, "To go to heaven, think what *that* is! to go to my Saviour who died that I might live! Lord, humble me, subdue every evil temper in me. May we meet in a robe of glory! Through Christ's merits alone can we be saved . . . Lord, I believe—I *do* believe with all the powers of my weak, sinful heart. Lord Jesus, look down upon me from Thy holy habitation; strengthen my faith, and quicken me in my preparation. Support me in that trying hour when I most need it! It is a glorious thing to die!" No vanity or self-praise on the ground of her life's labours ever found a place in her thoughts. Some one began to speak of her good deeds. "Talk not so vainly," she exclaimed; "I utterly cast them from me, and fall low at the foot of the cross." She sank gradually, and without pain, and on September 7, 1833, quietly passed away.

There are few thoughtful students who will hesitate to rank Hannah More with the leading religious and educational reformers of the eighteenth century. In essential matters she was a kindred spirit with Whitfield, Wesley, Raikes, and others, and worked, in the way marked out for her by God, for the regeneration of her country.

With regard to her books, she believed they would be little read after her death. To a considerable extent her judgment has been verified. Her writings were a continual seed-sowing, which later workers fertilised, and brought to maturity.

They were republished in eleven volumes in 1830. Besides the prominence given to their religious or moral purpose, most of them are remarkable for sustained fervour, persuasiveness of tone, and practical common sense. We give a few extracts from some of the principal works, to illustrate Hannah More's methods of appealing to the conscience and awakening spiritual concern.

"There are two things of which a wise man will be scrupulously careful—his conscience and his credit. Happily, they are almost inseparable concomitants; they are commonly kept or lost together; the same things which wound the one usually giving a blow to the other; yet it must be confessed, that conscience and a mere worldly credit are not, in all instances, allowed to subsist together . . .

"Between a wounded conscience and a wounded credit, there is the same difference as between a crime and a calamity. Of two inevitable evils, religion instructs us to submit to that which is inferior and involuntary. As much as reputation exceeds every worldly good, so much, and far more, is conscience to be consulted before credit—if credit that can be called, which is derived from the acclamations of a mob, whether composed of 'the great vulgar or the small'"—*Christian Morals* (chapter xxiv.).

"One cause, therefore, of the dulness of many Christians in prayer, is their slight acquaintance with the sacred volume. They hear it periodically, they read it occasionally, they are contented to know it historically, to consider it superficially; but they do not endeavour to get their minds imbued with its spirit. If they store their memory with its facts, they do not impress their hearts with its truths. They do not regard it as the nutriment on which their spiritual life and growth depend. They do not pray over it; they do not consider all its doctrines as of practical application; they do not cultivate that spiritual discernment which alone can enable them judiciously to appropriate its promises, and apply its denunciations to their own actual case. They do not use it as an unerring line, to ascertain their own rectitude, or detect their own obliquities."

* * * * *

"The discrepancies between our prayers and our practice do not end here. How frequently are we solemnly imploring of God that 'His kingdom may come,' while we are doing nothing to promote His kingdom of grace here, and consequently His kingdom of glory hereafter."

* * * * *

"Prayer draws all the Christian graces into its focus. It draws Charity, followed by her lovely train, her forbearance with faults, her forgiveness of injuries, her pity for errors, her compassion for want. It draws Repentance, with her holy sorrows, her pious resolutions, her self-distrust. It attracts Faith, with her elevated eye,—Hope, with her grasped anchor,—Beneficence, with her open hand,—Zeal, looking far and wide to serve,—Humility, with introverted eye, looking at home. Prayer, by quickening these graces in the heart warms them into life, fits them for service, and dismisses each to it appropriate practice. Cordial prayer is mental virtue; Christian virtue is spiritual action."—*The Spirit of Prayer* (chapters iii., viii., and xi.).

> "If good we plant not, vice will fill the place,
> And rankest weeds the richest soils deface.
> Learn how ungoverned thoughts the mind pervert,

And to disease all nourishment convert.
Ah! happy she, whose wisdom learns to find
A healthful fancy, and a well-trained mind.
A sick man's wildest dreams less wild are found
Than the day-visions of a mind unsound.
Disordered phantasies indulged too much.
Like harpies, always taint whate'er they touch.
Fly soothing Solitude! fly vain Desire!
Fly such soft verse as fans the dang'rous fire!
Seek action; 'tis the scene which virtue loves;
The vig'rous sun not only shines, but moves.
From sickly thoughts with quick abhorrence start,
And rule the fancy if you'd rule the heart:
By active goodness, by laborious schemes,
Subdue wild visions and delusive dreams.
No earthly good a Christian's views should bound,
For ever rising should his aims be found.
Leave that fictitious good your fancy feigns,
For scenes where real bliss eternal reigns:
Look to that region of immortal joys,
Where fear disturbs not, nor possession cloys;
Beyond what Fancy forms of rosy bowers,
Or blooming chaplets of unfading flowers;
Fairer than o'er imagination drew,
Or poet's warmest visions ever knew.
Press eager onward to these blissful plains,
Where life eternal, joy perpetual reigns."

The Search after Happiness.
HENRY JOHNSON.

SUSANNA WESLEY.

I.

PARENTAGE AND EDUCATION.

The mother of John Wesley was the daughter of Dr. Samuel Annesley, an eminent minister of the Church of England at the period of the great Civil War. He resigned his charge, being one of the two thousand who, after the Restoration, declared for Nonconformity, and preached their farewell sermons in the Established Church, on the 17th of August, 1662. He found his sphere in the meeting-house of Little St. Helen's, Bishopsgate.

Dr. Annesley's second wife, the mother of Susanna, was a woman of eminent piety, and beloved of all who knew her. "How many children has Dr. Annseley?" was a question asked of the eminent Puritan preacher Manton, who had just been officiating at the baptism of one of the number. "I believe it is two dozen, or a quarter of a hundred," he replied. Such was the family into which the mother of the Wesleys was born on the 20th of January, 1669. Of this crowded household, the majority were daughters, and Susanna was the youngest of these. In her own Journals, which form the only account of her childhood, we read of several instances of her "preservation from accidents," and once from a "violent death." The method of her education is not clearly stated, but "the tree is known by its fruits." There is evidence that it was sound and liberal, and up to the best standard of the day in any rank of society. French and music were evidently among her attainments, while in her letters and treatises there are abundant tokens that logic and philosophy were also held in effective possession and use. She tells us that which might have been expected when she says that she "was early initiated and instructed in the first principles of the Christian religion;" and in after days we find her giving to her son a rule which had proved to be a blessing to her own girlhood—"Never to spend more time in any matter of mere recreation in one day, than I spend in private religious duties."

The thoroughness of her own "private religious duties" is shown by the fact that in the year 1700 she made a resolution to spend one hour morning and evening in private devotion. This practice she kept up through life as far as circumstances would admit.

II.

THEOLOGICAL STUDIES.

Soon we find Susanna Wesley studying the works of Jeremy Taylor, of the early Puritan Divines, and the immortal Bunyan, till at length her vigour of intellect and enterprise in reading led her into danger. By reading Arian and Socinian authors of the period, her faith was shaken. This, however, was not to be for long, and the manner of her recall was marked by interesting circumstances.

It is at this juncture that Samuel Wesley, her future husband, first appears in the story as the friend of her soul. This young student, seven years her senior, had himself made "proof" of Socinianism. In the course of some literary work, he had been specially well paid for the translation of Socinian writings from the Latin; but his strong mind revolted from their principles, the task was resigned, and his faith became more firmly rooted in Christ as the eternal Son of God. In this frame of mind Mr. Wesley met Susanna Annesley, and by God's help, succeeded in accomplishing her complete extrication from the meshes of doctrinal error and distress.

It can be gathered from her writings, about this time, that the salutary change proceeded not out of complaisance to the lover, but by reception of a fulness of light from heaven. Clearness, zeal, and love mark her *Meditations and Disquisitions on the Holy Trinity; the Godhead and Atonement of the Lord Jesus Christ; the Personality and Work of the Holy Spirit.*

Another epoch in the girlhood of this remarkable young lady was the engagement, somewhat previously, of her mind in the controversy between the Church and Nonconformity. Here she had ample opportunity of being well-informed, for her father's house was the resort of many able men on both sides of the question. The result was that, with all due respect toward her beloved parent, she, renounced his ecclesiastical views and attached herself to the Established Church. "I was educated among the Dissenters," she writes, "and because there was something remarkable in my leaving them at so early an age, not being full thirteen, I had drawn up an account of the whole transaction, under which I had included the main of the controversy between them and the Established Church as far as it had come to my knowledge." Clearly, Susanna Wesley is not to be considered as having merely accepted the ecclesiastical situation, turning "Churchwoman" by marriage.

III.

MARRIAGE.

Dr. Annesley's daughters were remarkable for their personal beauty, and from all accounts it would seem that the subject of this narrative shared this "dower." She was of average stature and slight frame.

"Some time, late in 1689 or early in 1690," Susanna Annesley was married to Samuel Wesley. Mr. Wesley was at that time a curate at a salary of £30 a year, and with his newly-wedded wife, took lodgings in London till the autumn of 1690, when he received the living of South Ormsby, in Lincolnshire, through the presentation of the Marquis of Normanby.

While exercising, in his pastoral duties, a diligence and faithfulness such as to put him for the most part above censure, the young husband toiled hard in literary work for the support of his household, and by various publications of a theological character in verse and prose—at one time a metrical *Life of Christ*, at another a treatise on *The Hebrew Points*, and chiefly by articles in Dunton's *Athenian Oracle*—he earned the means of keeping his family at least above distress.

About the close of 1696 Samuel Wesley was presented to the parish of Epworth—a place destined to be irrevocably associated with his name. This promotion is said to have been awarded him by special desire of the Queen, to whom he had dedicated his *Metrical and Illustrated Life of Christ*.

IV.

EPWORTH.

Mr. and Mrs. Wesley, with their family of four children—one son and three daughters, the youngest of these being an infant in arms—duly took possession of their new sphere. The promotion proved to be a hard parish and a humble abode. The landowners were comparatively poor, and of small culture in mind or morals. The people were proportionately subject to hardships in their mode of life, and were rude and even "savage" in character, as events were soon to prove.

There were seven rooms in the straw-roofed parsonage requiring new furniture, which had to be procured with borrowed money—a beginning of things that formed a grievous burden for many a day. The trade of the place consisted chiefly in the dressing of flax, which was extensively grown in the fields of the river-island of Axholme, in-which the village of Epworth stood, with its population of two thousand. The parsonage shared in this trade; but misfortunes soon came thickly.

A fire broke out (not the one that has become so celebrated) in 1702, and destroyed a third part of the house. Mrs. Wesley and the children were in the study when the alarm was raised, and "the mother, taking two of them in her arms, rushed through the smoke and flame;" another was with difficulty saved, and happily none were lost. A year later the rector's whole crop of flax was consumed.

The famous fire took place in 1709. According to Mrs. Wesley's account—"When we opened the street door, the strong north-east wind drove the flames in with such violence that none could stand against them. But some of our children got out through the windows, the rest through a little door into the garden. I was not in a condition to climb up to the windows, neither could I get to the garden door. I endeavoured three times to force my passage through the street door, but was as often driven back by the fury of the flames. In this distress I besought our blessed Saviour for help, and then waded through the fire, as I was, which did me no further harm than a little scorching my hands and my face." The sequel is of undying interest to the Church and the world. One sweet child, six years of age, had been left sleeping upstairs: the father made frantic attempts to reach him by the burning staircase, but in vain, and finally fell on his knees in the passage, solemnly committing the child's soul to God.

The boy, awaking after some bewilderment with the glare that looked to him as daylight, climbed upon a chest at the window, and was seen. Men, rightly guided, did not lose the last chance by waiting for a ladder, but, mounting one upon the other's shoulders, some two or three in this way saved the child, who became the famous John Wesley.

When John had been saved, the father turned to the men who had saved the boy, with the words: "Come, neighbours, let us kneel down; let us give thanks to God; He has given me all my eight children. Let the house go; I am rich enough."

This terrible occurrence was attended by consequences which made the noble Christian mother anxious for her children, in another way. Being now dispersed among various households of the village for sleeping accommodation, the little ones were, for a time, in danger of those evil communications that corrupt good manners. From this the kindness of the few who sheltered them could scarcely defend them, for the malice of the many was great against their parish minister. The grounds of ill-will and persecution were political rather than personal. It is strongly suspected that these fires were, in every instance, the deed of incendiaries. The rector's cattle had been mutilated. The children had curses flung at them in the street, and on occasion of Mr. Wesley's absence at Lincoln to record his vote, many cowardly devices were resorted to by way of alarming the family at all hours of the night. One new-born child had been, owing to Mrs. Wesley's exhaustion and danger, committed to the care of a nurse. This poor woman, losing sleep by the cruel noises purposely raised outside, at last, far in the night, fell into a heavy slumber and "overlaid the child." Cold and dead, they brought it to the poor mother.

It was political spite, also, that was at the bottom of the conduct of a creditor, who caused the rector to be arrested for debt, at the church door, after a baptismal service, and hurried off to Lincoln Castle, "leaving his lambs among so many wolves." In prison Mr. Wesley engaged in an earnest work of evangelising his "brother jail-birds," as he called them; his conduct at this period more than realising the world-renowned picture which Goldsmith has drawn of his incarcerated Vicar of Wakefield. Susanna Wesley now strove to support herself and her children by means of the diary, but, fearing lest her husband should be pining in want, she sent to him her wedding-ring, beseeching him by this to get a little money for his comfort. He returned it with words of tender gratitude, saying that "God would soon provide." Indeed, being by this time regarded as a martyr to his political principles, he was approached by some brethren of the clergy seeking to deliver him, and an arrangement was made, after three months, by which he was liberated.

V.

THE SCHOOL IN THE HOME.

It would appear that, ultimately, the family of Susanna Wesley was almost as numerous as that of her father had been. A singular want of accuracy characterises all the records, but it is safe to say that her children were some eighteen or nineteen in number. Death came often during those years of persecution. John Wesley speaks of the serenity with which his mother "worked among her thirteen children;" but ten was the number of those who were spared to enjoy the blessing of that enlightened, affectionate, and admirable training on her part, which has been so fully recorded, and of which the fruits were witnessed especially in the eminence of her sons Charles and John. She paid the utmost attention to physical training. Punctuality in the hours of sleep was carefully carried out from infancy through the years that followed. The rules regarding food were all admirable, and the younger children were early promoted to a place at the parents' own table. Mrs. Wesley has committed all these matters to writing, and her own words are valuable for their wisdom. "In order to form the minds of children, the first thing to be done is to conquer the will. To inform the understanding is a work of time, and must, with children, proceed by slow degrees as they are able to bear it. But the subjecting the will is a thing which must be done at once, and the sooner the better." "Then a child is capable of being governed by the reason and piety of its parents, till its own understanding comes to maturity."

Again she writes: "Cowardice and fear of punishment often lead children into lying," and accordingly, to save her own from temptation, the rule was—"whoever was charged with a fault of which they were guilty, if they would ingenuously confess it and promise to amend should not be beaten." The most careful discrimination was made between inadvertent and deliberate falsehood.

"If they amended, they were never upbraided afterward." Kindly commendation was regularly awarded to obedience evidently done at a sacrifice. "When the thing crossed the child's own inclinations, and when any of them performed an act of obedience, or did any thing with an intention to please, though the performance was not well, yet the obedience and intention were kindly accepted, and the child with sweetness directed how to do better for the future."

Recreation was liberally allowed, and outdoor physical amusements encouraged. "High glee and frolic," so notably appearing in the narrative that, in after days, some writers thought to turn this matter against John Wesley, remarking that he had himself been indulged by his mother at home in amusements which he was now prohibiting to the students under him at college. He made the difference of age and the demands of duty his defence, rather than any difference of principle.

Here, surely, the motherly instinct of this remarkable woman may be of use to-day, in clearing the line of duty in the question of amusements.

"Your arguments against horse-races do certainly conclude against masquerades, balls, plays, operas, and all such light and vain diversions. I will not say it is impossible for a person to have any sense of religion who frequents these; but I never, throughout the course of my long life, knew as much as one serious Christian that did; nor can I see how a lover of God can have any relish for them."

"Take this rule—whatever weakens your reason, impairs the tenderness of your conscience, obscures your sense of God, or takes off the relish of spiritual things—in short, whatever increases the strength and authority of your body over your mind—that thing is sin to you, however innocent it may be in itself."

She fixed the age of five for the teaching to a child the letters of the alphabet; and tells us that in all cases except two, the first day saw the conquest of the alphabet. The birthday festivities over, next morning the child went to the schoolroom of the house, where no one must come into the room from "nine till twelve or from two till five," while the teacher devoted herself entirely to that one pupil. Another feature of the method was the abolition of the study of syllables, and the immediate and usually successful advance into words and sentences, such as the opening verses of the Bible, "In the beginning God created the heaven and the earth."

"It is almost incredible," said Mrs. Wesley, "what a child may be taught in a quarter of a year." To this period belongs the well-known incident—when one day Mr. Wesley said to his wife while engaged in repeating a lesson to a dull child, "I wonder at your patience: you have told that child twenty times that same thing," and the mother replied—"Had I satisfied myself by mentioning the matter only nineteen times, I should have lost all my labour; you see, it was the twentieth time that crowned the whole."

VI.

THE CHURCH IN THE HOME.

The children at Epworth were well grounded in the observance of Divine worship. We may look in vain in the records of many families for anything so deep and so beautiful as that one thing which is told of them—that before they could kneel or speak the little ones were taught to ask a blessing on their food by appropriate, signs. Repeating, as soon as they were able to articulate, the Lord's Prayer morning and evening, they were encouraged to add sentences of prayers of their own conceiving, petitions for their parents, and requests for things of their own earnest desire. From this period, in each case, the parental eye was already carefully looking forward, to the time when the mind should begin to think for itself; and to help them in this important matter, Mrs. Wesley, remembering her own mental struggles, prepared for her children a book of Divinity, written for their special edification.

In due time, as the children grew a little older, days of the week were allotted to each of them, for special opportunity of conversation with their mother, as distinct from being catechised by her. This was for the purpose of dealing with "doubts and difficulties." Of the well-recorded list of days and names the "Thursday with Jacky," and "Saturday with Charles," will mostly arrest the reader now. These days came to be fondly treasured in the memory of all the children.

Twenty years after John Wesley had left home, it is touching to hear him say—"In many things you have interceded for me and prevailed.

Who knows but in this too—a complete renunciation of the world—you may be successful?" "If you can spare me only that little part of Thursday evening which you formerly bestowed upon me in another manner, I doubt not it would be as useful now for correcting my heart, as it was then for forming my judgment."

Yet one more feature of Mrs. Wesley's plan of education was that of the children's appointed conversations with one another, the eldest with the youngest, the second eldest with the next in age, and so on. To this good purpose was devoted the better space available in the rooms of the "New Rectory," built after the fire.

VII.

STRUGGLES WITH POVERTY.

All this work of education, intellectual and spiritual, was conducted under severe pressure of poverty. When Mr. Wesley received the living of Epworth, it cost him fifty pounds to have the great seal affixed to his title, and to remove his family to the place. This unfortunately was but a specimen of the hard conditions under which he held his cure.

Lord Oxford wrote to the celebrated Dean Swift, soliciting his name as a subscriber to Mr. Wesley's book on Job—"The person concerned is a worthy, honest man; and by this work of his, he is in hopes to get free of a load of debt which has hung upon him some years. This debt is not owing to any folly or extravagance of his, but to the calamity of his house having been twice burnt, which he was obliged to rebuild. This is in short the case of an honest, poor, worthy clergyman, and I hope you will take him under your protection."

A wealthy brother of Mr. Wesley professed himself quite "scandalised" at the constant struggles of the family, and did a little for the wiping away of the reproach, but no more. "Tell me, Mrs. Wesley, whether you ever really wanted bread?" said the good Archbishop Sharp one day, by way of preface to a very generous donation on the spot. "My Lord," was the reply, "I will freely own to your grace that, strictly speaking, I never did want bread. But then I had so much care to get it before it was eat, and to pay for it after as has often made it very unpleasant to me. And I think to have bread on such terms is the next degree of wretchedness to having none at all."

"All this, thank God," said Mr. Wesley, "does not in the least sink my wife's spirits. She bears it with a courage which becomes her, and which I expected from her."

Mrs. Wesley's meditations on the matter carry with them an unchanging serenity of mind. "That man whose heart is penetrated with Divine love, and enjoys the manifestations of God's blissful presence, is happy, let his outward condition be what it will. This world, this present state of things, is but for a time. What is now future will be present, as what is already past once was. And then, as Pascal observes, a little earth thrown on our cold head will for ever determine our hopes and condition. Nor will it signify much who personated the prince or the beggar, since, with respect to the exterior, all must stand on the same level after death."

In a very dark hour she writes: "But even in this low ebb of fortune I am not without some kind interval . . . I adore and praise the unsearchable wisdom and boundless goodness of Almighty God for this dispensation of His providence towards me. For I clearly discern there is more of mercy in this disappointment of my hopes than there would have been in permitting me to enjoy all that I desired, because it hath given me a sight and sense of some sins which I had not before. I would not have imagined I was in the least inclined to idolatry, and covetousness, and want of practical subjection to the will of God . . . Again, the furnace of affliction which now seems so hot and terrible to nature, had nothing more than a lambent flame, which was not designed to consume us, but only to purge away our dross, to purify and prepare the mind for its abode among those blessed ones that passed through the same trials before us into the celestial paradise . . . How shall we then adore and praise what we cannot here apprehend aright! How will love and joy work in the soul! But I cannot express it; I cannot conceive it."

VIII.

A NEW DEPARTURE.

Where the great religious movement of the last century in England is to be traced to any human influence, the mother of John and Charles Wesley must have a large share of the sacred honour. This will be found to fall to her by right, not only on account of that profound religious education she imparted to her children, but also by reason of the peculiar direction which she gave it. Even in respect of their first institution of assemblies for the preaching of the Gospel outside the walls of churches or any stated places of worship, Susanna Wesley may be discovered to have led the way.

In the year 1711, during one of the protracted sojournings of Mr. Wesley in London attending Convocation, and also doing business with his publishers, his place at the parish church was supplied by a curate whose ministrations were not particularly efficient, although, as may be judged from things already told, the people of Epworth were not likely to be very exacting.

However, a notable reaction of feeling in favour of their minister had set in since the days of the fire, and the parishioners were, many of them, quietly attentive to Divine ordinances. Mrs. Wesley, without any pronounced hostility on her part toward the curate, felt a deep echo of the popular complaint in her own soul. Divine service at church had been cut down to one diet in the morning, and hence, to save her children and servants from temptation of mere idleness, the gifted mother felt herself called to set up a kind of service at the parsonage. Of this step she duly apprised her husband, saying: "I cannot but look upon every soul you leave under my care as a talent committed to me, under a trust by the great Lord of all the families of heaven and earth; and if I am unfaithful to Him or to you in neglecting to improve those talents, how shall I answer unto Him when He shall command me to render an account of my stewardship?"

As yet, all she had done was reading to, and instructing her own family. But the news of this spread in Epworth, and a hunger for the Word arose. The parents, brothers, and sisters of the servants dropped in till the audience was about thirty or forty. The services consisted of praise, prayer, and reading of a short sermon. At this time Mrs. Wesley's mind was greatly stimulated by the accounts she had been perusing of the devoted labours of two Danish missionaries in India. She felt impelled "to do somewhat" for Christ.

Conversation with the neighbours who had come to the parsonage-meetings shaped itself into meetings of inquirers. She now fell back upon the library, in quest of "more awakening sermons," which were found among her husband's stock of Puritan authors.

The attendance at the services now increased so as completely to fill the rooms. At length some three or four persons, headed by the curate, wrote to the rector in London concerning the doings of his wife and the danger of a "conventicle." Mr. Wesley was sufficiently interested and apprehensive to write to her and ask what had been done, and whether it did not look "particular." To this his wife, rather glad to be challenged, lost no time in replying; and her written explanation to the head of the house and parish has resulted in our possessing an ample account of the movement. "As to its looking particular," she said, "I grant it does, and so does almost everything that is serious, or that may any way advance the glory of God or the salvation of souls, if it be performed out of a pulpit or in the way of common conversation." After giving various reasons for her action, she proceeds: "Now, I beseech you, weigh all these things in an impartial balance . . . If you do, after all, think fit to dissolve this assembly, do not tell me that you desire me to do it, for that will not satisfy my conscience; but send me your positive command in such full and express terms as may absolve me from all guilt and punishment for the neglecting this opportunity of doing good, when you and I shall appear before the great and awful tribunal of our Lord Jesus Christ."

No wonder that all opposition on the part of the rector from this moment disappeared, and on returning to his charge he found many signs of a happy change, and that all things were as if freshened under the dew of the blessing of God.

IX.

RELATION TO HER SONS.

Susanna Wesley was the life-long counsellor of her children.

Amid those interesting conversations which were held with each member of the family on appointed days and hours, and which are frequently noted in Mrs. Wesley's private meditations, we are arrested by the heading of one of them—"Son John"—and we learn that he became a communicant at the Lord's table at eight years of age, this important step being taken by reason of his great seriousness and of the signs of grace that were seen in him.

His mother gives us another striking glimpse of him, in April 1712, when the scourge of small-pox attacked five of the children—"Jack bore his disease bravely like a man, and indeed a Christian without any complaint."

On recovering he was, through the influence of the Duke of Buckingham, to whom his father was known, sent to Charterhouse School; but at this period there is little or nothing recorded of correspondence with his mother. It is tolerably clear that the reason of this was that the boy was studious to a degree, and needed his father's injunction to see to it that he took regular exercise in the garden. The letters of Mrs. Wesley to her sons are best represented by those addressed to Samuel, now twenty years of age. After having distinguished himself at Westminster School, and won the special regard and friendship of those two eminent men, Bishops Sprat and Atterbury, Samuel repaired to Oxford. Following the fashion of the time, the youth had hitherto addressed his mother as "Dear Madam." His mother disliked the phrase, but had waited till the change should be made spontaneously to "Dear Mother," which instantly evoked the response, "Dear Sammy,—I am much better pleased with the beginning of your letter than with that you used to send me, for I do not love distance or ceremony; there is more of love and tenderness in the name of *mother* than in all the complimentary titles in the world . . . You complain that you are unstable and inconstant in the ways of virtue. Alas! what Christian is not so too? I am sure that I, above all others, am most unfit to advise in such a case: yet since I love you as my own soul, I will endeavour to do as well as I can."

Admirable advice is then given as to choice of company, with strictness yet with charity, for "we must take the world as we find it;" and the wholesome caution to beware "lest the comparing yourself with others may be an occasion of your falling into too much vanity," and "rather entertain such thoughts as these, 'Though I know my own birth and advantages, yet how little do I know of the circumstances of others!' 'Were they so solemnly devoted to God at their birth as I was?' You have had the example of a father who served God from his youth; and though I cannot commend my own to you, for it is too bad to be imitated, yet surely my earnest prayers for many years and some little good advice have not been wanting . . . If still upon comparison you seem better than others are, then ask yourself who it is that makes you differ: and let God have all the praise . . . I am straitened for paper and time, therefore must conclude. God Almighty bless you and preserve you from all evil. Adieu.

"SUSANNA WESLEY."

It is a striking fact that Mrs. Wesley's letters to her son John are for the most part concerning his secular affairs; the inference is not remote that, as regards his spiritual welfare, John Wesley appeared to his mother at all times to be in a satisfactory condition. At one time he presses her for an opinion on Thomas à Kempis, and receives an elaborate answer, at once philosophical and theological, in the course of which the remark is made—"I take à Kempis to have been an honest weak man, with more zeal than knowledge, by his condemning all mirth or pleasure as sinful or useless, in opposition to so many plain and direct texts of Scripture. 'Tis stupid to say nothing is an affliction to a good man; nor do I understand how any man can thank God for present misery, yet do I know very well what it is to rejoice in the midst of deep afflictions. Not in the affliction itself, for then it would cease to be one; but in this we may rejoice, that we are in the hand of a God who has promised that all things shall work together for good, for the spiritual and eternal good, of those that love Him." Evidently it is from an unshaken soul the concluding words of the letter proceed—"Your brother has brought us a heavy reckoning for you and Charles. God be merciful to us all!"

Much earnest and deeply discriminative advice is given to John on occasion of his entering the holy ministry. The letter then written to him abounds with traces of the fact that he had been in the habit of confiding much of his mind to his mother through those years. In 1727 she writes to him a profound and beautiful epistle, in terms which indicate that he had made her his *confidante* at the time, in his love for a young lady whom he had lately met in Worcestershire.

"What then is love? Oh, how shall we describe its strange, mysterious essence? It is—I do not know what! A powerful something; source of our joy and grief, felt and experienced by every one, and yet unknown to all! Nor shall we ever comprehend what it is till we are united to our first principle, and there read its wondrous nature in the clear mirror of uncreated love:"

Another letter belonging to the same year is solemnly prospective the topic being evidently the "cares of the world."

> "'Believe me, youth (for I am read in cares,
> And bend beneath the weight of more than fifty years).'

"Believe me, old age is the worst time we can choose to mend either our lives or our fortunes. Ah! my dear son, did you with me stand on the verge of life, and saw before your eyes a vast expanse, an unlimited duration of being, which you might shortly enter upon, you can't conceive how all the inadvertencies, mistakes, and sins of youth would rise to your view; and how different the, sentiments of sensitive pleasures, the desire of sexes and pernicious friendships of the world would be then from what they are now while health is entire and seems to promise many years of life."

X

WIDOWHOOD.

The Rector of Epworth had been slowly mastering his difficulties with the world. The circumstances of the family seem to have taken a favourable turn from the year 1724, when the small living of Wroote, four miles distant, and valued at £50 a year, was added to that of Epworth. The family removed to Wroote, and many of Mrs. Wesley's most interesting letters are dated from the parsonage there. Her husband continued to toil for some years at what he meant to be his great work—his commentary on the Book of Job—but the outer man was visibly perishing. His now palsied hand required the services of an amanuensis. "My eyes and my heart," he said, "are now almost all I have left; and bless God for them!" He died on the 25th of April, 1735, in the 72nd year of his age.

His death was marked by many utterances of faith and of joy in God, and by his memorable saying to his sons—"Be steady! The Christian faith will surely revive in this kingdom. You shall see it, though I shall not."

It was Samuel who was now for the most part charged with the support of his mother; but in this duty there was a generous rivalry among her children. The name of John appears in discharge of the last of his father's liabilities that had been cruelly pressed upon the very day of the funeral; and Charles writes to Samuel—"My mother desires you will remember that she is a clergyman's widow. Let the Society give her what they please, she must be still, in some degree, burdensome to you. How do I envy you that glorious burden, and wish I could share it with you."

Mrs. Wesley having now left the "old place," settled for a little in the neighbouring town of Gainsborough, and afterwards resided with Samuel at Tiverton from September, 1736, till July, 1737.

Her sons John and Charles had now set out upon their well-known Gospel enterprise to the State of Georgia in America. Their mother signalised the hour by a letter full of solemn and ennobling thought, in which she allows herself but slightly to touch upon the fact of separation, and gives her own personal version of the apostle's "strait betwixt two"— "One thing often troubles me: that notwithstanding I know that while we are present with the body we are absent from the Lord; notwithstanding I have no taste, no relish left for anything the world calls pleasure, yet I do not long to go home, as in reason I ought to do. This often shocks me. Pray for me that God would make me better, and take me at the best."

The Georgian mission of her sons having ended, to her joy, in their return home, a great work immediately opened for them in England. It now became apparent, in their consultations with their mother, that the views of Divine truth and even of the mode of propagating the Gospel, which were taking possession of their minds, had to her been long and deeply familiar as the desire of her heart. Her testimony was all the more valuable that it was given with much caution.

Samuel wrote to her complaining of the new ideas of his brothers John and Charles, and appealing confidently to her verdict in the matter. He found that she mainly coincided with the returned missionaries in those convictions regarding the Gospel doctrines of faith and instantaneous conversion that were so soon to move the world.

At the same time she shared his apprehensions regarding certain things in the work that bore an aspect of extravagance. "I should think that the reviving these pretentious to dreams, visions, etc., is not only vain and frivolous as to the matter of them, but also of dangerous consequence to the weaker sort of Christians. As far as I can see, they plead that these visions, etc., are given to assure some particular persons of their adoption and salvation. But this end is abundantly provided for in the Holy Scripture's, wherein all may find the rules by which we must live here and be judged hereafter. And if, upon a serious review of our state, we find that in the tenour of our lives we have or do now sincerely desire and endeavour to perform the conditions of the Gospel covenant required on our parts, then we may discern that the Holy Spirit hath laid in our minds a good foundation of a strong, reasonable, and lively hope of God's mercy through Christ."

To the communications of John and Charles regarding the fresh baptism of the Spirit that had come upon them, she wrote expressing her thankfulness for the glad tidings, only remarking to Charles that she thought he had surely fallen into an "odd way of thinking," in stating that till within a few months he had no spiritual life nor any justifying faith. "Blessed be God, who showed you the necessity you were in of a Saviour to deliver you from the power of sin and Satan, for Christ will be no Saviour but to such as see their need of one. Blessed be His holy name, that thou hast found Him a Saviour to thee, my son! Oh, let us love Him much, for we have much forgiven."

XI.

THE FOUNDRY AT MOORFIELDS.

Susanna Wesley came to London in April, 1739, to spend the rest of her days in a place that had been well prepared for her. John had found a centre at Moorfields for his work in the metropolis. Out of a disused Government foundry had been constructed a chapel, a house for the lay-preachers, and apartments for himself, where he wished to have his mother come and live with him. The new home, though but scantily furnished, proved to her a little paradise in the communion she now enjoyed with her son, in the easy access of all her children to her, and in the pleasure of seeing the great work and increase of the Gospel. Here also she received in her own soul a wonderful increase of blessing—so much surpassing all her experience hitherto as to cause her to make the reflection that "she had scarce heard, till then, such a thing mentioned as the having God's Spirit bear witness with our spirit." "But two or three weeks ago, while my son Hall was pronouncing these words in delivering the cup to me, 'The blood of our Lord Jesus Christ which was given for thee,' the words struck through my heart, and I knew God for Christ's sake had forgiven me all my sins."

It caused her no apparent pain a little after to receive a letter from her son Samuel, saying: "It was with exceeding concern and grief I heard you had countenanced a spreading delusion, so far as to be one of Jack's congregation. Is it not enough that I am bereft of both my brothers, but must my mother follow too? I earnestly beseech the Almighty to preserve you from joining a schism at the close of your life, as you were unfortunately engaged in one at the beginning of it. It will cost you many a protest, should you retain your integrity, as I hope to God you will." The new joy of his mother evidently so abounded in charity as to drown all bitterness and take away all fear of any real separation between them.

Samuel died in the autumn of the same year, during an illness of his mother, and John Wesley left the house that day rather than break the sad news to her, and one of his sisters was commissioned to do it with all gentleness. We find nothing but sweetness and hope in the letter which Susanna Wesley was enabled to write to her son Charles:—"Your brother was exceedingly dear to me in this life, and perhaps I have erred in loving him too well. I once thought it impossible to bear his loss, but none know what they can bear till they are tried. I rejoice in having a comfortable hope of my dear son's salvation. He is now at rest, and would not return to earth to gain the world. He hath reached the haven before me, but I shall soon follow him. He must not return to me, but I shall go to him, never to part more."

Many Christian friends continued to visit her at Moorfields; her conversation was prized by all, and her presence on the scene and at the centre of evangelism was a power for good. In true consistency with the memorable season at Epworth, and her own institution of the Church in the Home, Mrs. Wesley was privileged to give her testimony in favour of lay-preaching. To John Wesley the field was now indeed "the world," and his labours were multiplying past his strength. While he went from place to place, Mr. Thomas Maxfield, "a young man of good sense and piety," took charge of the work at Moorfields. His appointed duty extended to "the reading and explaining of the Scriptures to bands and classes;" but Maxfield soon went the length of public preaching, which he did with much ability and unction. John Wesley lost no time in coming home to check this "irregular proceeding." But his mother urged:—"John, you know what my sentiments have been. You cannot suspect me of readily favouring anything of this kind. But take care what you do with respect to this young man, for he is as surely called to preach as you are. Examine what have been the fruits of his preaching, and hear him yourself." This was done; and John Wesley said, "It is the Lord; let Him do what seemeth Him good. What am I that I should withstand God?"

Thus fitly, as became her already historic part in it, Susanna Wesley may he said to have launched the important institution of lay-preaching in the Church that bears her name.

XII.

LAST DAYS AND DEATH.

The life at Moorfields, which had been, to this venerable mother in Israel, of the character of a peaceful haven after a rough voyage, was now drawing rapidly to a close. Her bodily illnesses much resembled those of her husband's later years, and were, no doubt, to be in some measure attributed to the penury and hardship she had shared with him so long.

But we do not hear so much about her maladies us of the many signs of triumph over them, till by the month of July, 1742, the vital power is ebbing low, and her daughters gather round her. The sons were out in the field. Charles had bent over her with filial attentions, till, concluding in his own mind that her strength would hold out for a few days, he departed to his work, hoping soon to return.

John Wesley was at Bristol on Sunday evening the 18th of July, and had just ended preaching to a large congregation, when the message came that his mother was apparently near death.

He rode off immediately for London, which he reached on the 20th, and, as he says in his Journal, "I found my mother on the borders of eternity; but she has no doubt or fear, nor any desire but, as soon as God should call her, to depart and be with Christ." She enjoyed a quiet sleep on the evening of the 22nd, and awoke in the morning in a joyful frame of mind. Her children heard her say, "My dear Saviour, art Thou come to help me in my extremity at last?"

Utterances of praise at intervals filled the hours that remained, At four o'clock in the afternoon her son had left her for a little, that he might snatch some hasty refreshment in the adjoining room, when he was called back again to offer the commendatory prayer. "She opened her eyes wide and fixed them upward for a moment. Then the lids dropped, and the soul was set at liberty, without one struggle or groan or sigh, on the 23rd of July, 1742, aged seventy-three. We stood round the bed and fulfilled her last request, uttered a little before she lost her speech, 'Children, as soon as I am released, sing a psalm of praise to God.'"

There was a vast crowd at the funeral, at Bunhill Fields, on the 1st of August. John Wesley's voice faltered as he pronounced the words, "The soul of our dear mother here departed"—and the grief of the multitude broke out afresh. A hymn was sung, and he then stood forth and preached one of the most moving sermons that ever came from his lips, turning not upon the pathos of the funeral, but upon the Bible picture of the last judgment. Of the occasion he himself has said—"It was one of the most solemn assemblies I ever saw or expect to see, on this side eternity." The stone at the head of her grave was inscribed with her name, and with verses from the pen of her son Charles:—

HERE LIES THE BODY
OF
MRS. SUSANNA WESLEY,
YOUNGEST AND LAST SURVIVING DAUGHTER OF
DR. SAMUEL ANNESLEY.

In sure and stedfast hope to rise,
And claim her mansion in the skies,
A Christian hero her flesh laid down,
The cross exchanging for a crown;

True daughter of affection she,
Inured to pain and misery;
Mourned a long night of grief and fears—
A legal night of seventy years.

The Father then revealed His Son;
Him in the broken bread made known
She knew, and felt her sins forgiven,
And found the earnest of her heaven.

Meet for the fellowship above,
She heard the call, "Arise, My love!"
"I come," her dying looks replied,
And lamb-like, as her Lord, she died.

XIII.

CONCLUSION.

The title "Founder of Methodism," humanly speaking, must be shared between mother and son. To many minds this will seem to have been a question settled by the action of Mrs. Wesley at Epworth.

But her part in the matter shows a deepening beauty from the first in fulfilment of the words of her Journal concerning John, with special reference to his remarkable rescue from the fire, "I do intend to be more particularly careful of the soul of this child, that Thou hast so mercifully provided for."

When, at college, he and his brother, with their young companions, owing to their living by rule, first won the name of "Methodists," amid sneers and persecutions, his mother cheered him on. At that juncture, subsequently, when he was in a state of hesitancy as to entering the holy ministry, and his father had encouraged the idea of delay, his mother said, "The sooner you are a deacon the better"—and broke the spell of what might have been a fatal backwardness. On that evening, at Aldersgate Street, 24th May, 1738, so memorable in the spiritual history of Methodism, when John Wesley stood up in his newly-found fulness of the assurance of grace, and encountered much sharp rebuke on the spot, he had been well fortified beforehand with his mother's sympathy, saying, "She was glad he had got into such a just way of thinking." She also saw eye to eye with him in his position in the controversy between Calvinism and Arminianism.

The beginning of lay-preaching dates, as we have seen, from her support of Thomas Maxfield, and the leading features of the mode of preaching which John Wesley recommended to his followers may be found, long before, in his mother's counsels to himself—"to avoid nice distinctions in public assemblies"—to exalt Christ and the work of the Spirit. "Here you may give free scope to your souls," and "discourse without reserve, as His Spirit gives you utterance." Well does her son call her "in her measure and degree a preacher of righteousness."

So shines the bright light of Susanna Wesley all along the upbuilding of that great Christian society which bears the name of her sons. Her example must surely also be of special value at the present day, when, alike in the Church and in the world, the place of woman rises in importance, and the demand is for further opportunity of usefulness. For the life of this gifted and saintly woman is characterised by a modesty that is above criticism, and, at the same time, shows no lack of the greatness of power and achievement in the work of the Lord.

JAMES CUNNINGHAM, M.A.

MRS. HEMANS.

Mrs. Hemans is fully entitled to a place in the ranks of Excellent Women, not only on account of her personal character, but also on account of the work she did—a work removed from the "stunning tide," but not the less effectual.

There is no doubt that Mrs. Hemans exerted a distinct influence and made a distinct impression on the national character. She left the world unmistakably better for her having lived in it. Many do not realise what great abiding results flowed from her work. And one chief way in which she was productive of so much good to her race was this: she raised the standard of popular poetry, raised it at a time when it sadly needed raising, to a higher level and tone. "Though she wrote so much and in an age when Byron was the favourite poet of Englishmen, not a line left her pen that indicated anything but a spotless and habitually lofty mind." It was no mean achievement to establish the popularity of a poetry which was by its purity a rebuke to much that had hitherto passed current and received applause.

How well she succeeded in accomplishing the ends which, as we learn in that beautiful piece of hers, "A Poet's Dying Hymn," she had set before herself and others who gave expression to their thoughts in verse!

> "And if Thy Spirit on Thy child hath shed
>   The gift, the vision of the unsealed eye,
> To pierce the mist o'er life's deep meanings spread,
>   To reach the hidden fountain-urns that lie

Far in man's heart—if I have kept it free
And pure, a consecration unto Thee,
    I bless Thee, O my God!

* * * * *

Not for the brightness of a mortal wreath,
    Not for a place 'midst kingly minstrels dead,
But that, perchance, a faint gale of Thy breath,
    A still small whisper, in my song hath led
One struggling spirit upwards to Thy throne,
Or but one hope, one prayer—for this alone
    I bless Thee, O my God!"

    Many a straggler in life's perplexities found sympathy and help in the sweet verses of this poetess. They felt that there was one struggling by their side, one who could rest on God's promises, and could almost insensibly "weave links for intercourse with God."

I.

EARLY DAYS.

Felicia Dorothea Browne was born in Duke Street, Liverpool, on the 25th of September, 1793. She was the second daughter and the fourth child of a family of three sons and three daughters. Her father, who was a native of Ireland, was a merchant of good position. Her mother, whose maiden name was Wagner, was the daughter of the Venetian consul in Liverpool. The original name was Veniero, but as the result of German alliances it had assumed this German form. Three members of the family had risen to the dignity of Doge. The first six years of Felicia's life were spent in Liverpool. Then commercial losses compelled her father to break up his establishment in that city and remove to Wales. The next nine years of her life were spent at Gwyrch, near Abergele, in North Wales. The house was a spacious old mansion, close to the seashore, and shut in on the land side by lofty hills. Surely a fit place for the early residence of a poetess of Nature. Besides this advantage of situation, she had the privilege of access to the treasures of a large library. The records of her early days show her to have been a child of extreme beauty, with a brilliant complexion and long, curling, golden hair. But her personal beauty was not the only thing that arrested attention. Her talents and sweetness of disposition retained the notice which her attractiveness had obtained. The old gardener used to say that "Miss Felicia could 'tice him to do whatever she pleased." And he was not the only one who fell under her gentle constraint. She was a general favourite.

This girl of many hopes had no regular education. She was never at school. Her mother's teaching and her own avidity for information were almost her only means of instruction. Mrs. Browne was a woman of high acquirements, both intellectual and moral, eminently adapted for the training of so sensitive a mind. For a time the child was taught French, English grammar, and the rudiments of Latin by a gentleman who used to regret that she was not a man, to have borne away the highest honours at college! A remarkable memory was of great benefit to her. Her sister states that she could repeat pages of poetry from her favourite authors after having read them over but once. On one occasion, to satisfy the incredulity of one of her brothers, she learned by heart the whole of Heber's poem of "Europe," containing four hundred and twenty-four lines, in an hour and twenty minutes. She repeated it without a single mistake or a moment's hesitation. Long pieces of both prose and poetry she would often recite after having twice glanced over them. This power of memory stood her in good stead in her later life, when physical weakness prevented her from writing down what she had composed. Her thoughts had to be retained in her mind, and then dictated.

When Felicia Browne was about eleven years old she spent the winter in London with her father and mother. But this visit had not the charm for her that it has for most young people. She saw nothing in the metropolis to compensate for the loss of the country. The sights and scenes of the busy throng were not so congenial as the sights and scenes of the quiet little Welsh home. "She longed to rejoin her younger brother and sister in their favourite rural haunts and amusements—the nutting wood, the beloved apple-tree, the old arbour, with its swing, the post-office tree, in whose trunk a daily interchange of letters was established, the pool where fairy-ships were launched (generally painted and decorated by herself), and, dearer still, the fresh, free ramble on the seashore, or the mountain 'expedition' to the Signal Station, or the Roman Encampment." Town parties and town conventionalities had little in them to gain favour in the eyes of this bonnie free country lass. Not that she did not sometimes derive pleasure from the sights she was taken to. Especially was she impressed by her visits to some of the great works of art. On entering a gallery of sculpture, she involuntarily exclaimed, "Oh, hush:—don't speak!"

II.

FIRST POEMS.

The first appearance in print! What an event in life is this! What a new world it seems to open out to the writer! Felicia Browne was fourteen years old when a collection of her poems was published. The earliest of these early compositions was written when she was only eight years of age.

The volume of poems appeared in 1808. Perhaps it would have been a more judicious course on the part of her friends if they had prevented them from appearing. The young girl of fourteen years was by her youth ill-fitted to face the criticisms of the literary world.

At this time there came across her path the person whose name she was afterwards to bear—Captain Hemans, of the King's Own Regiment. He was on a visit in the neighbourhood of Gwyrch, and soon became an intimate friend in the family which contained Felicia amongst its members. Before he was called upon to embark with his regiment for Spain, an impression had been created which three years' absence did not efface on either side. The friends of both parties hoped that it might be otherwise, and that nothing would come of this attachment. But their hopes were not to be realised.

III.

MARRIAGE.

In 1809 the Browne family removed to Bronwylfa, near St. Asaph. Her self-education and her literary work went on side by side.

Captain Hemans returned to Wales in 1811, and in the following year he was married to Miss Browne. His appointment as adjutant to the Northamptonshire Militia caused them to take up their residence at Daventry, a neighbourhood by its tameness strangely contrasting with her "own mountain-land." But she was not to be long away from her old home. The next year, on the reduction of the corps, a return was made to Bronwylfa. Mrs. Hemans was never again, until death parted them, to leave her mother, "by whose unwearied spirit of love and hope she was encouraged to bear on through all the obstacles which beset her path." A period of domestic privacy in association with literary occupation and study followed. Five children, all sons, were given to her. One can easily understand how many calls there were now on her, as, her marriage being not altogether a happy one, she had to arrange the education of her children. How well she trained them, not only in temporal wisdom, but in the highest of all wisdom, many evidences show. We may anticipate and insert an anecdote of one of her boys at the age of eleven. She had been reading to him Lord Byron's magnificent address to the sea:—

"Roll on, thou deep and dark-blue ocean, roll."

He listened with breathless attention, and at the close broke out with these words—"It is very grand indeed!—but how much finer it would have been, mamma, if he had said at the close, that God had measured out all those waters with the hollow of His hand!" On another occasion she was explaining to her eight-year-old boy the meaning of the title of a story he was reading, "The Atheist." His argument was real and ready: "Not believe in a God, mamma? Who does he expect made the world and his own body?"

IV.

WORK AND FRIENDS.

The plentiful contributions from her pen were becoming increasingly popular, and it may be added increasingly useful. There is no doubt that she was a distinct moral power for good.

As almost every one thinks that he or she can compose poetry, and that better than others, it often happens that in a prize poem competition there is no lack of persons ready to enter the lists. So it was when a patriotic Scotchman offered a prize of £50 for the best poem on "The meeting of Wallace and Bruce." The number of competitors was astounding, and the mass of matter sent in overwhelming, one production being as long as "Paradise Lost." Quality prevailed over quantity, and the award was made to Mrs. Hemans. This was not the only occasion on which she was adjudged the prize in a competition. In 1821 she obtained that awarded by the Royal Society of Literature for the best poem on "Dartmoor."

One of her poems, which was destined to be almost more useful than any of the others, was "The Sceptic." A reviewer's testimony to the elevating influence of the work, after complaining of the grave defect in some of the most popular writers of the day, in that "they are not sufficiently attentive to the moral dignity of the performances," concludes with this encomium on Mrs. Hemans' work:—"With the promise of talents not inferior to any, and far superior to most of them, the author before us is not only free from every stain, but breathes all moral beauty and loveliness; and it will be a memorable coincidence if the era of a woman's sway in literature shall become co-eval with the return of its moral purity and elevation." A more gratifying testimony to the worth of "The Sceptic" was given in a visit of a stranger to Mrs. Hemans. It occurred many years after "The Sceptic" was published; indeed, a very short time before her death. The visitor was told that she was unable to see him, as she was only just recovering from an illness. He entreated for a few minutes' interview with such importunity that it was granted to him. On his admission he explained with the utmost feeling that the object of his visit was to acknowledge the deepest debt of obligation; "that to her he owed, in the first instance, that faith and those hopes which were now more precious to him than life itself; for that it was by reading her poem of 'The Sceptic' he had been first awakened from the miserable delusion of infidelity and induced to 'search the Scriptures.'" This was not the only time she received a comforting assurance of this kind with regard to the poem.

The warm friendship of the Bishop of St. Asaph, Dr. Luxmoore, was a great boon to Mrs. Hemans. He was always ready with his advice and his support; and she found them of singular benefit in her comparatively lonely position. The bishop's palace was like a second home. There she and her children were always welcome. Of like value was the friendship of another who was also destined to have a place on the episcopal bench. Reginald Heber was a frequent visitor at the residence of his father-in-law, the Dean of St. Asaph. He soon became deeply interested in the welfare of Mrs. Hemans. She found in him one whose counsel, especially in literary matters, was of the utmost value. His suggestions and encouragement supplied just what she wanted. Any one who reads his hints with regard to her contemplated poem "Superstition and Revelation" will know how full and painstaking was the trouble he took to assist his friend.

The design of the poem to which reference has just been made was a grand one. It is best described in her own words: "Might not a poem of some extent and importance, if the execution were at all equal to the design, be produced, from contrasting the spirit and tenets of

Paganism with those of Christianity? It would contain, of course, much classical allusion; and all the graceful and sportive fictions of ancient Greece and Italy, as well as the superstitions of more barbarous climes, might be introduced, to prove how little consolation they could convey in the hour of affliction, or hope in that of death. Many scenes from history might be portrayed in illustration of this idea; and the certainty of a future state, and of the immortality of the soul, which we derive from revelation, are surely subjects for poetry of the highest class." The poem was commenced, but never completed. It was pressed out by other undertakings.

V.

THE HOME IN WALES.

Mrs. Hemans found peculiar pleasure in reading and speaking German. "I am so delighted," she wrote, "when I meet with any one who knows and loves my favourite *scelenvolle* (full of soul) German, that I believe I could talk of it for ever." Her sister remarks that her knowledge of the language seemed almost as if it had been born with her.

The poetess could write humorous prose as well as serious verse. Some of her letters written in 1822 give a very amusing description of the inconveniences she had to put up with whilst certain alterations were being made at Bronwylfa. She describes how at last she was driven to seek refuge in the laundry, from which classical locality, she was wont to say, it could be no wonder if sadly *mangled* lines were to issue. "I entreat you to pity me. I am actually in the melancholy situation of Lord Byron's 'scorpion girt by fire'—her circle narrowing as she goes—for I have been pursued by the household troops through every room successively, and begin to think of establishing my *métier* in the cellar; though I dare say, if I were to fix myself as comfortably in a hogshead as Diogenes himself, it would immediately be discovered that some of the hoops or staves wanted repair." "There is a war of old grates with new grates, and plaster and paint with dust and cobwebs, carrying on in this once tranquil abode, with a vigour and animosity productive of little less din than that occasioned by 'lance to lance and horse to horse.' I assure you, when I make my escape about 'fall of eve' to some of the green quiet hayfields by which we are surrounded, and look back at the house, which, from a little distance, seems almost, like Shakespeare's moonlight, to 'sleep upon the bank,' I can hardly conceive how so gentle-looking a dwelling can continue to send forth such an incessant clatter of obstreperous sound through its honeysuckle-fringed windows. It really reminds me of a pretty shrew, whose amiable smiles would hardly allow a casual observer to suspect the possibility of so fair a surface being occasionally ruffled by storms."

The lyric "The Voice of Spring" was written in 1823. It was followed by "Breathings of Spring." The season of spring had a marked influence upon her. It was, with all its joy and beauty, generally "a time of thoughtfulness rather than mirth." It has been well observed that autumn in one way is a more joyous time than spring. It reminds us that "we shall go to them," while in spring everything seems to say "they will not return to us."

> "But what awakest thou in the *heart*, O Spring!
>   The human heart, with all its dreams and sighs?
> Thou that givest back so many a buried thing,
>   Restorer of forgotten harmonies!
> Fresh songs and scents break forth where'er thou art—
>   What wakest thou in the heart?
>
> Too much, oh, then too much! We know not well
>   Wherefore it should be thus, yet, roused by thee,
> What fond, strange yearnings, from the soul's deep cell,
>   Gush for the faces we no more may see!
> How are we lamented, in the wind's low tone,
>   By voices that are gone?"

In 1825 there appeared one of her principal works—the one she considered as almost, if not altogether, the best—*The Forest Sanctuary*. It related to the sufferings of a Spanish Protestant in the time of Philip II., and is supposed to be narrated by the sufferer himself, who escapes with his child to a North American forest. The picture of the burial at sea was the passage of whose merits she had the highest opinion.

VI.

MOTHER AND DAUGHTER.

Another change of home took place in 1825. The new home was not more than a quarter of a mile from the old one. Rhyllon could be seen from the windows of Bronwylfa. It was a very different house. The former is described as a tall, staring brick house, almost destitute of trees; the latter as a perfect bower of roses, peeping out like a bird's-nest from amidst the foliage in which it was embosomed. The contrast is playfully depicted in a dramatic scene between Bronwylfa and Rhyllon. The former, after standing for some time in silent contemplation of Rhyllon, breaks out into the following vehement strain of vituperation:—

> "You ugliest of fabrics! you horrible eyesore!
> I wish you would vanish, or put on a vizor!
> In the face of the sun, without covering or rag on,
> You stand and outstare me, like any red dragon."

And so on through many amusing and spirited lines, showing the lighter side of the authoress's character. Her sister describes this part of her life as perhaps the happiest of all, and this was produced to a great extent by her seeing the happiness of others, especially that of her boys. She was always ready to join them in their rambles and their sports. The mornings were spent in the instruction of her children, then in answering countless letters and satisfying the demands of impatient editors. And this done, she would revel in the enjoyment of fresh air. "Soft winds and bright blue skies," she writes, "make me, or dispose me to be, a sad idler." For this reason she delighted in the rigour of winter, as being most conducive to literary productiveness.

A heavy sorrow was overshadowing this happy home. Between Mrs. Hemans and her mother there was the strongest bond of affection. In her poems there may be traced the intensity of this love. It is found in the simple lines, "On my Mother's Birthday," when the child was only eight years old, and, after incidentally appearing in many a poem, it is shown in all its intensity in the "Hymn by the Sick-bed of a Mother."

> "Father, that in the olive shade,
>   When the dark hour came on,
> Didst, with a breath of heavenly aid,
>   Strengthen Thy Son;
>
> Oh, by the anguish of that night,
>   Send us down blest relief;
> Or to the chastened, let Thy might
>   Hallow this grief!"

And if the flame of passionate affection shone out in the time of fear and impending sorrow, no less was it seen after the dread hour had come. What beauty there is in the lines entitled "The Charmed Picture":—

> "Sweet face, that o'er my childhood shone,
>   Whence is thy power of change,
> Thus ever shadowing back my own,
>   The rapid and the strange?

> Whence are they charmed—those earnest eyes?
>   I know the mystery well!
> In mine own trembling bosom lies
>   The spirit of the spell!"

This mother patiently bore sickness for eight months, and then passed away. Something of what this blow meant to the loving daughter may be gathered from her letters. But she knew where true comfort was to be found, and in alluding to the words of another setting forth the Divine consolation, she says, "This is surely the language of real consolation; how different from that which attempts to soothe us by general remarks on the common lot, the course of Nature, or even by dwelling on the release of the departed from pain and trial."

It was not surprising that her health, for a long time delicate, now showed signs of an alarming nature. She often had a complete prostration of strength, succeeded by a wonderful reaction.

VII.

REMOVAL FROM WALES.

The place of Mrs. Hemans in the literary world was established. As might be expected, friendships were formed with those who had tastes in common. Amongst the number were Miss Baillie, Miss Mitford, Mrs. Howitt, Miss Jewsbury, and Dean Milman. From her friends she sought sympathy rather than praise. Always appreciative of words of encouragement, she gave back good exchange in the artless way into which she entered into the pursuits of her correspondents.

Her health continued to give great anxiety to her friends, and matters were not improved by the unconquerable dislike of the patient to the adoption of the necessary precautions and remedies. But in the midst of all her suffering her imagination was busy. Compositions were dictated to friends who sat by her bedside. Her amanuensis record—how the little song "Where is the Sea" came to her like a strain of music whilst lying in the twilight under the infliction of a blister.

In 1828 she published the *Records of Woman*, the work into which she said she had put her heart and individual feelings more than in anything else she had written. One verse amongst many others indicates the pressure put upon her feeble frame by the intensity of her activity of mind.

"Yet I have known it long;
Too restless and too strong

Within this clay hath been the o'ermastering flame;
  Swift thought that came and went,
  Like torrents o'er me sent,
Have shaken as a reed my thrilling frame."

A severe trial was at hand. The home must again be changed and the beloved Wales left. The marriage of her sister and the appointment of her brother to an official post were the immediate cause. In which direction should she turn her steps with most advantage? The choice was determined by the consideration that at Wavertree near Liverpool she had several attached friends, that there she would meet with advantages for the education of her boys and also with more literary communion for herself.

The wrench from the "land of her childhood, her home, and her dead," was a hard one. She wrote, telling her friends how she literally covered her face all the way from Bronwylfa until her boys told her they had passed the Clwyd range of hills. Then she felt that something of the bitterness was over.

"The sound of thy streams in my spirit I bear;
  Farewell, and a blessing be with thee, green land!
On thy hearths, on thy halls, on thy pure mountain air,
  On the chords of the harp, and the minstrel's free hand,
From the love of my soul, with my tears it is shed,
As I leave thee, green land of my home and my dead."

Her love for the people of Wales was not an unreciprocated love. Many of them rushed forward to touch the posts of the gate through which the poetess had passed; and when, three years later, she paid a visit to St. Asaph, came and wept over her, and entreated her to make her home among them again.

VIII.

WAVEETEEE.

Wavertree had its advantages, but it certainly had its disadvantages too. She was brought into a scene where all her precious time might have been absorbed in the trivialities of society. She was overwhelmed with offers of service and marks of courtesy. All the gaiety of a large town was open to her. Gladly would she, as one who had made her mark, have been received on all hands. But consideration of both time and inclination demanded that her life should be spent in a more retired way. She had a great distaste to "going out." And so the frivolous soon gave her up, and went their own way. Her dress was not rigorously correct; she seemed to have motives and pursuits unlike theirs. And so they did not desire her company any more than she found satisfaction in theirs. In the society of those with whom she had no interest in common she well describes her state as feeling herself more alone than *when* alone. There was much to try her in the curiosity which prompted so many to call upon the strange poetess; but she treated this experience in a cheerful manner. She was pursued by albums, their possessors all anxious to have something written on purpose for themselves. We can understand her humorous appeal to a friend "to procure her a dragon, to be kept in her courtyard."

The life at Wavertree was very different from that in Wales in many respects. She had to face the cares and vexations of domestic life, now that she lived alone in her own house. She had to bear her part in general society. The change was not a palatable one. "How I look back upon the comparative peace and repose of Bronwylfa and Rhyllon—a walk in the hayfield—the children playing round me—my dear mother coming to call me in from the dew—and you, perhaps, making your appearance just in the 'gloaming,' with a great bunch of flowers in your kind hand! How have these things passed away from me, and how much more was I formed for their quiet happiness than for the weary part of *femme célèbre* which I am now enacting."

A visit to Scotland in 1829 was a great event in her life. She seemed to gain fresh energy and vigour. Edinburgh was ready with a hearty welcome. Admiration was in danger of degenerating into adulation; as, for example, when a literary man, on his introduction to her, asked "whether a bat might be allowed to appear in the presence of a nightingale." On another occasion a man of eminence in the book world was honoured with a visit from her. Afterwards he was asked whether he had chanced to see the most distinguished English poetess of the day. "He made no answer," continued the narrator, "but taking me by the arm, in solemn silence, led me into the back parlour, where stood a chair in the centre of the room, isolated from the rest of the furniture: and pointing to it, said, with the profoundest reverence, in a low earnest tone. 'There *she* sat, sir, on that chair!'" One of the brightest parts of this bright tour was that spent with Sir Walter Scott. The recollection of her walks and talks with the great man was always a treasured memory. And so were the words with which he parted from her. "There are some whom we meet, and should like ever after to claim as kith and kin; and *you* are one of these."

In 1830 Mrs. Hemans published her volume of *Songs of the Affections*. The principal of the poems, "A Spirit's Return," was suggested as the result of a favourite amusement—that of winding up the evenings by telling ghost stories. A discussion arose as to the feelings with which the presence and the speech of a visitant from another world would be most likely to impress the person so visited. Mrs. Hemans contended that the predominant sensation would partake of awe and rapture, and that the person visited must thenceforward and for ever be inevitably separated from this world and its concerns—that the soul which had once enjoyed so strange and spiritual communion must be raised by its experience too high for common grief to perplex or common joy to enliven.

> "The music of another land hath spoken.
> No after-sound is sweet; this weary thirst!—
> And I have heard celestial fountains burst.
> What *here* shall quench it?"

IX.

HOME IN THE LAKE COUNTRY.

A visit to the Lakes of Westmoreland in 1830 was a source of great enjoyment to Mrs. Hemans. The beauty of the district was one attraction, but the prospect of sharing the society of Mr. Wordsworth was a greater attraction. Wearied out with the "glare and dust of celebrity," she was longing for the hills and the quiet peacefulness of the Lake country. It is needless to say that the first poetess of Nature was charmed with the first poet of Nature, and the poet with the poetess. Her letters were full of expressions of delight and keen appreciation of the privilege she was enjoying. Wordsworth was kindness itself. "I am charmed with Mr. Wordsworth, whose kindness to me has quite a soothing influence over my spirits. Oh! what relief, what blessing there is in the feeling of admiration when it can be freely poured forth! 'There is a daily beauty in his life,' which is in such lovely harmony with his poetry, that I am thankful to have witnessed and *felt* it."

Mrs. Hemans, after staying a fortnight at Rydal Mount, took a little cottage called Dove's Nest near the lake. Here she was joined by her children, into whose pursuits she heartily threw herself. This was a season of grateful rest to her. "How shall I tell you of all the loveliness by which I am surrounded, of all the soothing and holy influence it seems shedding down into my inmost heart! I have sometimes feared within the last two years, that the effect of suffering and adulation, and feelings too highly wrought and too severely tried, would have been to dry up within me the fountains of such peace and simple enjoyment; but now I know—"

'Nature never did betray
The heart that loved her.'

"I can think of nothing but what is pure, and true, and kind; and my eyes are filled with grateful tears even whilst I am writing to you." But even to this sweet retirement she was pursued by curious tourists, "hunting for lions in doves' nests," and by letters which threatened "to boil over the drawer to which they were consigned."

She had made up her mind that it was a wise step to leave Wavertree. At one time Edinburgh was thought of as a fit place for her residence. But finally Ireland, and not Scotland, became the home of her latter days, one reason for this choice being that her brother would be near to give his advice and guidance as to her sons. In 1831 she took up her abode in Dublin, where, whilst entering very little into general society, she much enjoyed intercourse with many kindred spirits whom she gathered around her. Amongst her most valued friends were the Archbishop of Dublin and Mrs. Whately, from whom she met with marked kindness. These years in Dublin have been described as the happiest as well as the last of her life. Reading was perhaps more than ever a delight to her, especially of works of religious instruction and consolation. Bishop Hall, Leighton, and Jeremy Taylor, and other old divines afforded her great strength and refreshment, whilst the Scriptures were her daily study and delight. Wordsworth was the poet she loved best and read oftenest, never a single day during the last four years of her life being passed, unless sickness prevented, without her reading something of his.

X.

ASPIRATIONS DURING FAILING HEALIH.

"Nervous suffering" is a phrase that describes Mrs. Hemans' state of health. But still her mind was busy and her pen active, especially on subjects of a religious character. "I now feel as if bound to higher and holier tasks which, though I may occasionally lay aside, I could not long wander from without some sense of dereliction. I hope it is not self-delusion, but I cannot help sometimes feeling as if it were my true task to enlarge the sphere of sacred poetry, and extend its influence." In 1834 *Hymns for Childhood* and *National Lyrics* appeared in a collected form, and soon after the long-contemplated collection of *Scenes and Hymns of Life*. The aim of these may be best expressed in her own words. It was to enlarge the sphere of sacred poetry "by associating with its themes, more of the emotions, the affections, and even the pure imaginative enjoyments of daily life, than had hitherto been admitted within the hallowed circle."

Two last works were to issue from her mind and heart. The lyric "Despondency and Aspiration" was hoped to be her best production, as it was certainly her most laborious effort. On it she was anxious to concentrate all her powers. It was meant to be the prologue to a poetical work which was to be called *The Christian Temple*. It was her purpose, "by tracing out the workings of passion—the struggle of human affection—through various climes, and ages, and conditions of life, to illustrate the insufficiency of any dispensation, save that of an ill-embracing Christianity, to soothe the sorrows, or sustain the hopes, or fulfil the desires of an immortal being whose lot is cast in a world where cares and bereavements are many." She was never to carry out this design.

She dictated *Thoughts during Sickness* in the intervals of sickness, when concentrated thought was possible. Their shortness tells of the shortness of those intervals. Who is not better for thinking over these sonnets, recalling as they do a peaceful spirit of resignation and calmness at the approach of the last hour?

> "Let others *trembling* bow,
> Angel of Death, before thee;—not to those
> Whose spirits with Eternal Truth repose
> Art thou a fearful shape. And, oh, for *me*,
> How full of welcome would thine aspect shine,
> Did not the cords of strong affection twine
> So fast around my soul, it *cannot* spring to thee."

The last of the series is entitled a "Sabbath Sonnet." It was composed by Mrs. Hemans a few days before her death, and dictated to her brother. It ends in these words—fit words for the last utterances of a Christian poet:

> "I may not tread
> With them those pathways—to the feverish bed
> Of sickness bound; yet, O my God, I bless
> Thy mercy, that with Sabbath peace hath filled
> My chastened heart, and all its throbbings stilled
> To one deep calm of lowliest thankfulness."

But we are anticipating. At the end of 1834 Mrs. Hemans was recommended to try change of air. Most kindly Archbishop Whately placed at her disposal his country seat of Redesdale, where she had every comfort. But there was a comfort she had that was not of man's making or man's giving. "Far better than these indications of recovery is the sweet religious peace which I feel gradually overshadowing me with its dove-pinions, excluding all that would exclude thoughts of God."

All around her delighted to ease her suffering and to minister to her comfort. Especially thoughtful was her faithful attendant. And well was that attendant repaid in hearing the words which fell from her mistress's lips. How bright was the testimony of the dying poetess! "I feel like a tired child wearied, and longing to mingle with the pure in heart! I feel as if I were sitting with Mary at the feet of my Redeemer, hearing the music of His voice, and learning of Him to be meek and lowly." "Oh, Anna, do not you love your kind Saviour? The plan of redemption was indeed a glorious one; humility was indeed the crowning work. I am like a quiet babe at His feet, and yet my spirit is full of His strength. When anybody speaks of His love to me, I feel as if they were too slow; my spirit can mount alone with Him into those blissful realms with far more rapidity."

XI.

"THE BETTER LAND" REACHED.

Mrs. Hemans left Redesdale to return to Dublin, so as to be near her physician. She could only leave her bed to be laid upon a couch. The sufferings were great, but there was no complaint. She would never allow those around her to speak of her state as one calling for pity. She seemed to live partly on earth, partly in heaven. "No poetry could express, nor imagination conceive, the visions of blessedness that flitted across her fancy, and made her waking hours more delightful than those even that were given to temporary repose." She would ask to be left perfectly alone, in stillness and darkness, to commune with her own heart and reflect on the mercies of her Saviour. Her trust in the atonement was entire, and often did she speak of the comfort she derived from dwelling upon that central fact. She assured a friend that the tenderness and affectionateness of the Redeemer's character, which they had often contemplated together, was now a source not merely of reliance, but of positive happiness to her—*"the sweetness of her couch."*

As is often the case under such circumstances, her thoughts were busy with the haunts of her childhood, the old home and the old walks. Her memory appeared unweakened. Its powers, always so great, seemed to be greater than ever. She would lie hour after hour, repeating to herself chapters of the Bible and pages of Milton and Wordsworth. When delirium came upon her, it was observed how entirely the beautiful still retained its predominance over her mind. The one material thing that gave her pleasure was to be surrounded with "flowers, fresh flowers."

Often did she thank God for the talents He had entrusted to her, and declared how much more ardently than ever her powers would have been consecrated to His service had life been prolonged. On March 15th she received the Holy Communion for the last time, one of her sons being a partaker of that feast for the first time. But the end was not to come at once. There was another flicker of life. The days that remained were spent in pious preparation, one of her favourite occupations being the listening to the reading of some of her most valued books. The *Lives of Sacred Poets* and the *Lives of Eminent Christians*, in both of which her life was soon to be worthy of a place, were especially enjoyed. In the latter book she earnestly recommended the perusal of the account of the death of Madame de Mornay, as showing in bright yet not exaggerated colours "how a Christian can die."

On the 26th of April she dictated to her brother the last strain, the "Sabbath Sonnet," to which reference has already been made. From this time she began to sink slowly but steadily. On the 12th of May she was able to read part of the 16th chapter of St. John, her favourite among the evangelists, which was the Gospel for the day, and also the Collect and Epistle. She delighted to hear passages from a book she dearly loved—a selection from the works of Archbishop Leighton. "Beautiful! beautiful!" she exclaimed. To her faithful attendant she said that "she had been making her peace with God; that she felt all at peace within her bosom."

On Saturday the 16th May, 1835, she slumbered nearly all the day: and at nine o'clock in the evening, without pain or struggle, her spirit passed away to the "Better Land."

'I hear thee speak of the better land,
Thou callest its children a happy band;
Mother, oh, where is that radiant shore?

Shall we not seek it, and weep no more?
Is it where the flower of the orange blows,
And the fire-flies glance through the myrtle boughs?'
   'Not there, not there, my child!'

'Is it where the feathery palm-trees rise,
And the date grows ripe under sunny skies?
Or 'midst the green islands of glittering seas,
Where fragrant forests perfume the breeze,
And strange, bright birds, on their starry wings,
Bear the rich hues of all glorious things?'
   'Not there, not there, my child!'

'Is it far away, in some region old,
Where the rivers wander o'er sands of gold?
Where the burning rays of the ruby shine,
And the diamond lights up the secret mine,
And the pearl gleams forth from the coral strand?
Is it there, sweet mother, that better land?'
   'Not there, not there, my child!'

'Eye hath not seen it, my gentle boy,
Ear hath not heard its deep songs of joy;
Dreams cannot picture a world so fair—
Sorrow and death may not enter there:
Time doth not breathe on its fadeless bloom,
For beyond the clouds, and beyond the tomb,—
   It is there, it is there, my child!'

Her remains were laid to rest in a grave within St. Anne's Church, Dublin. A tablet records her name, her age—forty-one years—and the date of her death. There are added the following lines of her own:—

"Calm on the bosom of thy God,
   Fair spirit, rest thee now;
E'en while with us thy footsteps trode,
   His seal was on thy brow.
Dust to its narrow home beneath,
   Soul to its place on high;
They that have seen thy look in death,
   No more may fear to die."

XII.

ABIDING WORDS.

Though many of the productions of the gifted poetess will soon be forgotten, there is no doubt that some will live. The subjects are those which gain an admittance to the hearts of all classes. We have already given in full that beautiful poem "The Better Land." There is no danger of "Casabianca" passing into oblivion. Children delight to commit it to memory, and are all the better for the lesson of devotion to duty they have learnt.

> "Yet beautiful and bright he stood,
>   As born to rule the storm;
> A creature of heroic blood,
>   A proud, though childlike form.
> The flames rolled on—he would not go
>   Without his father's word;
> That father, faint in death below,
>   His voice no longer heard."

Mrs. Hemans was at her best in treating of such matters as those dealt with in "The Homes of England" and "The Landing of the Pilgrim Fathers." Any one is to be pitied who can read without admiration these lines from the former:—

"The merry homes of England!
 Around their hearths by night
What gladsome looks of household love
 Meet in the ruddy light!
There woman's voice flows forth in song,
 Or childhood's tale is told,
Or lips move tunefully along
 Some glorious page of old.

The blessed homes of England!
 How softly on their bowers
Is laid the holy quietness
 That breathes from Sabbath hours!
Solemn, yet sweet, the church bell's chime
 Floats through their woods at morn;
All other sounds in that still time
 Of breeze and leaf are born."

There is little danger of "The Landing of the Pilgrim Fathers" being forgotten. How well the poetess indicated the, motive which led them from their native country to the unknown land!—

"What sought they thus afar?
 Bright jewels of the mine?
The wealth of seas, the spoils of war?
 They sought a faith's pure shrine!

Ay, call it holy ground,
 The soil where first they trod!
They have left unstained what there they found—
 Freedom to worship God!"

As an example of Mrs. Hemans' treatment of sacred subjects, we may quote the concluding verses of "Christ's Agony in the Garden":—

> "He knew them all—the doubt, the strife,
>   The faint perplexing dread,
> The mists that hang o'er parting life,
>   All darkened round His head;
> And the Deliverer knelt to pray,
>   Yet passed it not, that cup, away.
>
> It passed not—though the stormy wave
>   Had sunk beneath His tread;
> It passed not—though to Him the grave
>   Had yielded up its dead.
> But there was sent Him from on high
>   A gift of strength for man to die.
>
> And was *His* mortal hour beset
>   With anguish and dismay?—
> How may *we* meet our conflict yet,
>   In the dark, narrow way?
> How, but through Him, that path who trod?
>   Save, or we perish, Son of God!"

We are thankful to find that the poetess had such clear views of the atonement as those to be met with in her *Sonnets, Devotional and Memorial,* for example, in "The Darkness of the Crucifixion."

The last quotation shall be one from "The Graves of a Household," the opening and the closing verses of a literary gem which will never lack appreciation:—

"They grew in beauty side by side,
    They filled one home with glee;—
Their graves are severed far and wide.
    By mount, and stream, and sea.

The same fond mother bent at night
    O'er each fair sleeping brow;
She had each folded flower in sight—
    Where are those dreamers now'?

* * * * *

And parted thus they rest, who played
    Beneath the same green tree;
Whose voices mingled as they prayed
    Around one parent knee!

They that with smiles lit up the hall,
    And cheered with song the hearth!
Alas, for love! if *thou* wert all,
    And nought beyond, O Earth."

The lyrics of Mrs. Hemans will ever keep her memory fresh. "In these 'gems of purest ray serene,' the peculiar genius of Mrs. Hemans breathes, and burns, and shines pre-eminent; for her forte lay in depicting whatever tends to beautify and embellish domestic life, the gentle overflowings of love and friendship, home-bred delights and heartfelt happiness, the associations of local attachment, and the influences of religious feelings over the soul, whether arising from the varied circumstances and situations of man, or from the aspects of external Nature."

S.F. HARRIS, M.A., B.C.L.

MADAME GUYON

I.

HER BIRTH AND BRINGING-UP.

Jeanne Marie Bouvières de la Mothe, afterwards Madame Guyon, was born at Montargis, about fifty miles south of Paris, on April 13, 1648. Her father, who bore the title of Seigneur de la Mothe Vergonville, was a man of much religious feeling. Although Jeanne was a child of delicate health, her mother does not seem to have bestowed much trouble upon her, sending her, when only two years and a half old, to an Ursuline seminary a short time, and then committing her almost entirely to the care of servants, from whom, as a matter of course, her mental and moral culture at that highly-receptive age did not receive much attention. When four years old, she was transferred to the care of the nuns in a Benedictine convent. "Here," she says in her autobiography,[1] "I saw none but good examples; and as my natural disposition was towards the good, I followed it as long as I met with nobody to turn me in another direction. I loved to hear of God, to be at church, and to be dressed up as a nun."

---

1 *La Vie de Madame J.M.B. de la Mothe-Guyon, écrite par elle-même,* première partie, ch. ii., 6. The edition from which I quote was published at Paris, in three volumes, by the "Associated Booksellers," in 1791. See also Life by J.C. Upham (Sampson Low & Co., 1872).

Now, as her opening mind drank in such instruction as came to her, she deeply felt the claims of God upon her love and service. Under the influence of a remarkable dream, she openly expressed her determination to lead a religious life; and one day, with unguarded frankness, she avowed her readiness to become a martyr for God. Her fellow-pupils at the convent, like Joseph's brethren, did not appreciate either her dream or her avowal. With girlish jealousy they laid her devout aspirations at the door of pride, and proceeded to test her professions in a cruel manner. They persuaded her that God had taken her at her word and called her suddenly to undergo the martyrdom for which she had declared her readiness. Her courage did not give way at their summons. So, after allowing her a short time for preparatory prayer, they led her into a room made ready for the purpose, where a cloth was spread on the floor, and an older girl stood behind her, lifting a large cutlass, and seemingly prepared to chop off the child's head. Who can wonder that at this too realistic sight the little girl's valour gave way? She cried out that she must not die without her father's leave. The girls triumphantly asserted that this was a paltry excuse, and let her go, with the scornful assurance that God would not accept as a martyr one who had so little of a martyr's courage.

Poor little Jeanne Marie! This unjust ordeal had a painful effect on her joyous spirit. Child though she was, she saw clearly that, like Simon Peter, she had been too ready and bold in her avowals of devotedness to her Lord. She thought that by her cowardice she had offended God, and that now there was little likelihood of winning His favour and enjoying His support. Her health, always delicate, could not but be injured by this unpleasant episode, and after a while she was taken home and again left to the care of the servants. Placed a second time at the Ursuline convent, she was happy in being under the care of her half-sister,—a good creature, who devoted her excellent abilities to the loving training of Jeanne in learning and piety. While here, the little girl was often sent for by her father; and at his house, on one occasion, she found Henrietta Maria, the widowed queen of England, who was so much pleased with her pretty ways and sprightly answers that she tried to induce M. de la Mothe to place his daughter in her care, intimating that she would make her maid of honour to the princess. The father, much to the queen's annoyance, declined the honour, and Madame Guyon, in after years, considered that perhaps she owed her salvation to his judicious refusal.

At this Ursuline seminary she remained, under her sister's care, until she was ten years old, when she was taken home again, and then placed in a Dominican convent, where she stayed eight months. Here she was left much to herself, but was so happy as to find an abiding companion, a heaven-sent gift, in a copy of the Bible, which had been "providentially" left in the apartment assigned to her. "I read it," she says, "from morning to night; and having a very good memory, I learnt by heart all the historical parts." Whatever were the immediate results of this close acquaintance with the Book of books, it is certain that in after years, when the true light had shined into her soul, her early intimacy with the Bible was of great service to her progress, and helped to qualify her in some measure for writing her *Explanations and Reflections* on the sacred volume. On her return home once more her religious state seems to have fluctuated considerably. Family jealousies and jars deadened the fervour of her devotion. Preparations for her first Sacrament under her sister's guidance, and the actual participation in that ordinance, had for a time a beneficial effect. But the solemnity of the Supper passed away without permanent influence on her heart.

She was now growing up a fine tall girl, of remarkable beauty and of equal fascination of speech and manner. Her mother became proud of her loveliness, and took great interest in her dress and appearance. Accomplished and attractive, she was welcome in every circle, and her wit and gaiety made her company much sought after. Her serious impressions passed away, and her heart was hot in the chase after pleasure. That it was still tender and susceptible we learn from a little incident at this period. She had gone for a walk with her youthful companions, and during her absence a young cousin, De Toissi, who was going as a missionary to Cochin China, called for a short time at her father's house. On her return home she found that he had already departed, and she heard such an account of his sanctity and of his pious utterances that she was deeply affected and was overcome with sorrow, crying all the rest of the day and night. Once more she sought earnestly "the peace of God, which passeth all understanding," but sought it by deeds of charity and by bodily austerities, instead of by the simple way of faith. At this time, in the fervour of her devotion, she resolved to enter a convent and become a nun. Her father, however, believed that his daughter, whom he tenderly loved, might be truly religious without taking such an irrevocable step. But soon—whether through some juvenile attachment or not we cannot tell— her good desires and resolves grew faint, she left off prayer, and lost such comfort and blessing as had been granted her from above. "I began," she says, "to seek in the creature what I had found in God. And Thou, O my God, didst leave me to myself, because I had first left Thee, and Thou wast pleased, in permitting me to sink into the abyss, to make me feel the necessity I was under of maintaining communion with Thyself in prayer."

In 1663 her father removed his household to Paris, and Jeanne Marie was transferred to a larger and more brilliant arena for the display of her beauty and accomplishments. Louis XIV. was on the throne, and Paris was at the very height of its gaiety and celebrity. The influence of its dissipation and distraction on the spirit of Mademoiselle de la Mothe was of course unfavourable to religion. Her parents found themselves not merely in a fashionable circle, but in a highly-intellectual centre. The *grand monarque* posed as the great patron of literature and the arts; and society presented splendid opportunities for the exercise of the young lady's conversational powers. She tells us that she began to entertain extravagant notions of herself, and that her vanity increased. In such surroundings it could hardly be otherwise. Her faith and love, such as they were, had died away, and her devotion had dwindled down to nothing. The dazzling world before her was in her eyes something worth conquering; and she set herself to gain its acclamation, and was to a great extent successful. From this high state of worldly gratification, and low state of religious principle and enjoyment, she was aroused and rescued in a very rough and painful manner.

II.

MARRIED LIFE.

Early in 1664, when not quite sixteen, Jeanne Marie de la Mothe was given in marriage to M. Jacques Guyon, a man of thirty-eight, possessed of great wealth, whom she had seen for the first time only a few days before the ceremony took place. Many ladies no doubt envied her, but for her it was an unhappy change. Several suitors had appeared, with whom she felt she could have been content and happy; but M. Guyon's riches and perseverance had carried the day with her parents, and marriage, to which she had looked forward as the period of liberation from restraint, and of freer enjoyment of the gay Parisian life, proved but the commencement of a dreary spell of dulness and misery. Her friends, who came to congratulate her the next day after the wedding, were surprised to find her weeping bitterly, and, in answer to their raillery, were told by her, "Alas! I used to have such a desire to be a nun: why, then, am I married now? and by what fatality has this happened to me?" She was overwhelmed with this regret, this longing to be a *religieuse*. The sudden transition from being the admired of all beholders, "the cynosure of neighbouring eyes," the witty belle whose every word and look were treasured up, to the hopeless condition of a bird pining in a gilded cage, was very hard to bear.

The details of the poor girl's sufferings in her new home are painful to read; but as Madame Guyon relates these early trials, she devoutly regards them as the means employed by her Heavenly Father to wean her affections from the world and turn them towards Himself. Beset with sore afflictions, guarded and illtreated by a servant devoted to her mother-in-law, cut off from the innocent pleasures of friendly intercourse, perpetually thwarted and misrepresented, she bethought herself of the possibility of getting help from above, and once more turned her mind towards God and heavenly things, doing her best, according to her imperfect light, to propitiate the Divine favour. She gave up entirely the reading of romances, of which formerly she had been passionately fond. The *penchant* for them had already been deadened, some time before her marriage, by reading the Gospel, which she found "so beautiful," and in which she discerned a character of truth which disgusted her with all other books. She resumed the practice of private prayer; she had masses said, in order to obtain Divine grace to enable her to find favour with her husband and his mother, and to ascertain the Divine will; she consulted her looking-glass very seldom; she regularly studied books of devotion, such as *The Initiation of Jesus Christ*, and the works of St. Francis de Sales, and read them aloud, so that the servants might profit by them. She endeavoured in all things not to offend God.

Her mind, shut off from all earthly comfort, was now driven in upon itself. Her lengthy meditation, though it helped to give her some degree of resignation, did not produce true peace and joy Though quite natural under the circumstances, it was an unhealthy habit, and doubtless tended to foster the mystic dreaming which grew upon her in riper years. Changes of circumstances now came to her relief. Soon after the birth of her first child, a heavy loss of property called her husband to Paris, to look after his affairs; and she, after a while, was permitted to join him there. This made a pleasant break in the dreary round of her married life. She cared nothing for losses, so long as she could gain from her stern and surly mate some token of affection and acknowledgment; and this, though in very small fragments, she had now occasionally the satisfaction of getting. While at Paris she had a severe illness, and the learned doctors of the city brought her to death's door by draining her of "forty-eight pullets" of blood.

Sad to say, as she regained her health, her husband resumed his moroseness and violent tempers, and her feeble strength was tried to its utmost. But she records, "This illness was of great use to me, for, besides teaching me patience under very severe pains, it enlightened me much as to the worthlessness of the things of this world. While detaching me to a great extent from myself, it gave me fresh courage to bear suffering better than I had done in the past." When at last she regained her health, the loss of her mother and the crosses of every-day life served still further to solemnize her mind, and to turn her aspirations heavenwards. She followed strictly her plan for private prayer twice a day; she kept watch over herself continually, and in almsgiving and other ways endeavoured to do as much good as she could.

III.

LIGHT BREAKS IN.

About this time a pious lady, an English exile, came to reside at her father's house; and though she could but imperfectly understand her devout conversation, Madame Guyon saw in her face a sweet satisfaction which she herself had not as yet attained. Then her cousin De Toissi arrived from the East, and, with sincere concern for her welfare, encouraged her in her search after happiness in God. To him she unburdened her soul, giving him a full account of all her faults and all her wants. He tendered the best counsel he could. She now tried to meditate continually on God, saying prayers and uttering ejaculatory petitions. But all was in vain. The advice of these excellent persons led her to look too much inwardly upon her own heart, instead of upward to the Saviour as revealed in His word. So she still laboured along in deep darkness and depression.

It was with a sudden brilliance that light and joy broke in upon her spirit. In July, 1668, she was once more at the parental home, to nurse her father, who was dangerously ill. Knowing well his daughter's unhappiness, M. de la Mothe recommended her to consult his confessor, an aged Franciscan, who had been of service to himself. This good man, after listening for some time to the story of her restless wanderings after peace, said, "Madame, you are seeking outside what you have within. Accustom yourself to seek God in your heart, and you will find Him there." These few and simple words turned her gaze from her own efforts and feelings to see that peace was a thing to be found not in outward deeds but in a heart right with God; and so she was enabled to realise the bounteous love of God, which at that instant was broadening her heart by the Holy Spirit. The next morning when she told the old Franciscan of the effect of his words, he was much astonished.

"These words," she observes, "brought into my heart what I had been seeking so many years; or rather they made me discover what was there, but what I had not been enjoying for want of knowing it. O my Lord, Thou wast in my heart, and didst require of me only a simple turning inward to make me perceive Thy presence. O Infinite Goodness, Thou wast so near, and I went running hither and thither in search of Thee, and did not find Thee. My life was wretched, yet my happiness lay there within me. I was poor in the midst of riches, and I was dying of hunger close by a table spread and a continual feast. O Beauty, ancient and new, why have I known Thee so late? Alas! I sought Thee where Thou wast not, and did not seek Thee where Thou wast. It was for want of understanding these words of Thy Gospel, where Thou sayest, 'The kingdom of God is not here or there; but the kingdom of God is within you.'"[1]

There can be no doubt that her heart now realised something of the great fundamental truth that "God is Love." She had been trying to propitiate Him, as a Being of awful majesty and purity, by good works, strict conduct, severe penances. Now she saw at a glance the mistakes of her former conceptions of the Divine Being, and all her faculties drank in the grand verity of the boundless love of God.

Her own account of this vital change is as follows: "I told this good father that I did not know what he had done to me; that my heart was totally changed; that God was there, and I had no more difficulty in finding Him; for from that moment was given me an experience of His presence in my soul; not by mere thought or intellectual application, but as a thing which one really possesses in a very sweet manner. I experienced these words of the spouse in the Canticles: 'Thy name is as ointment poured

---

1 *La Vie*, première partie, ch. viii., 7.

forth: therefore do the virgins love thee.' For I felt in my soul an unction which like a healing balm cured in a moment all my wounds, and which even spread itself so powerfully over my senses that I could scarcely open my mouth or my eyes. That night I could not sleep at all, because Thy love, O my God, was for me not only as a delicious oil, but also as a devouring fire, which kindled in my soul such a flame as threatened to consume all in an instant. I was all at once so changed as not to be recognisable either to myself or to others. I found neither the blemishes nor the dislikes (which had troubled me): all appeared to me consumed like a straw in a great fire."[1]

These extracts from her autobiography are important as giving a key to her subsequent life. We see here the intensity of her affections and emotions, the excitability of her temperament, the tendency to wander into regions of spiritual imagination, the liking for strong dramatic expression, which, though not in themselves blamable, yet gave to the outside world, and even to those about her who were open to adverse prepossessions, false impressions as to the depth and reality of her religion. They, close at hand, could not make the allowance which we can easily make for the extravagances of a soul which had just emerged from the prison gloom of depression and distrust into this realisation of the Divine love and favour. When her enthusiastic spirit led her to subject herself to the severest penances, she joyed in their infliction and could not make them severe enough. And here at once comes out prominently a primary error of judgment in this good woman at the very outset of her Christian life. She gives us details of a specially disgusting penance which she inflicted on herself. In this, as in the rest of her self-imposed tortures and degradations, the impulse manifestly came not from above, but from the mistaken imaginings of an over-wrought mind encased in a frail and delicate frame; and these morbid fancies were based on her intense passion for self-abasement. We must remember that at this critical time,

---

[1] *Ibid.*, ch. viii., 8.

when she most needed counsel, she had really no one to guide her—no one, that is, who possessed spiritual wisdom and common sense.

Though Madame Guyon was much absorbed in a mystical ecstasy, which she describes as prayer without words or even thoughts, she was no mere visionary. Her love to God, her intense devotion to her Saviour, led her to earnest endeavours to do good to those around her. The poor and the sick, young girls exposed to temptation, all who needed temporal or spiritual help, were the special objects of her care and benevolence. In leading others to Christ she was remarkably successful. She had indeed exceptional qualifications for this missionary work. Just over twenty years of age, her youthful beauty and grace, the tender, yearning love which lit up her expressive features, the ready utterance and sweet voice, and the charm of manner which never left her, were no unfitting media to convey the tidings of mercy to many a benighted seeker after rest and peace.

IV.

AFFLICTIONS AND GLOOM.

At this time she found great benefit from the counsel of her friend Geneviève Granger, the prioress of the Benedictine convent, who encouraged her in her determination to avoid all conformity to the world, and to live wholly to God. She once more made progress in the Divine life, and the trials which now came thickly upon her were the means of blessing her soul with increase of purity and peace. Hers were no light trials. Besides the constant annoyance from her implacable mother-in-law and the ill-tempered behaviour of her husband, heavy afflictions befell her. The terrible small-pox attacked her, and spoilt her beautiful face, though it left her alive. Her cruel mother-in-law, instead of tenderly nursing her, basely neglected her, debarred her from medical attendance, and imperilled her life. The loss of her beauty alienated her husband's affection—such as it was—from her, and he became still more open to unfavourable influences. Burdened as she was with these troubles, yet another was added. Her younger son, a lovely boy four years of age, was carried off by the same fearful disease. Yet in all these afflictions she showed a spirit of holy resignation.

In the summer of 1671 she made the acquaintance of Father La Combe, who came with an introductory letter from her half-brother Father La Mothe. He was in search of inward peace, and Madame Guyon's counsels, the outcome of deep thought and Divine enlightenment, were of great service to him. The next year was marked by other trying losses.

Her little daughter, who latterly had been her one source of human comfort, died rather suddenly. This was probably the severest trial of her life. In the same month she lost her affectionate father. Yet in these bereavements also she charged not God foolishly, but took them as a part of the discipline wisely ordered to knit her soul in closer union to Him.

On July 22, 1672, the fourth anniversary of the day on which she first found peace, at the suggestion of her correspondent Geneviève Granger, she put her signature and seal to a covenant which that lady had drawn up. "The contract," she says,[1] "ran thus: 'I N. promise to take as my husband our Lord Jesus Christ, and to give myself to Him as His spouse, although unworthy.' I asked of Him, as the dowry of my spiritual marriage, crosses, contempt, confusion, disgrace, and ignominy; and I prayed Him to give me grace to entertain dispositions of littleness and nothingness with regard to everything else." Though we cannot consider such covenants in general as wise in themselves, nor this one in particular as appropriate in its language, yet for a time it seemed to give greater strength to her holy resolutions and increased stability to her pious frame of mind. But about eighteen months afterwards she fell into a state of depression, or absence of joy, which lasted nearly six years.

Probably this state of "privation," as she terms it, was in great measure the result of physical causes. She had for many years tried her bodily strength to the utmost by her severe self-denying treatment of herself. And now the death of her intimate friend, the above-mentioned Geneviève Granger, no doubt exercised a lowering effect on her spirits. It was a testing time for her faith, and it is a signal proof of the depth and reality of her piety that through all this trying season she held fast her trust in God, and kept on her way, though uncheered for a time by the joyous emotions with which she had so long been favoured. It was well that her mind, which had been overtaxed and strained by the intensity

---

1 *La Vie de Madame Guyon*, première partie, ch. xix., 10.

of her religious fervour, and by its unbroken continuity of introspection, should be brought into a more healthful state by this bitter tonic of joylessness.

In 1676 her husband's health, never very good, completely broke down, and after a long illness he died, leaving her, at the age of twenty-eight, a widow, with three children. As the solemn hour of parting drew near, she swept away all the wretched interference which had helped to cloud the happiness of their married life, and, kneeling by his bed, she begged him to forgive anything she had done amiss. The better nature of the man now at length prevailed, and he said—what he had never said before—"It is I who ask pardon of you. I did not deserve you:" which was perfectly true. He left a large amount of property, but his affairs were in a perplexing state of entanglement, and his young widow, unused to business, had to do her best to make all straight. She proved equal to the occasion, and soon, with her quick perception and uncommon powers of direction and persuasion, she reduced the complicated tangle to order, and then retired to a house of her own, where she was free from the annoying devices of her irreconcilable mother-in-law, and could devote herself to the education of her children, the perfecting of her own education, and the visitation of the sick and poor.

It was in 1680, after nearly seven years of comparative darkness and depression, that her spiritual gloom was broken in upon by a letter from Father La Combe, in which he took the sensible view that by this sore deprivation God was teaching her not to lean on her state of feeling, but to look to Him alone for comfort and strength. On the 22nd of July—a day several times marked in her history as one of signal blessing—her prayers were heard, and God again lifted up the light of His countenance upon her. "On that happy day," she writes, "my soul was fully delivered from all its distresses. It began a new life," a life of steady peace and joy, guarded from dependence on the joy itself by the painful experience from which she had just emerged.

From this time forth she devoted her life to the spread of the knowledge of the love of God. After much deliberation and consultation with others, she left Paris in July, 1681, to commence work in the south-east of France. The preceding winter had been passed in making necessary preparations, in relieving the necessities of the famished poor of Paris, and in other works of charity.

V.

HER PUBLIC WORK.

On that July morning, when Madame Guyon embarked on the Seine secretly, for fear of the interference of her half-brother, she was really embarking on the chief business of her life, the work of spreading the doctrine of inward holiness. She had felt drawn to the district of Geneva by a desire to give temporal and spiritual help to the poor people at the foot of the Jura range. And now, having consulted at Paris the Bishop of Geneva, she was making her way, in company with her little daughter, a nun, and two servants, to the little town of Gex. Passing through Annecy and Geneva, she reached her destination on July 23, and took up her residence at the house of the Sisters of Charity. This was for a time the centre of her labours of love. Besides her works of charity, she felt impelled to tell others of the spiritual blessings which she herself enjoyed.

Situated as she was, a Protestant without herself suspecting it, and that in the very heart of the Roman Catholic Church; a devout reader of the Bible, and one who valued the ministrations of priests as advisers and "confessors," rather than as transacting the penitent's own work for him, her superior intelligence, and her happy art of carrying conviction to the listeners, raised the jealousy of the clergy, just as her pure life was a silent rebuke to all lax livers, whether monk, nun, or priest. D'Aranthon, the bishop, had welcomed her to his diocese, and at first received her doctrines with appreciative favour. But he was a man easily persuaded, swayed by the last person who talked to him, and as her opinions became more pronounced, he began to perceive that they were dangerous to the stability of the corrupt, priest-ridden Church of which he was an "overseer." He had appointed Father La Combe as Madame Guyon's "director," her spiritual guide and instructor. But in practice the position was reversed, and it was she who led La Combe into higher regions of thought and experience, of which he soon became the eloquent exponent.

La Combe's preaching attracted great attention at Thonon, on the other side of the Lake of Geneva; and the bishop was anxious lest these new doctrines should spread, and he himself should get into trouble at Rome on their account. He now wanted to circumscribe Madame Guyon's sphere of influence by getting her to become prioress of a convent at Gex. He evidently thought that by having her here under some restraint, and by keeping her close to the duties of the cloister, he would be able to put a stop to the propagation of her heretical opinions. But though she gave a little too much heed to visions and dreamy imaginings, she had lost no whit of the practical common-sense and clearness of sight which had distinguished her in many mundane emergencies. She absolutely refused to make over her property for the good of the sisterhood, and would not undertake an office which would shut her up from her mission of proclaiming far and wide, as the Divine Hand opened the way, the message of the Saviour's love and the Holy Spirit's sanctifying power. This refusal brought much persecution and annoyance both to herself and to Father La Combe, who had manfully refused to obey the bishop when he ordered him to use his influence in making Madame Guyon comply with his expressed wishes.

A party was now formed at Gex specially for the persecution of Madame Guyon, and after much annoyance and suffering she felt she was providentially called to leave a town where she had many disciples, whose lives she had been the means of brightening and elevating. In the spring of 1682 she crossed the Lake of Geneva to Thonon, where she pursued the same missionary career, and was the means of raising up a little church of believers in the midst of dense bigotry and superstition. She never "preached" in public, but in private she conversed and prayed with individual seekers after salvation, and at times had conferences with several together in a small room. By these means, and by her excellent letters, she effected an amazing amount of good in all that region. For a time, a short and happy time, all went rightly; but she knew only too well that persecution must ensue. It could not but come to this good woman, who devoutly fulfilled what she esteemed to be the lawful commands of her Church, but who took as her highest authority and director the open Bible, explained not by priest or friar, but by the Holy Ghost working upon her own acute intellect and devout heart. It is worthy of notice that under her guidance several small societies or communities were formed by poor girls who had become decided Christians. These young people helped each other in secular matters, and held little meetings for reading and prayer and loving fellowship. Their associations were soon broken up by the priestly party, as, indeed, was to be expected; the girls were deprived of ordinary church privileges, and some of them were driven out of Thonon altogether. Another indication of the rising tide of persecution was that the dominant party ordered all books relating to the inner life to be brought to them, and publicly burnt in the market-place the few which were given up.

At length, through the influence of her enemies, Madame Guyon received from the bishop notice that she must go out of his diocese, and Father la Combe was similarly warned to depart. All espostulation was in vain, and leaving Savoy, in which her labours had been so much blessed, she set out on a wearisome journey into Piedmont, crossing the perilous Mont Cenis on a mule, and came to Turin.

In spite of many annoyances, she had spent two happy years at Thonon in work for her Divine Master; and she would have been more than human if she had not felt, though in a spirit of sweet resignation, the wrench which these frequent changes of habitation inflicted. No wonder that she called to mind the pathetic words in Matthew viii. 20: "The foxes have holes, and the birds of the air have nests; but the Son of Man hath not where to lay His head." "This," she writes,[1] "I have since experienced to its full extent, having had no sure abode where I could remain more than a few months, and every day in uncertainty where I should be on the morrow, and besides, finding no refuge, either among my friends, who were ashamed of me and openly renounced me just when there was an outcry against me, or among my relations, most of whom have declared themselves my adversaries and been my greatest persecutors, while the others looked on me with contempt and indignation."

At Turin she found temporary refuge and rest in the house of the Marchioness of Prunai, but appears to have spent only a few months of 1684 in that city. She longed to return to evangelistic work in France. Accordingly in the autumn she went to Grenoble, and had great success in her labours, but, through the hatred of her enemies, was obliged to quit the place secretly, leaving her little daughter in charge of her faithful maid La Gautière. She had already commenced authorship, at Thonon, by writing, during an interval of much-needed rest, her book entitled *Spiritual Torrents*. At Grenoble she began her commentaries on *The Holy Bible*, and here she published her famous work, *A Short and Very Easy Method of Prayer*, which speedily ran through several editions. So, by word of mouth, and by pen, she taught, and "the new spirit of religious inquiry," as she calls it, spread and prevailed. It was indeed the *old* spirit of inquiry, as old as the days of the apostles, and its basis was the principle which she clearly enunciates, "that man is a sinner, and that he must be saved by repentance and faith in Christ, and that faith in God through Christ subsequently is, and must be, the foundation of the inward life." Such a bold proclamation of Gospel truth could not but rouse the anger of the clerical party at Grenoble. The persuasive missioner was soon the centre of a storm of wrath and indignation, which the friendly Bishop Camus,

---

1 *La Vie*, seconde partie, ch. xiv., 1.

afterwards a cardinal, was unable to allay. Early in 1686 she left Grenoble for Marseilles, where she hoped to find refuge for a while. But her fame had preceded her. "I did not arrive in Marseilles," she records, "till ten in the morning, and it was only a few hours after noon when all was in uproar against me."

In this excitable city she remained only eight days; but in that short space some good was effected. Now began a series of wanderings in search of a home. Arriving at Nice, she felt acutely her desolate state. "I saw myself without refuge or retreat, wandering and homeless. All the artisans whom I saw in the shops appeared to me happy in having an abode and refuge." After a stormy voyage to Genoa, she reached Verceil, on the Sessia, and after a stay of a few months amongst kind friends, but precluded from public work by ill-health, she decided to return once more to Paris, and there pursue her labours.

Unaware of the king's despotic intolerance, she arrived in the French capital on July 22, 1686, after an absence of five years, and soon became the centre of an enlightened circle of friends, of high rank, who were glad to listen to her teaching and to learn the way of the Lord more perfectly. For a while all was quiet. But her enemies—among whom her half-brother, Père La Mothe, was ever the most virulent—were meantime very busy, and at length a charge was laid against her before the king. She was seized by warrant of a *lettre de cachet*, and consigned to solitary imprisonment in the convent of Sainte Marie, in the suburb of St. Antoine. Louis XIV. was now posing as a defender of the faith, and was glad to show his Catholic zeal in the punishment of a lady who was said to hold opinions similar to those of Molinos, whom he had recently induced the Pope to condemn. Nearly four months previously her eloquent disciple, Father la Combe, had been committed to the Bastille for life.

VI.

IN PRISON.

On January 29, 1688—the first month of a year specially dear to English lovers of civil and religious liberty—Madame Guyon was taken to her cell in Sainte Marie. It was a room in an upper story of the convent, with a barred door, and an opening for light and air on one side. Here she was shut up from her friends; her gaoler, a crabbed, hard-hearted nun, who treated her with the greatest rigour, regarding her not only as a heretic, but as a hypocrite and out of her senses as well. Feeble in body and in bad health, her mind was much troubled about her beloved daughter, whom interested persons were trying to force into a marriage of which Madame Guyon strongly disapproved. But though, under harsh treatment, she became very ill, and was nigh unto death, her peace and joy proved their heavenly origin by unbroken continuance in this trying season. As she recovered, she found occupation in writing her autobiography, and in composing hymns and sacred poems. Amongst the latter is the charming *cantique* given at the end of her Life, and beginning—

"Grand Dieu! pour Ton plaisir
Je suis dans une cage,"

which has been happily Englished as follows:—

"A little bird I am,
    Shut from the fields of air;
And in my cage I sit and sing
    To Him who placed me there;
Well pleased a prisoner to be,
Because, my God, it pleases Thee.

Nought have I else to do,
    I sing the whole day long,
And He whom well I love to please
    Doth listen to my song.
He caught and bound my wandering wing,
But still He bends to hear me sing.

Thou hast an ear to hear,
    A heart to love and bless,
And though my notes were e'er so rude.
    Thou would'st not hear the less,
Because Thou knowest, as they fall,
That love, sweet love, inspires them all.

My cage confines me round,
    Abroad I cannot fly;
But though my wing is closely bound,
    My heart's at liberty.
My prison walls cannot control
The flight, the freedom of the soul.

Oh, it is good to soar
    These bolts and bars above,
To Him whose purpose I adore,
    Whose providence I love,

And in Thy mighty will to find
The joy, the freedom of the mind."

Her liberation from this imprisonment came from a remarkable quarter. Madame de Miramion, a pious lady, often visited the convent with charitable intent. Having heard much about Madame Guyon, she asked to see her; and having seen her and conversed with her, she soon became her warm friend, and pleaded her cause with Madame de Maintenon, who was now at the height of her power and possessed supreme influence with the king, whose wife she had become, by a private marriage, in 1685. Madame de Miramion, having in this way procured Madame Guyon's release from her convent prison, took her to her own house. It was a happy change for this much-tried woman. She was once again among friends, and had the society of her daughter. She went to St. Cyr—a royal institution for the education of the daughters of the poorer aristocracy, in which Madame de Maintenon took interest—to thank the great lady for her kindness. The latter was charmed with the bright, saintly ex-prisoner, whose devout spirit shone out in her countenance and breathed in her fascinating speech. She had many conversations with her, and begged her to give instruction to the girls of St. Cyr.

It was at this time that Madame Guyon first met the great Fénelon, who was a director of St. Cyr, as well as one of the most noted characters of the age. She won his lasting regard. He was cheered by the warmth of her piety and her unwavering faith, while his more logical and better disciplined mind would no doubt moderate and tone down her excess of introspection and rapt emotion. She spent three happy years in Paris, consulted by many persons on religious matters, admired and honoured by several distinguished people, and sheltered from storm in the house of her daughter, now married to the Count de Vaux. But the sunshine was not to last long. Godet, Madame de Maintenon's confessor and one of the directors of St. Cyr, was possessed with a jealous hatred of his co-director, Fénelon, and also disliked Madame Guyon. Breathing into the mind of the great lady—who, though of Huguenot descent, was nothing if not "orthodox"—doubts as to Madame Guyon's correctness of belief, he caused Madame de Maintenon to withdraw her countenance from her *protégée*, and to discontinue her own visits to St. Cyr. Now was the time for Madame Guyon's enemies to attack her, when they saw the court favourite's countenance withdrawn. An attempt was made to poison her, and so far succeeded that her health was impaired for many years.

Then Bossuet appeared on the scene. In September, 1693, he came to see her in Paris, feeling, doubtless, that he was the man to settle all these Pietistic commotions. At Madame Guyon's request he consented to examine her numerous writings; and when, in the course of some months, he had performed this task, and had also perused her MS. autobiography, he had another long conversation with her, which brought out fully the peculiarities of her doctrine. In this interesting discussion he seems to have adopted a bullying tone somewhat incompatible with his remarkably mild Christian name, Jacques *Bénigne*, and to have forgotten the courtesy due to a lady who, whatever her errors might be in his eyes, was one of the brightest lights and purest saints in the Roman Catholic Church of that day. Finally, the matter became an affair of State, and the king appointed a commission to sit, at Issy, upon her orthodoxy—Bossuet, De Noailles, and Tronson. The two latter were charmed with her mild and teachable spirit. But the fierce Bossuet was not yet satisfied; and as she put herself under his special direction for a time, he consigned her to a convent at Meaux, and at length required her to sign certain doctrinal articles, and a decree condemning her books. To this last, however, a qualifying clause was appended, to the effect that she had never intended to say anything contrary to the spirit of the Church, not knowing that any other meaning could be given to her words. In fact, while conceding to her Church the right to condemn whatever it did not approve in her tenets, she held much the same position as Galileo when his theory as to the movements of our planet was condemned as heretical, and he capped his enforced retractation with the quiet protest, *"E pur si muove."*

In her letter to her three ecclesiastical judges, dated "in August, 1694," she courageously tells them, "I pray you, my lords, to remember that I am an ignorant woman; that I have written my experiences in all good faith, and that if I have explained myself badly, it is the result of my ignorance. As regards the experiences, *they are real.*"[1]

Bossuet at length appeared to be satisfied, and gave her a certificate of her filial submissiveness to the Roman Catholic faith, and she thought herself free to return to Paris. It was not perhaps the wisest step to take; the bishop was displeased at it, as was also the bigoted Madame de Maintenon. Madame Guyon went to live in privacy in a small house in the Faubourg St. Antoine, where she hoped to be left in peace. But her enemies got scent of her hiding-place, arrested her, and shut her up in the Castle of Vincennes, whence, after a few weeks at Vaugirard, she was transferred to the Bastille.

Of her life in this famous prison we have little or no detail. Like all its unfortunate inmates, she was forbidden to reveal its secrets; but we gather from her own words that, amid sickness and the many hardships of her prison life, one of her severest trials was found in the rumours which reached her of "the horrible outcry," outside the walls, against herself and her sympathisers. But in this dark season she held fast her confidence in God, and her spirit found utterance and relief in some of those songs, full of love and trust, which are included in the four volumes of her poetical works.

---

1 *La Vie*, troisième partie, ch. xvi., 6.

VII.

LAST YEARS.

She was confined in the Bastille for four years, and when at last, in 1702, she was released, her health was completely ruined by the privations she had suffered, the bitter cold of winter, and in the warmer weather the poisonous exhalations from the stagnant waters of the moat. When once more she issued into the sweet air of liberty, "My afflicted spirit," she says, "began to breathe and recover itself; but my body was from that time sick and borne down with all sorts of infirmities." Even now, however, she was not free to go where she liked. After a brief visit to her daughter in Paris, she was required to take up her residence at Blois, a hundred miles south-west, and there, in complete retirement, she spent her remaining days, still writing cheery words of counsel to her disciples in France and other lands, and enjoying spells of happy converse with the steadfast friends who sought her out in her exile.

She lived on in peace and quiet, though often in pain and weakness, for fifteen years after her release from the Bastille. Her final release from all earthly trials and sorrows took place on June 9, 1717, when she had entered about three months into her seventieth year. That her beautiful spirit of resignation was maintained to the last, and that her faith was pure and steadfast, we have proof in these expressions in her will, written a short time before her death: "Thou knowest that there is nothing in heaven or in earth that I desire but Thee alone. In Thy hands, O God, I leave my soul, not relying for my salvation on any good that is in me, but solely on Thy mercies and the merits and sufferings of my Lord Jesus Christ."

We find here no trace of that reliance on the Virgin Mary, or that frequent clamouring for her interest and intercession, which then formed and still forms so integral a portion of the daily routine of Romish worship. It is a remarkable feature of Madame Guyon's religious life that, in an idolatrous age, her faith constantly soared straight up to God, ignoring the mediation of the Virgin and the saints, and regarding the priests themselves, not as intermediaries between Christ and her soul, but simply as her appointed counsellors and guides on the road to heaven. We need not wonder that such bitterness was shown towards her, and that no effort was spared to suppress teaching so dangerous to the very foundations of the ancient edifice of error.

VIII.

HER TEACHING.

On a previous page I have given extracts from her autobiography which show pretty plainly the mistakes into which Madame Guyon fell at the outset of her Christian career. They had their root in the idea that her communion with God was so close and intimate that all her thoughts were not merely devout and God-ward, but even Divine, coming direct from God. So she fell into the Quietist error of intense introspection, looking for guidance, not solely to the written Word, but chiefly to her own inward impressions, or "inspirations," as she considered them to be.

But was it at all wonderful that this good woman, brought up in the bondage of corrupt doctrine and deeply-incrusted prejudices, should entertain some theological errors? The only wonder is that she attained so much of the truth, and, in that age of mingled intolerance and licentiousness, lived a life of purity and charity, of holy aspirations and devout performance. And though her excessive introspection is not at all to be imitated, and many of her views are such as we with our greater light cannot, of course, endorse, yet her mistakes in metaphysics and in theology did not affect the beauty of her life, which was chiefly spent in acts of charity and earnest endeavours to spread the knowledge of her Lord and Saviour. If her benevolent efforts at evangelisation did not always show the successful results she desired, if disappointments crowded some of her later years, yet to her case we can rightly apply the words of the poet:

> "Yet to the faithful there is no such thing
> As disappointment; failures only bring
> A gentle pang, as peacefully they say,
> 'His purpose stands, though mine has passed away.'"

Her Works, amounting in all to forty volumes, were published in Paris in several editions. Her *Poems and Spiritual Songs* occupy four volumes. Some of these simple utterances of a devout heart were beautifully translated by Cowper, and with one of the most characteristic of these renderings this sketch may fitly be concluded:—

"THE ENTIRE SURRENDER.

> Peace has unveiled her smiling face,
> And woos thy soul to her embrace,
> Enjoyed with ease, if thou refrain
> From earthly love, else sought in vain.
> She dwells with all who truth prefer,
> But seeks not them who seek not her.
>
> Yield to the Lord with simple heart
> All that thou hast and all thou art;
> Renounce all strength but strength Divine,
> And peace shall be for ever thine.
> Behold the path which I have trod,
> My path till I go homo to God."

WILLIAM NICHOLS.

ANN JUDSON.

CHAPTER I.

EARLY YEARS.

Ann, a daughter of John and Rebecca Hasseltine, was born in Bradford, Massachusetts, on December 22, 1789. The quiet daily life of the simple New England people from whom she sprang, and amongst whom she was brought up, was as beneficial a training for her future career as could have been found for her. The feverish activity and never-ceasing struggle to be first, which have now taken possession of the American people, were then almost unknown, and the descendants of the Puritan fathers spent their days in peaceful toil. Most of the New Englanders were engaged in farming or small manufactures, and there was a deeply religious spirit throughout the whole of the Northern States.

Of the early life of Ann Hasseltine we know comparatively little. Her family was evidently in moderately easy circumstances, and the Hasseltine household was a happy and closely-united one. The parents, with wise foresight, were careful to give their children as good an education as could be obtained in the neighbourhood, and kept them at school till well advanced in their teens. Ann was distinguished among her sisters for her gay, joyous, and somewhat emotional temperament. There was no half-heartedness about her, and whatever she took up she would throw her whole soul into. As was to be expected in a community where religious matters occupied so prominent a place, the urgent need of a personal faith in Christ was placed before her at an early age. She could not suppress a vague longing after something, she knew not what; and every now and then her conscience would be aroused, and she would quicken her efforts to be good.

When she was sixteen, affairs reached a crisis. A series of religious conferences had been held in Bradford during the early months of 1806, and she regularly attended them. Each meeting deepened the impression on her mind as to the need of a higher life. Her old amusements seemed now utterly distasteful to her, and the fear of being for ever lost weighed heavily on her soul. She was invited to a party by an old friend; but her heart was too sad to care for such things, so on the morning of the party she stole off to the house of one of her aunts, who, she thought, might be able to help her in her trouble. Her aunt spoke seriously to her of the necessity of obtaining salvation while she could, and the poor girl became more downcast than ever. "I returned home with a bursting heart," she afterwards said, "fearing that I should lose my impressions with the other scholars, and convinced that if I did so my soul was lost."

She shut herself in her bedroom, refused to touch any but the plainest food, and for some days pleaded with God for pardon. Gradually the light came in her soul. "I began to discover a beauty in the way of salvation by Christ," she said. "He appeared to be just such a Saviour as I needed. I saw how God could be just in saving sinners through Him. I committed my soul into His hands, and besought Him to do with me what seemed good in His sight. When I was thus enabled to commit myself into the hands of Christ, my mind was relieved from that distressing weight which had borne it down for so long a time. I did not think that I had obtained a new heart, which I had been seeking, but felt happy in contemplating the character of Christ, and particularly that disposition which had led Him to suffer so much for the sake of doing the will and promoting the glory of His Heavenly Father."

With so deep an experience it was only natural that the whole course of her outward life should be completely changed. She soon made an open profession of religion by becoming a member of the Congregational Church at Bradford; and her friends could see the reality of her conversion by her consistent daily walk.

She now threw herself with greater zeal into her ordinary studies, and this soon resulted in her being requested to take temporary charge of a small school at Salem. When the work there was done, a teachership was found for her in another place near at hand, and it was while thus engaged that she became acquainted, with her future husband, Adoniram Judson.

Mr. Judson, who was some sixteen months her senior, was the eldest son of a Congregational minister at Malden, near Boston, and had from his youth been noted for possessing intellectual powers far above the average. When a boy, he diligently read every book that he could get hold of, and at Brown University he graduated head of his class. For a time during his college course he became affected with the sceptical views which were then fashionable; but the death of a friend brought him back to the old faith, and as an outcome of his conversion he became a student at the Theological College at Andover.

While at college, Judson and three fellow-students had their interest deeply aroused in the conversion of heathen nations. They petitioned the General Assembly of their church on the matter, and solicited its advice as to whether "they ought to renounce the object of missions as visionary or impracticable;" and if not, what steps they should take to translate their longings into action.

The importance of this appeal was at once recognised by the churches, and as an immediate consequence the "Board of Commissioners for Foreign Missions" was formed, a society which has grown until it is now one of the greatest missionary organisations in the world. Judson went on a visit to England in order to expedite matters, and to consult with the officials of the London Missionary Society. After some delay, caused by the capture of the vessel in which he was sailing by a French privateer, he reached London and saw the directors. They agreed to support him and his companions should the American Board be unable to do so, and with this assurance Judson returned to America.

He now made Miss Hasseltine a formal offer of marriage, and she knew that if she accepted she must of course accompany him abroad. For a time she not unnaturally hesitated. She was asked to do what no American woman had before attempted, and the life of a foreign missionary seemed full of unknown horrors. It meant to leave home and probably never to see friends or native land again, to be worn out in the unhealthy climate of some tropical land, to suffer "every kind of want and distress, degradation, insult, persecution, and, perhaps, a violent death." Friends, with few exceptions, advised her to decline, and public opinion was strongly opposed to such a "wild, romantic undertaking" as a woman going out to the heathen. "O Jesus," she prayed in her perplexity, "direct me, and I am safe; use me in Thy service, and I ask no more. I would not choose my position of work or place of service; only let me know Thy will, and I will readily comply!"

After some weeks of hesitation she definitely made up her mind. "I have at length come to the conclusion," she wrote, on October 28, 1810, "that if nothing in Providence appears to prevent, I must spend my days in a heathen land. God is my witness that I have not dared to decline this offer that has been made me."

Her decision surprised many of her acquaintances. "I hear," said one lady to another, "that Miss Hasseltine is going to India. Why does she go?" "Why, she thinks it her duty. Would you not go if you thought it your duty?" "But," replied the first speaker emphatically, *"I would not think it my duty."*

On February 6, 1812, an ordination service was held at the Tabernacle Church in Salem, when Adoniram Judson and four others were set apart for foreign missionary work. On the previous day he and Ann Hasseltine had been made man and wife at Bradford; and a few days later Mr. and Mrs. Judson, accompanied by Mr. Newell and his wife, set out in the brig *Caravan* for Calcutta.

CHAPTER II.

THE ROAD TO RANGOON.

After a four months' voyage the missionary party reached Calcutta, and there they received a warm welcome from Dr. Carey and his fellow-workers. They were invited to the missionary headquarters at Serampore, a spot some few miles from Calcutta, in possession of the Danish Government, where the Baptist missionaries resided in order to avoid the interference of the English authorities. At that time the British rulers of India were opposed to all missionary work, and discouraged it by every means in their power. Foreign preachers were not allowed to reside in India even for a few weeks, and English missionaries were not suffered to remain unless they could obtain special permission from the East India Company. The American missionaries had not been many days in India before they discovered this. They were summoned from Serampore to Calcutta, and there formally commanded, in the name of the Company, to leave India at once and return to America. To do this would have ruined all their plans, so they asked and obtained permission to go instead to the Isle of France (Mauritius), whither a vessel was about to sail. But as it would only accommodate Mr. and Mrs. Newell, the Judsons perforce remained in Calcutta waiting for another ship.

They were allowed to stay in peace for a couple of months; but when the authorities learnt that they had not yet departed, an urgent order was issued, commanding that they should be immediately sent to England in one of the East India Company's vessels. There seemed no possibility of their evading the order this time, but they learned that another vessel was just going to set out for the Isle of France. Unfortunately it was impossible for them now to obtain permission to go there; but the captain of the vessel, on hearing the circumstances, offered to take them without leave. So they quietly got on board. But on the second day of their journey down the river a Government dispatch arrived, ordering the pilot to stop the vessel, as it had among its passengers persons who had been ordered to go to Europe. In consequence of this demand Mr. and Mrs. Judson were at once hurried on shore, and the ship went on its way.

They were landed at the village of Fultah, and here they remained for four days, not knowing what to do. If they returned to Calcutta they would be at once sent to England, and they could not remain where they were for any time without discovery and arrest. Every day their perplexity increased. The sight of a boat coming down the river or a stranger entering the village would fill them with alarm, for they expected at any moment to be seized by Government agents sent after them. At the end of the fourth day relief came in a most unexpected way. A letter was handed to Mr. Judson containing an official permit for them to go on to the Isle of France in the vessel from which they had a few days before been removed. How this permit was obtained, or who had sent it to them, they could never discover; and there was no time then to speculate on the matter. The ship was now at least seventy miles away, in the Saugur Roads, and had probably already set out to sea. In the hope that it might possibly have been delayed in starting, and that they might catch it, they at once started down the river in boats. After being rowed all night and all next day, they found on reaching the roads that they were in time, as owing to the absence of some of the crew the vessel had been delayed. It may be imagined how thankfully they found themselves once more on board.

Before leaving Calcutta an important change had taken place in Mr. and Mrs. Judson's views about the question of infant baptism. While on the voyage from America, Mr. Judson, knowing that he would come in contact with the Baptist missionaries at Serampore, had studied the subject in order to be able to defend his position to them. The result had been that doubts had gradually arisen in his mind as to the correctness of his own point of view, and he spoke on the subject to his wife. She deprecated any hasty action, but they both resolved to give careful attention to the matter. Every consideration of human interest would have led them to cling to their old belief, for, as Mrs. Judson pointed out, "If her husband should renounce his former sentiments he must offend his friends at home, hazard his reputation, and, what was still more trying, be separated from his missionary companions."

"I hope that I shall I be disposed to embrace the truth," she wrote, "whatever it may be. It is painfully mortifying to my natural feelings to think seriously of renouncing a system which I have been taught from infancy to believe and respect... We must make some very painful sacrifices. We must be separated from our dear missionary associates, and labour alone in some isolated spot. We must expect to be treated with contempt and cast off by many of our American friends—forfeit the character we have in our native land, and probably have to labour for our support where we are stationed."

After prayerful consideration they both applied to Carey for baptism, much to the surprise of the great English missionary, who had known nothing of their struggles. This step necessarily involved their separation from the Congregational Board of Commissioners who had sent them out, and there was then no American Baptist Missionary Society to which they could look for help; but Mr. Judson wrote to the American Baptist churches stating what he had done, and appealing to them to support him in his labours. The Baptists soon afterwards responded to his appeal by forming a Missionary Union, and they appointed Mr. and Mrs. Judson two of their agents. Thus was Mr. Judson an important though indirect instrument in causing another great American denomination to throw itself into the work of evangelising the world.

The first news that Mrs. Judson heard on reaching the Isle of France was that Mrs. Newell, her companion from America, had died a few weeks previously, before even being allowed to commence the work to which she had dedicated her life. The governor of the island had been warned about the coming of the Americans, and advised "to keep an eye on them;" but he gave them a warm welcome, and expressed a hope that they would settle in the place and work among the natives and the soldiers. But the Isle of France hardly seemed to offer a sufficiently extensive field for their energies, and there were other places more in need of their services. Mr. and Mrs. Judson specially wished to go to Burmah, where, with a population of many millions, there was hardly a single Christian teacher. But the character of the people and of the government was such that any strangers going among them must take their lives in their hands, Notwithstanding this they determined, after due inquiry, to go to Penang, and thence to attempt to find access to the country. It was necessary first to go to Madras, in order to find a vessel which would take them eastwards. But on arriving at Madras they found that it would be impossible to procure a passage to Penang; so they took passage in a ship that was going to Rangoon, and after some adventures reached the field of their future work in July, 1813. "We cannot expect to do much in such a rough, uncultivated field," wrote Mrs. Judson, "yet if we may be instrumental in clearing away some of the rubbish and preparing the way for others, it will be sufficient reward."

CHAPTER III.

PREPARATION TIME.

Mr. and Mrs. Judson might well have been excused had they hesitated to settle in Rangoon, for the prospects before them in that place were anything but hopeful. The Emperor of Burmah was an absolute monarch, and rumour gave him the credit of being unjust, tyrannical, grasping, capricious and cruel. The people were described as "indolent, inhospitable, deceitful and crafty;" and in spite of the natural wealth of the land the majority of the inhabitants were miserably poor. This was largely due to the fact that all property was held on the most uncertain tenure, everything being liable to be seized at any time by the emperor or by some of his officials.

More than one unsuccessful attempt had been made to form a missionary settlement in Rangoon previous to the arrival of the Judsons. Preachers had been sent out from Serampore, and by the London Missionary Society; but none of them had been able to occupy the field for any length of time. When the Judsons arrived there was only one other Christian teacher in Burmah, Mr. Felix Carey, who was then at Ava, the residence of the emperor. Mrs. Carey, a native of the country, was staying at Rangoon, in a house built by the Serampore Baptist missionaries, and she welcomed the new-comers to her home, where they stayed for some months.

The first work to which the Judsons set themselves was the study of the Burmese tongue. This was a task of extreme difficulty, for the only part of the language put into writing which would help them was a small portion of a grammar and six chapters of St. Matthew's Gospel, which had been translated by Mr. Felix Carey. Even with all the aids at present in use, Burman is anything but easy to acquire. It has been called the "round O language," on account of each word being made up of a number of small circles; and to an untrained eye the words seem almost exactly alike. "The letters and words are all totally destitute of the least resemblance to any language we have ever met with," Mr. Judson wrote to a friend in Salem, "and these words are not fairly divided and distinguished as in Western writing by breaks, and points, and capitals, but run together in one continuous line, a sentence or paragraph seeming to the eye but one long word; instead of clear characters on paper, we find only obscure scratches on palm leaves, strung together and called a book. We have no dictionary and no interpreter to explain a single word, and must get something of the language before we can avail ourselves of the assistance of a native teacher . . . It unavoidably takes several years to acquire such a language in order to converse and write intelligibly on the truths of the Gospel."

Mr. and Mrs. Judson obtained a native teacher, and settled down to a daily struggle with their task. The man was at first unwilling to have Mrs. Judson as a pupil, thinking it below his dignity to instruct a woman: but when he saw that she was determined to persevere he abandoned his opposition. As the teacher knew no English and the pupils knew no Burman, progress was of necessity very slow. "Our only mode of ascertaining the names of objects which met our eye," wrote Mrs. Judson, "was by pointing to them in the presence of our teacher, who would immediately speak the names in Burman; we then expressed them as nearly as possible by the Roman character, till we had sufficiently acquired the power of the Burman."

In order to get more in contact with the people, they left Mr. Carey's hospitable roof and took up their residence in the centre of the town. This obliged Mrs. Judson to commence housekeeping on her own account, and consequently she had less time to devote to study; yet to her surprise she made faster progress now than she had ever done before. She thus described her daily life, in a letter home: "We are busily employed all day long. Could you look into a large open room, which we call a verandah, you would see Mr. Judson bent over his table covered with Burman books, with his teacher at his side, a venerable-looking man in his sixtieth year, with a cloth wrapped round his middle and a handkerchief on his head. They talk and chatter all day long with hardly any cessation.

"My mornings are busily employed in giving directions to the servants, providing food for the family, etc. At ten my teacher comes, when, were you present, you might see me in an inner room at one side of my study table, and my teacher the other, reading Burman, writing, talking, etc. I have many more interruptions than Mr. Judson, as I have the entire management of the family. This I took on myself for the sake of Mr. Judson's attending more closely to the study of the language; yet I have found, by a year's experience, that it is the most direct way I could have taken to acquire the language, as I am frequently obliged to speak Burman all day. I can talk and understand others better than Mr. Judson, though he knows more about the nature and construction of the language."

It was impossible to do any direct evangelistic work until the language had been more fully mastered, and Mrs. Judson was continually spurred on in her studies by the desire to speak to the natives about the Lord Jesus Christ. "O Thou Light of the world," she prayed, as she realised more fully the ignorance of the people, "dissipate the thick darkness which covers Burmah, and let Thy light arise and shine!"

CHAPTER IV.

A HEAVY AFFLICTION.

When Mrs. Judson had been in Rangoon six months she was taken somewhat seriously ill, and it was deemed advisable that she should go to Madras, both for the sea voyage and in order to obtain skilled Medical advice, which could not be had in Rangoon. She met with nothing but kindness all the way. The Viceroy granted her special permission to take a native woman as her attendant, a thing which was deemed a very great favour indeed, as no native woman was usually allowed to leave the country. The captain of the vessel in which she sailed refused to accept any money for the passage; and when she sent the physician who attended to her seventy rupees in payment for his advice, he returned them with an expression of pleasure in having been of any service to her. She went back to Rangoon renewed in health, and a few months later she became the mother of a little boy.

For a short time the baby was the treasure of the mission-house. In their loneliness and separation from all friends, the hearts of the father and mother went out to their little one, and he became even more to them than an only child usually is to its parents. The Burmans regarded him as quite a curiosity, for he was the only purely white infant in the place. The baby would lie quietly for hours on a mat in the study, while his parents were poring over their books, and when work was done they would throw the palm leaves on one side, take up the boy, and carry him in state around the house and garden. His presence seemed to light up the home with a new and sacred joy; but he was not to be there long. When he had completely twined himself around his parents' hearts he was taken away, for after a few days' illness he died when only eight months old.

This sore affliction was the means of drawing out much sympathy from many of the natives. The chief wife of the Viceroy had been greatly attracted by the little lad when he was alive, and on hearing of his death she paid a visit of condolence to his parents, accompanied by her official attendants, numbering some two hundred people. "Why did you not send me word, that I might come to the funeral?" she asked, smiting her breast and showing every sign of sorrow. The heart-broken mother replied that her grief was so great that she did not think of it, and the Burman lady then did her best to comfort her, and strove with warm, womanly sympathy to make her forget her loss.

CHAPTER V.

SOWING TIME.

For three years Mr. and Mrs. Judson devoted themselves solely to the study of Burman, and did not even attempt any directly evangelistic work, beyond the opportunity afforded by casual conversation with a few individuals. They well knew that any impatient attempts to push forward the work would probably result in closing the country against Christianity for many years to come.

It was not without heavy hearts that they saw the years passing away and nothing apparently being done. They had half expected, before leaving America, that it would require little more than a plain proclamation of the Gospel to win converts; but a short experience of the reality of missionary life showed them that the work was not so easy as had been imagined. The people were careless and indifferent, and no permanent impressions seemed to be produced upon their minds. They would listen politely while the missionaries pleaded with them for Christ, and then would lightly dismiss the matter with the remark that all religions were good.

One reason why preaching had not been attempted was because Mr. and Mrs. Judson felt it would be well at first to devote their energies more especially to the printing and circulation of Christian literature. In Burmah almost every man could read, and it would be possible to reach far more through the printed page than by public speaking. A portion of a gospel had been translated by Mr. Felix Carey, but this was lost in a wreck, so Mr. Judson started a fresh translation of the New Testament, and prepared one or two tracts. In 1815 he wrote to Dr. Carey, asking if he could print some Burmese tracts at the Serampore press; the doctor replied that it would be far better for Judson to start a press of his own in Rangoon, and in order that he might do so he sent him a complete outfit, including a press, a supply of type, and other necessary stock.

When the printing press reached Rangoon, there came with it two new helpers, Mr. and Mrs. Hough, sent out by the American Baptist Missionary Society. Mr. Hough had been a printer before leaving America, and so he was able to render practical assistance almost from the day of his arrival, by taking charge of the printing department. Two small tracts were issued as quickly as possible, one a Summary of Christian Doctrine, and the other a catechism; and Mr. Judson hurried on with his translation of the New Testament. The printing of these was the first thing of the kind that had ever been done in Burmah, and the missionaries rejoiced that the art of printing should be introduced into the country directly through Christianity.

Their first serious inquirer was brought to them through these tracts. One day in March, 1817, a man, evidently of good position, came to the mission-house and astonished Mr. Judson with the question, "How long a time will it take me to learn the religion of Jesus?" The surprised missionary replied that it all depended on whether God gave him light and wisdom, and asked how he came to know anything of Jesus. Had he been there before? "No." Had he seen any writings concerning Jesus? "I have seen two little books." "Who is Jesus?" Judson asked, to test his knowledge. "He is the son of God who, pitying creatures, came into the world and suffered death in their stead." "Who is God?" "He is a being without beginning or end, who is not subject to old age or death, but always is."

Mr. Judson was delighted beyond measure to hear these words proceed from the lips of a Burman. He handed him a tract and catechism, but these the man had read, and specially wanted another book. Judson had told him that he was preparing another book, but had not got it ready yet. "Have you not a little of that book done which you would be graciously pleased to give me?" the man asked; and Judson, thinking it better not to let the opportunity pass by, gave him two half sheets which had been already printed, and which contained the first five chapters of Matthew.

The man did not come again to them for some time, but they learned that he was appointed governor of some villages a distance away. The following January he had to visit Rangoon, and once more called at the mission-house. Mr. Judson was away just then, having gone for a short time to India, but Mrs. Judson had a long talk with him, and asked him if he had yet become a disciple of Jesus. "I have not yet," he replied, "but I am thinking and reading in order to become one. I cannot yet destroy my old mind, for if I see a handsome cloth or handkerchief I still desire them. Tell the great teacher when he returns, that I wish to see him, though I am not a disciple of Christ." He requested more books and then left.

Up to this time the rulers had been most friendly, but in 1818 a little event occurred which indicated to the missionaries what might at any time happen. The former Viceroy had left, and a new one was appointed in his stead. It was the time when Mr. Judson was away in India, and one morning Mr. Hough received a command, written in most threatening language, ordering him to at once appear at the court-house to give an account of himself. He went, and was ordered to come next day for examination, and the officials assured him that, "If he did not tell all the truth about his situation in the country, they would write it with his heart's blood."

For two days he was subjected to a severe cross-examination, and the officials seemed to delight in annoying and threatening him in every possible way. He could not appeal to the Viceroy, for he was not sufficiently acquainted with the language; so the native teacher drew up a petition, and Mrs. Judson herself presented it to the Viceroy. He received it kindly, and at once gave orders that Mr. Hough was not to be troubled further. They afterwards found out that the thing had been arranged by the minor officials, in order to extort money from the missionaries.

Before Mr. Judson returned a severe epidemic of cholera broke out in Rangoon, and Mr. Hough was very anxious to take his wife and Mrs. Judson out of the place and go back to India. It was a trying and troubled time, and all missionary-work was necessarily at a standstill. Mrs. Judson was very reluctant to leave Burmah, and for long refused to depart; she had not heard from her husband for many months, and did not know on what day he might return. But Mr. Hough was so persistent that she at last consented, and allowed her luggage to be taken on board a vessel, she herself following. But at the last moment, when the ship was on the point of sailing, she felt that she could not leave, and ordered her things to be taken back to the city again. Mr. and Mrs. Hough went on, and she was left alone, but within a few days her husband returned, and her greatest trouble was over.

CHAPTER VI.

INQUIRERS AND CONVERTS.

Soon after the retirement of Mr. Hough, two other missionaries and their wives came out to Rangoon, and the Judsons felt it was time to commence a more aggressive work. A little house of public worship, or zayat, was erected in one of the main roads and opened to all who liked to come in. The work had to be done very quietly, in order not to arouse the opposition of the Government, for there was much uncertainty at the time about the course the officials would take should any converts be made. When the zayat was finished, Mr. Judson called together some of the people living around, and held his first public service in the Burmese tongue. From this time meetings were held several times a week, and during the day Mr. Judson would sit in the house, talking and arguing with all who chose to come in to him.

Every Wednesday evening, at seven o'clock, Mrs. Judson met a class of women, numbering generally from twelve to twenty. To these she would read the Scriptures and talk in a simple way about God. "My last meeting was very animating," she said when describing one of these classes, "and the appearance of the females (thirteen in number, all young married women) very encouraging. Some of them were inquisitive, and after spending two hours seemed loth to go. One said she appeared to herself like a blind person just beginning to see. And another said she believed in Christ, prayed to Him daily, and asked what else was necessary to make her a real disciple of Christ. I told her she must not only say that she believed in Christ, but must believe with all her heart. She again asked what were some of the evidences of believing with the heart. I told her the manner of life would be changed, but one of the best evidences she could obtain would be when others came to quarrel with her and use abusive language, if, so far from retaliating, she felt a disposition to bear with, to pity, and to pray for them. The Burman women are particularly given to quarrelling, and to refrain from it would be most decided evidence of a change of heart."

During the daytime, while Mr. Judson was talking with any man who called, Mrs. Judson would sit in another part of the place and see all the women visitors. By this plan she was enabled to preach the Gospel to many. What time she could spare from this work she now devoted to a study of Siamese. A number of people in Rangoon knew only that language, so she learned it sufficiently well to be able to converse with them, and to translate a gospel and several tracts into their tongue.

In 1819 the hearts of the missionaries were cheered by a native, Moung Hau, coming out and openly professing Christianity—the first fruit gathered after seven years of labour. Many had partly accepted their teachings, and had been evidently impressed by their message; but up to that time no real, definite converts had been made.

Moung Hau soon showed that a real work of grace was progressing in his heart. He told the missionaries that he had found no other Saviour but Jesus Christ, from all the darkness and uncleanness and sins of his whole life, that he could look nowhere else for salvation, and that therefore he proposed to adhere to Christ for ever. "It seems almost too much to believe that God has begun to manifest His grace to the Burmans," the members of the little mission band said one to another; but the sincerity of Moung Hau was such that they could not doubt it, and after a time of probation he was publicly baptized.

There were signs that this convert was only the first of an abundant harvest. In the autumn of the same year, two more men requested baptism, but this time the rite had to be performed privately, for the

Viceroy had begun openly to avow himself hostile to Christianity. Dark rumours of persecution were heard, and one inquirer was summoned before the authorities and warned to beware of what he did. So serious did matters become that public preaching had for a time to be abandoned, and many inquirers ceased their visits to the mission-house, and were heard of no more.

The missionaries thought that if they could only appeal to the Emperor, and obtain his permission to carry on their work, all might be well again; so after much deliberation Messrs. Judson and Colman went on a journey to the royal city of Ava, and obtained an audience of the Emperor. They humbly requested that his subjects might be permitted to become Christians without incurring the wrath of the authorities; but when the monarch heard their petition he treated it with open disdain, and they had to return to Rangoon saddened and disappointed beyond measure.

The news that nothing must be expected from the Government but persecution seemed to give strength to the three converts and to several really earnest inquirers. When the missionaries spoke of going to another part of Burmah, where they could have more liberty, their disciples implored them to remain. "It is useless to remain under present circumstances," Mr. Judson said. "We cannot open the zayat; we cannot have public worship; no Burman will dare to examine this religion, none can be expected to embrace it." "Teacher," one of the converts replied, "my mind is distressed; I can neither eat nor sleep since I find you are going away. I have been around among those who live near us, and I find some who are even now examining the new religion. Do stay with us a few months. Do stay till there are eight or ten disciples; then appoint one to be teacher of the rest." Many others said the same, and at last it was decided that Mr. and Mrs. Judson were to remain in Rangoon, while Mr. and Mrs. Colman, the other missionaries there at the time, should move to Chittagong, a place near at hand under British protection, and try to form a station there.

Within a few weeks after this, several who had long been inquirers came and requested baptism, although they were well aware that by doing so they were making themselves liable to death by most horrible torture. One man, a prominent native in good circumstances, and well known as a great orator and metaphysician, who had for a long time been arguing with Mr. Judson about Christianity, now openly declared himself a follower of Jesus. Others did the same, and God seemed to reward His servants by showing them such results from their labours as they had hardly hoped ever to obtain.

The threats of persecution for a time ceased, and the prospects of the mission improved in every way. By early in 1821 the number of baptized disciples had increased to nearly twenty, and among them were several professional men of great influence in the city and some women. Many others, although not professed disciples, showed by their acts that they sympathised with the Christians and would do what they could for them.

In December, 1821, Dr. Price, a medical missionary, arrived with his wife from America, and soon afterwards Mr. and Mrs. Hough returned. Though the missionaries were left in comparative peace, they well knew that severe measures might at any time be taken against them. Every now and then there came rumblings of the threatened storm, and one of the chief converts was obliged to flee from the city on account of proceedings being started against him for his change of faith.

A few months before the arrival of Dr. Price, Mrs. Judson had so broken down in health that her husband decided to send her to America for the long sea voyage. She first went to England, where she received a warm welcome from many Christians, and then she proceeded to the United States, where she spent the winter. Medical men in America were unanimous in advising her not to return to the East, as they said her state of health was such that she would probably die before long if she went there. But nothing could keep her back from what she felt to be the post of duty. "I cannot prevail on myself to be any longer from Rangoon than is absolutely necessary for the preservation of my life," she said; so in June, 1823, she started on the return journey, accompanied by another missionary and his wife.

CHAPTER VII.

PRISONERS OF WAR.

When Mrs. Judson reached Calcutta on her return voyage to Rangoon, she was informed that war might break out at any time between England and Burmah, and was strongly advised not to attempt to go on. But she was determined to rejoin her husband at once, and finding that a vessel would start for Rangoon in a few days, she took a passage in it. She was not to stay long in Rangoon, however, for the Emperor had ordered Dr. Price and Mr. Judson to take up their residence in Ava. Dr. Price was already there, and Mr. Judson had only stayed at Rangoon to meet his wife, on the understanding that he should set out for the capital as soon as possible.

The missionaries attempted to carry on their work at Ava in the same way as they had previously done at Rangoon, but the public mind was in too excited a state just then to permit of much progress being made. The Emperor had for some time treated the English Government with open disdain, and had collected an army together for the avowed purpose of invading Bengal. He even caused a pair of golden fetters to be made, to bind the Governor-General of India when he should be led as captive to Ava. But before the Emperor could carry out his plan, the English took the initiative and invaded his country. He was confident of victory, but information was soon brought to him that the English had captured Rangoon, and this was followed by news of various other English victories.

The foreign residents at Ava naturally felt that their position there was somewhat precarious. At first the Emperor assured them that "as they had nothing to do with the war, they should not be molested;" but when tidings of English triumphs followed one another in rapid succession, the attitude of the natives grew more and more menacing.

Some Englishmen formerly in the employ of the Court were seized, and their belongings examined. In the account book of one of them were items recording certain sums having been paid to Mr. Judson. This money had been given to him in exchange for circular bankers' orders, sent from America; but the Emperor did not understand this. He concluded that Judson had been paid to be an English spy, and at once gave orders for the arrest of both the missionaries.

The scene can best be described in Mrs. Judson's own words. "On the 8th of June, just as we were preparing for dinner, in rushed an officer holding a black book, with a dozen Burmans, accompanied by one whom, from his spotted face, we knew to be an executioner, and a 'son of the prison.' 'Where is the teacher?' was the first inquiry. Mr. Judson presented himself. 'You are called by the King,' said the officer—a form of speech always used when about to arrest a criminal. The spotted man instantly seized Mr. Judson, threw him on the floor, and produced the small cord, the instrument of torture. I caught hold of his arm. 'Stay,' said I, 'I will give you money.' 'Take her too,' said the officer, 'she also is a foreigner.' Mr. Judson, with an imploring look, begged they would let me remain till further orders. The hardened executioner drew tight the cords, bound Mr. Judson fast, and dragged him off I knew not whither. In vain I entreated the spotted face to take the silver, and loosen the ropes; but he spurned my offers and immediately departed."

Mr. Judson was hurried away to the death prison, and his wife found herself a captive in her own house. She was exposed to many insults from the guard of soldiers set over her, and for three days she was unable to go out. Then, by a judicious bribe, she obtained a certain measure of liberty. She at once went to the governor of the city and sought to obtain the release of her husband. This could not be gained, but she purchased permission to see him. He crawled to the door of the prison, as fast as his trebly-bound limbs would allow, and spoke for a minute to her; but before they could exchange many words Mrs. Judson was peremptorily ordered away by the jailer.

The Government officials came again to the mission-house and seized all the silver they could find in it; but Mrs. Judson had received warning of their visit, and before they arrived had hid as much money as she could. Had she not done this, she and her husband must inevitably have starved during the following months. As it was, she had something now with which to mollify the officials, and she succeeded in getting her husband and Dr. Price taken out of the common prison for a time, and placed in an open shed.

Day by day she worked incessantly, petitioning every one of influence, from the Queen downwards, for her husband's release. Many sympathised with her, but one and all declared themselves unable to do anything. The governor of the city, who had chief control of the prison, happily became their friend, and did all he dared for them. Three times he was informed by a near relative of the Emperor, that if he would cause all the white prisoners to be privately put to death it would be pleasing to the monarch; but every time he managed to avoid doing it.

For seven months Mrs. Judson strove daily on her husband's behalf, and spent what time she could with him in the gaol. "Sometimes," she said, "I could not go into the prison till after dark, when I had two miles to walk in returning to the house. Oh, how many times have I returned from that dreary prison at nine o'clock at night, solitary and worn out with fatigue and anxiety, and endeavoured to invent some new scheme for the release of the prisoners."

After her husband had been in prison for some months, she gave birth to a little daughter, and for a few weeks was unable to get about to look after the captives as before. During this time news came to Ava of further great defeats of the Burmese troops, and the treatment of the captives was at once made harsher. They were again shut in the inner prison, among all the common malefactors of the place, and were each bound with five pairs of fetters. The hottest season of the year had now arrived, and the situation of the prisoners was far more terrible than any words can describe. The room in which they were confined was occupied by about a hundred native criminals; there was no ventilation beyond that afforded by the cracks in the walls, and the continual stench and heat were almost unbearable. As soon as she could get about, Mrs. Judson built herself a small bamboo hut by the gate of the prison, and lived there, to be as near as possible to her husband. After he had been a month in this black hole Mr. Judson was taken ill with fever, and after much entreaty she was permitted to move him to a little bamboo cell by himself, and to go in daily to feed him and to give him medicine.

CHAPTER VIII.

"THROUGH MUCH TRIBULATION."

The darkest hour had not yet come! Two or three days after she had secured the removal of her husband from the common prison, he and all the white men were suddenly seized and hurried out of the city. Mrs. Judson was engaged elsewhere at the time, and for some hours she was unable to learn where the prisoners had been taken; but a servant who had seen them leave gave her a clue, and she at once followed it up. She deposited her books and medicines with the friendly governor, and set out with her babe on her arm, and two orphan children she had adopted by her side, seeking her husband. After a wearisome journey she found him in a wretched prison at Oung-pen-la, almost dead from weakness and the torture he had undergone on his forced march, and was greeted with the pathetic words, so illustrative of Adoniram Judson's utter unselfishness, "Why have you come? I hoped you would not follow, for you cannot live here." The prison was placed in a lonely spot, far away from any village. There was no accommodation for Mrs. Judson, and no food could be obtained near at hand. She was refused permission to build herself a little hut, but the jailer found her a small, dirty store-room in his own house, and here she and the three children lived for the next six months. Day by day she searched for food, not only for her husband, but for the other white prisoners; and though worn out with pain and sorrow, cheered them, looked after their every want, and continually applied to the officials for some improvement in their lot. The untold privations she was suffering soon told on a frame that had never been very strong. Her two adopted children were taken with small-pox, and when they had partly recovered the baby was also attacked. Mrs. Judson had now to look after them in addition to her other work, and would often spend the day attending to the prisoners, and the night in nursing the children. The watchings and fatigue at last broke her down, and for two months she was unable to leave her bed. She had for most of the time no attendant except a common Bengalee cook, but this man proved an invaluable aid. He worked almost without ceasing, nursing Mrs. Judson, searching for provisions, and feeding the prisoners. The little baby was in a most deplorable state. It had no nurse, Mrs. Judson could not feed it on account of her fever, and the only way it existed was by her husband obtaining permission from the jailer to go out for a short time each day, carry the child around the village, and beg a little nourishment for it from those mothers who had young children. "I now began to think the very afflictions of Job had come upon me," wrote Mrs. Judson. "When in health I could bear the various trials and vicissitudes through which I was called upon to pass; but to be confined with sickness, and unable to assist those who were so dear to me, when in distress, was almost too much for me to bear; and had it not been for the consolations of religion, and an assured conviction that every additional trial was ordered by infinite love and mercy, I must have sunk under my accumulated sufferings."

Meanwhile the English army was daily coming closer and closer to the capital, and Mr. Judson was taken out of prison and sent down to the Burmese camp, to act as translator in the negotiations which were going on between the two forces. The victorious British general, Sir Archibald Campbell, ordered the Burmese to pay a heavy war indemnity, and to cede a large part of their territory to the English; and he also stipulated that all foreign prisoners who wished should be handed over to him. Consequently the Judsons found themselves once more free, after a year and seven months' imprisonment, and were made the honoured guests of the English general.

But the relief came too late, for Mrs. Judson's constitution was completely undermined by the privations she had endured. She and her husband settled in Amherst, a new town in British Burman territory, and hopefully looked forward to carrying on a useful work there. They had not been many months in the place before Mrs. Judson had a bad attack of fever, at a time when her husband was away helping the English general. She seemed temporarily to get better, but she had no strength left to resist the disease, and gradually sank. "The teacher is long in coming, and the new missionaries are long in coming," she murmured in a moment of relief from her delirium. "I must die alone, and leave my little one; but as it is the will of God I acquiesce in His will. I am not afraid of death; but I am afraid I shall not be able to bear these pains. Tell the teacher the disease was most violent, and I could not write; tell him how I suffered and died; tell him all that you see; and take care of the house and things until he returns." For most of the time she lay unconscious, and on October 24, 1827, after about sixteen days of illness, and at the age of thirty-seven, she passed away before her husband could return. Soon afterwards her baby followed her.

And so went home one of the noblest women who have laboured in the mission field. Her brave spirit, her undaunted trust in God and in the power of prayer upheld her, when the courage of the bravest men would have failed. Not a little of the remarkable success of the work of God in Burmah is due to the indomitable perseverance and the wise devotion to God and to her husband of Ann Judson; and wherever the Gospel is preached, that also which this woman hath done shall be spoken of for a memorial of her.

Was her life thrown away? Were the labours and sufferings she had bodily undergone wasted? Not so. The story of her life has been and still is a precious heritage for the whole Church militant, a lesson which ever appeals to Christians to rouse themselves from self-seeking and apathetic lives, and consecrate their talents to the Master's use. Though she was taken up higher, the work in Burmah did not stop, and before many years had passed, hundreds and thousands of the people among whom she had laboured were professing to serve the true God; so true is it that "the blood of the martyrs is the seed of the Church."

FRED. A. McKENZIE.

MARY LOUISA WHATELY.

I.

PARENTAGE AND CHILDHOOD.

Mary Louisa Whately came of a distinguished family. Her father, Dr. Richard Whately, for many years Archbishop of Dublin, was one of the most remarkable and prominent men of the first half of the nineteenth century, a voluminous writer, a strenuous thinker, and a statesmanlike ecclesiastic. Her mother, Elizabeth, daughter of Mr. W. Pope of Uxbridge, was, says Miss E.J. Whately, a woman of "grace and dignity of character, delicacy of mind and sensitive refinement, which were united with high powers of intellect and mental cultivation and a thirst for knowledge seldom exceeded."[1] She was an ardent Christian, and devoted herself to works of beneficence and Christian service among the poor, as far as her delicate health would allow.

Mary was born at Halesworth in Suffolk, of which parish her father was then the rector, on August 31, 1824. The following year her father was appointed Principal of St. Alban Hall, and removed with his family to Oxford. In 1831 he accepted the Archbishopric of Dublin, and thus at the age of seven Dublin became, what it remained for thirty years, Mary Whately's home. She was the third of a family of five, four girls and one boy, who all inherited something of their mother's delicacy

---

1 *Life of Archbishop Whately*, by his daughter, vol. 1. p. 43.

of constitution and a good share of their father's strength of intellect and character. They were near enough to each other in age to share one another's studies and games, and, living a very retired life, depended largely on each other for companionship. For a portion of the year they resided in the archiepiscopal palace in Dublin. But on account of the many social demands made on him in the city, the place became distasteful to Dr. Whately, and he engaged a charming country residence called Redesdale, some four or five miles out of town. Here he resided the larger portion of the year, living a quieter life than was possible in the city, and driving into Dublin on most mornings to attend to his official duties. In the intervals of study and the discharge of public duty he devoted himself to his garden, in the cultivation of which he displayed much skill and ingenuity. Redesdale was the children's home, though the life there was occasionally varied by a stay in London (where their father usually spent a few weeks each spring to attend the House of Lords), at Tunbridge Wells, where they had relatives, or at the seaside, and later by visits to the Continent.

The Archbishop had very decided views on the training and education of children, and his wife also, as her *English Social Life* shows, had thought much on the subject. One of the Archbishop's rules was that children should never learn anything by rote. "When Mrs. Whately and I first married," he observed on one occasion, "one of the first things we agreed on was, that should Providence send us children, we would never teach them anything they did not understand. 'Not even their prayers, my lord?' asked the person addressed. 'No, not even their prayers,' he replied."[1] Mary's education was conducted mainly by a governess, under the superintendence of her parents. Her brother, Archdeacon Whately, thus refers to her early life: "Our life in Ireland was on the whole a very retired one. For the greater part of our sojourn there we saw very little society, nor had my sisters a sufficient vent for a craving, which in some of them

---

1 *Life of Archbishop Whately*, by his daughter, vol. 1. p. 62.

was very strong, for social intercourse and active work . . . In early life she showed the germs of that vigour and energy of character for which she was afterwards so distinguished. In all our youthful games she was fond of taking the lead, and generally succeeded in obtaining it . . . Like most young persons of a sanguine and imaginative temperament, she lived very much in an ideal future of her own creation . . . It was well for my sister that we were not allowed in our younger days to read any unwholesome trash in the way of fiction. We were not indeed unduly restricted in works of imagination, but we read nothing which was foolish or sensational, and a higher taste than the taste for mere stories was cultivated in us. Mary Whately had a strong predilection for works of travels, history, and adventures. Perhaps these tastes were a foreshadowing of her future destiny, and prepared her for it."[1] Her sister adds, "Mary was from her earliest years ardent and impulsive, hot-tempered and generous. She was quick at lessons, and possessed of a retentive memory, though the active brain and lively imagination made schoolroom routine somewhat irksome to her."[2]

---

1 *The Fireside* for 1889, pp. 817, 818.
2 *Life of Mary J. Whately*, by E.J. Whately, p. 10.

II.

THE BEGINNINGS OF CHRISTIAN LIFE AND SERVICE.

Dr. and Mrs. Whately gave their children a careful religious and moral training, and sought to instil into their minds the highest motives for right doing, and to set before them a high standard of conduct. Mrs. Whately early associated her daughters with herself in visiting among the poor in the village of Stillorgan, which adjoined the grounds of Redesdale, and in teaching in the village school. The poor of Dublin also were not forgotten, and especially at Christmas time Mary shared with her mother in the distribution of gifts among the deserving poor in the city, and in the entertainment of many of them in the servants' hall of the palace.

It is not known, perhaps she could not herself tell, exactly at what period the light of the Gospel first dawned upon her heart, but a subsequent time at which her spiritual life was much deepened and intensified was very marked. In 1849 the health of her brother broke down, and he was ordered by the physicians to spend the winter on the Continent. Mary accompanied him. They went first to Nice, but the climate disagreeing with them, they passed on to Florence and Pisa, and subsequently spent some time among the Waldensian valleys. This tour was in many ways a preparation for Mary's future life. She took lessons in painting, which was to be the chief recreation of her later years; she attained some proficiency in Italian, which led her a few years afterwards to engage in mission work among the poor Italians in Dublin; and her visit to the Waldensian valleys gave her her first insight into evangelical work abroad. But most important of all, she became acquainted with M. Meille, a young Waldensian pastor, and his wife, through her intercourse with whom her religious convictions became intensified and her spiritual horizon widened. When she returned to Dublin the great Irish famine was still continuing. The distribution of food and other efforts to relieve the distress were occupying the attention of all philanthropic persons. Mrs. Whately had become actively engaged in this work, and she and her daughters henceforward took a more prominent part in aggressive Christian work than they had hitherto done. Famine relief paved the way for greatly extended effort to spread Gospel knowledge among the Roman Catholic population. Industrial and Bible schools, refuges, and other Christian institutions sprang up in various parts of the country. Protestant missions to Roman Catholics were greatly extended. In this work Mary Whately found opportunity for the expression of her deepened spiritual experience. She taught in the adult classes at the Townsend Street Mission Hall joined her sisters and other ladies in founding a ragged school for boys—the first in Ireland—and afterwards in instituting a work among destitute girls, which issued in the Luke Street Girls' Home where hundreds of poor girls were taught to live respectable and Christian lives. These various forms of Christian service gave her tact and experience in dealing with the poor, which proved invaluable in her subsequent work in Egypt. As her sister says, "The Irish Church Mission work was the preparatory training to which she always especially looked back with thankfulness. The admirable manner of teaching and explaining Scripture employed in their schools she felt to have been the most valuable education for her subsequent life-work."[1]

In 1856, as she was in ill health, it was recommended that she should spend the winter in a warmer climate. Egypt was chosen, and, accompanied by a friend, she landed at Alexandria and proceeded to Cairo, where she

---

1 *Life of Mary L. Whately*, by E.J. Whately, p. 15.

remained several months. This was her first acquaintance with what was to be the land of her adoption. Before returning home in the spring of 1857 she made a prolonged tour in Syria and Palestine. She took much note of the mission work carried on in various places, and so greatly interested was she in the work among Jewesses then carried on in Jerusalem that she had some thoughts of giving it for a time her personal assistance.

III.

FIRST EFFORTS IN CAIRO.

The year 1860 was one of sorrow and bereavement to Mary Whately. She lost first her youngest sister, then her mother. Under the strain of nursing and sorrow her own health was seriously affected, and she was ordered by the doctors to spend the winter in a warmer climate. Her thoughts recurred to Egypt and her former pleasant sojourn there; accordingly she selected Cairo as her residence, purposing in her heart to make an attempt to bring the Gospel within reach of the Moslem women and girls. Egypt was then very different from what it is now. Railways were but just beginning to make their appearance, the Suez Canal was not yet cut, European customs, now so prevalent, had scarcely begun to invade the age-long usages of the upper classes. English residents in Cairo and tourists up the river were alike few in number. Few outside influences had been brought to bear on the Mohammedan population to moderate their extreme bigotry and hatred of anything called *Christian*—a word which they invariably associated with the picture and image worship of the members of the Greek or Roman Church with whom they had come in contact, or with the irreligious pleasure-seeking of tourists, or travellers by the overland route to India. The Copts, or descendants of the early Egyptian Christians, were almost without exception buried in the profoundest ignorance of the Scriptures and of Christian truth, given over to superstitious beliefs and practices, and destitute of any real spiritual life. Education for boys was of the most primitive character; for girls it was never thought of, nor had any educational effort ever been made for them during the twelve centuries which had elapsed since the rise of Mohammedanism. Christian missionary operations were almost non-existent. The American Presbyterians had recently commenced missionary effort, but their work was mainly, as it still is, among the Copts, and they had not yet opened a station in Cairo. Since 1827 indeed the Church Missionary Society had maintained a missionary—sometimes two—in Cairo, but their work had not issued in the formation of a Protestant Christian Church.

"It was laid on my heart," says Mary Whately, "to try and do something for the girls and women of the land, especially those of the Moslem poorer classes, far the most numerous, of course. The only schools hitherto opened for the children of the land had no scholars except from the Copts or native Christians; others were considered quite out of reach, and many of my friends endeavoured to dissuade me from an attempt which was sure to end in failure, as they said. However, it seemed best to make an effort, at all events. But it was begun in prayer, and therefore difficulties and delays did not greatly discourage me."[1]

Mary Whately, accompanied by a cousin, resided for a time with Mrs. Lieder, of the Church Missionary Society. But in order to open a school she had to engage a house for herself; and after great difficulties one was secured in a suitable position. It was but a comfortless abode, and only rude furniture and inefficient domestic help were obtainable. But Miss Whately held outward comforts in light regard. Even in later days, when she had built for herself a capacious and comfortable house, it was furnished in the simplest, even rudest fashion, and all her personal expenses were cut down to the lowest possible point, that she might have the more to spend the work to which she gave both her heart and her life. As as she was settled in her new house she endeavoured to make acquaintance of her neighbours.

---

1 *Life of Mary L. Whately*, pp. 21, 25.

Miss Whately was but just beginning to learn Arabic, and the only assistants she could get for starting her school were a Syrian matron—who could speak but a few words of English and read with difficulty the New Testament—and her daughter of thirteen. Accompanied by the Syrian matron, Miss Whately went out into the surrounding lanes and invited the women to send their little girls to her to be taught to read and sew. She met with many curt refusals and received many fallacious promises; but when at last, in February 1861, a start was made, nine little girls were present the first morning "No recruiting sergeant," she says, "was ever so pleased with a handful of future soldiers, for it was beating up for recruits for the Lord." [1] The numbers gradually increased, though from time to time they were seriously affected by the spreading of malicious reports and the opposition of bigoted relatives and the only way to keep up the attendance was to go round visiting to obtain recruits, and to cultivate an acquaintance with the parents of the old scholars. In three months the children had been reduced to some sort of order, taught the alphabet and the way to sew; they could repeat a few texts, and sing a few hymns with some approach to sweetness. But perhaps of more importance still, they had learned to love and obey their teacher. Before her return to England for the summer she took them for an early morning feast in the public gardens of Cairo: and when the simple repast was finished, while "the little ones danced and waved boughs in a perfect ecstacy of merriment," the elder girls, she says, "seemed to find no pleasure so great as following us about, pointing to the flowers, and frequently throwing their arms round us, exclaiming, 'I love thee! I love thee much!' with eyes really overflowing with affection. How often had it been said 'You can make nothing of Moslem girls!' but the key of love is wonderfully powerful, and equally so in every land in opening the doors of young hearts."[2]

---

1 *Bagged Life in Egypt*, new ed., p. 29.
2 2 *Ibid.*, p. 110.

Meanwhile the beginnings of other Christian work had been made by Miss Whately. In the early mornings she would drive or ride a few miles out of the city, and seating herself near to some hamlet would enter into conversation with the women and girls, and seek to instil into their dark minds some drops of divine truth. Much of her time also was spent in visiting the poorer women of the city.

When, at the end of May, both the heat of the climate and family claims necessitated her return home, she placed her little school under the care of a teacher whom the Society for Promoting Female Education in the East provided.

The following winter was passed with some friends at Pau. After a trip to the north of Spain she spent another summer at home. In the autumn of 1862 she again arrived in Cairo, to re-open her school, which had for some time been suspended through the departure of the teacher. Many of her former scholars, hearing of her return, came to give her a very hearty greeting, and were willing to come back to school, bringing their younger sisters with them. They had, however, forgotten nearly all they had learned, and were at first very unruly. No assistance beyond that of an ignorant woman to help keep order and teach a little sewing was obtainable, while Miss Whately's still imperfect acquaintance with Arabic increased the difficulties which are everywhere experienced in the conduct of a ragged school. The younger children were especially difficult to deal with. The parents of the Mohammedan children objected to the use of pictures, being accustomed to see them the objects of reverence on the part of the Copts and other Eastern Christians, while the Coptic children were inclined to worship them. Amusing songs in Arabic, suitable for young children, there were none; and when a little marching about was attempted for the sake of variety, the mothers said, "We send our children to *learn*, and you teach them to *play*! If that is what they go to school for, they may as well be at home."[1] After a time a young

---

1 *Among the Huts*, p. 269.

woman was found who could do a little teaching. Miss Whately had to continue to give all the religious instruction herself. Yet, despite the many difficulties, the school was firmly established and continued to make slow but steady progress.

When her scholars were about to start for the "school-treat" to which reference has been made, a little boy, looking on with envious eyes, had exclaimed in a piteous voice, "I wish I were a girl."[1] "It was indeed a triumph," says Miss Whately, "to the little school that it caused an Egyptian boy even for a moment to wish himself a girl." Other boys had expressed their desire to come to school; so, as the 'girls' school did not meet on Sundays, Miss Whately started a Sunday class for boys. This was all it was possible for her to do by herself. But just at that time she became acquainted with one who, with other members of his family, was henceforth to be closely associated With all her work in Egypt. This was Mansoor Shakoor, a young Christian Syrian of good family and education, who, after working for some years as teacher and evangelist in Syria, had become agent in Cairo for the Moslem Mission Society, recently established in England. First of all Yousif Shakoor, brother of Mansoor, came to help her in work.[2] Later Mansoor also entered her employ, and she maintained both the brothers from her private resources. Thus she was provided with devoted and efficient helpers. Under their superintendence a regular school for boys was established, and when in 1863 she again returned to England she left the charge of all her work in their hands. On the 8th of October in that year Archbishop Whately died, and Mary Whately's Irish home being broken up, she determined henceforth to fix her permanent abode in Cairo. She now hired another house near to her own residence for the accommodation of the increasing schools.

---

1 *Ragged Life in Egypt*, new ed., p. 167.
2 *Life of Mansoor Shakoor*, pp. 58, 59.

Very few English people can stand the intense heat of the Egyptian summer, and Mary Whately being disinclined in 1864 to come so far as to England, spent a short time instead in Syria. When she returned to Cairo she took with her to educate and train Fereedy Naseef, the young cousin and betrothed of Mansoor Shakoor. For this young girl there sprang up in Mary Whately's heart a deep and warm affection; she called her and treated her as her daughter, and both before and after her marriage in the summer of 1868 she resided under Miss Whately's roof. When in 1872 her husband died, she still remained, and Miss Whately shared with her the care and training of her young son and daughter, while she in return gave great assistance in the conduct and work of the mission.

IV.

MISSION WORK IN CAIRO AND ON THE NILE.

Is it possible to convert Moslems to Christianity? are they ready to receive it? No one perhaps is more competent to answer these questions than Mary Whately, and this is what she says: "To say, as has been sometimes rashly declared, that the Moslems are ready to receive Christianity, and that the faith of the false prophet is crumbling away, is what I would not venture for a moment to assert. But I can state as a fact, that in the neighbourhood of Cairo the peasant population both men and women, are willing, and many of them eager to *listen* to the Word of God when it is brought before them judiciously and discreetly, as well as with kindness and zeal."[1]

Subsequent experience confirmed this view, and more than twenty years later she remarks "It is necessary to be discreet in dealing with Mohammedans, for if the spirit of bitterness is once aroused, the door is shut, for the time at least, against good influences."[2] To awaken to an experience of vital religion the ignorant, superstitious, and spiritually lifeless Copts is a difficult task; to bring to personal faith in Christ the bigoted Moslems is more difficult still. "A Moslem's religion," she says, "is twined up with his political, social, domestic life so minutely, that the whole rope, as it were, has to untwisted before he can be free from error,

---
1 *More about Rugged Life in Egypt*, p. 210.
2 *Life of Mary L. Whately*, p. 109.

and the very admixture of truth in their book makes it harder in some respects to refute than if, like the heathen doctrines, it was all wrong throughout. Perhaps the intense self-righteousness of Moslems is after all the hardest point about them; their notion that in the end all who are Islam are safe strengthens them in this belief."[1] Nevertheless, the points of contact between the Mohammedan faith and the Christian a wise teacher can use as pegs to hang Christian teaching upon; and this Mary Whately's previous experience among the ignorant and bigoted Roman Catholics of Ireland enabled her to do with much tact. When peasants said to her, "Your book is Christian—we don't like Christian books," she would explain that it was God's book, and that the Koran did not forbid it to be read; and that she wanted to tell them about Seidna Eessa (the Lord Jesus), whom Mohammed acknowledged to be a prophet. In this way many an initial difficulty would be overcome, and the reading, with simple explanation, of stories from the Gospels would elicit the response, "The words are good," and the request for the gift of a New Testament.

As soon as Miss Whately had settled in Egypt she began visiting the poorer women of Cairo. Usually she was received with courtesy, and when she became known, with gratitude; and though this work was arduous and consumed much time, through it an entrance was made for the Gospel into many homes. Into the houses of the rich she penetrated but seldom, partly because her work lay in other directions, and partly because these were occupied by numerous slave-wives, who, being chiefly Circassians or Georgians, spoke Turkish, and did not understand Arabic. In earlier years Miss Whately did all the visiting herself, and her books bear abundant testimony to the skill with which she could turn the conversation to spiritual matters; in later years she was much assisted in it by Mrs. Shakoor and by a Bible-woman whom she employed.

---

1 *A Glimpse behind the Curtain*, p. 117.

Mansoor and Yousif Shakoor engaged in similar work among men. They often found men at the coffee-houses willing to listen to the reading of the Scriptures. When this was put a stop to through the opposition of the Moslem priests, a book depot was opened, which did good service for some years. Evening meetings were also established, but these were attended almost exclusively by Copts, though occasionally a Moslem would brave the real danger of being present at a Christian service.

Beside the early morning rides to which reference has been made, which afforded opportunities for religious conversation, Miss Whately would occasionally stay for a week or two at some farmhouse or by the seaside, and find opportunities of teaching the people around something of the Gospel. The following is an incident connected with this work in the country: "At an open spot just outside the village a barber was shaving a peasant's head, and, as usual, a group were assembled near him chatting and smoking. Mr. Shakoor took advantage of this and resolved to join the party of men, and get into conversation, while I went a little further in search of some women. I soon found four or five with some little girls, all sitting upon a dust-heap! They looked very dirty, as well they might, but I remembered 'who can raise up the beggar from the dung-hill and make him to sit among princes.' I saluted the poor women in a friendly way, and though looking astonished they replied civilly. After a little chat and a few questions on both sides, I asked if they had ever heard about our first parents, Adam and Eve, and how sin came into the world. They just knew the names, but no more, and were pleased to listen while I related the story. Before I had finished, an old woman who had come up interrupted me. A young man who was standing near and listening, desired her not to interrupt the lady, for he could see she was learned, and 'thou art ignorant,' he added, with more truth than politeness. 'But you are not well placed here,' he said, pointing to the heap on which they were seated. 'Come to the roof of my house, my mother will show you the way, and these women can come too if they like.' I acceded to this courteous invitation, and followed the mother and son up the mud-brick steps leading to the rude terrace; and though anything but clean, it was a great improvement on what we had left, and with genuine kindliness the old woman brought out an old but well-preserved carpet and spread it for me. The others had followed, and sat round to hear what the stranger could have to read to them. They really seemed interested, though sometimes interrupting me with remarks not at all to the purpose. I managed to bring them back to the stories I read, of course choosing the simplest possible, and trying to explain a little as we went."[1]

Miss Whately would occasionally make an excursion into the desert, making the acquaintance of the wild Bedouin tribes, and reading to them the Scriptures. "Lady," once said a Bedouin, lifting the curtain of a tent in which she and her sister were seated, "I saw your horse at the water, and my comrade and I are come to hear some of your book." They listened attentively while she read to them the ninth chapter of John's Gospel.

An important part of her work was the missionary tours which she made each year in the winter or early spring. The first of these journeys was in 1861, the last within a few weeks of her death. The spiritual condition of those she visited is thus described by Miss Whately: "The mass of the peasants are little, if at all, different from what they were in the days of Pharaoh. Instead of praying to gods of stone and revering brutes, it is true they now call on the Almighty, but know scarcely anything about Him, neither His Word nor His laws. Much of the religion of the *fellah* consists in prostrations, and his *spontaneous* prayers are usually invocations to dead men, as we see with Nile boatmen and other labourers; when in a fatiguing work, they call on the 'Lord Hosseen or Zeid,' &c. to 'stretch out a hand and help.' Buffaloes and sheep are frequently sacrificed at the shrines of sheiks of reputed sanctity, or at the mosque dedicated to Lady Zeynab. A pilgrimage to Mecca and the performance of certain ceremonies there are supposed to cleanse the pilgrim from sin. The Copts

---

1 *Among the Huts*, pp. 181-184.

(who form the minority of the population) have always preserved their veneration for Scripture, but neglected it, and were extremely ignorant, till in some degree aroused by the efforts of missionaries to seek more after education, and to read more of the Word of God." She proceeds thus to describe the work among these people: "On our yearly Nile excursion we had great cause for encouragement, both among the Copts and the far more numerous Moslems. The coast of the river is dotted with numbers of villages—some almost large enough to be considered towns, boasting a few houses with windows, a mosque, and a small primitive school; others are mere hamlets, consisting of mud huts crowded closely together, and built in and out of the palm-trees. We brought to several of these places both medicine for the sick and books for those who desired them, and were heartily welcomed as the peasants' friends; indeed every year the welcome grows warmer. Dr. Azury, the skilful medical man of the Mission, has always numerous patients; and after their bodily ailments have been attended to, they and their friends and neighbours assemble on the shore to hear him read from the Bible. Mrs. Shakoor and myself are at the same time occupied in visiting the poor women in their homes or in reading and speaking to troops of both men and women in the open air. When we are going to leave, the boat is besieged by men and lads asking for Bibles or portions of Scripture, which are given to those only who can read. The last sight as we sail away is often that of a circle gathered round one who reads aloud to those who cannot read for themselves."[1]

---

1 *Report of the English-Egyptian Mission* for 1887.

V.

PROGRESS OF THE SCHOOLS.

The boys' school, which had begun with a few ragged Moslem children in a room which was little better than a stable, increased rapidly. In 1870 the pupils numbered one hundred and sixty in daily attendance. About half were Moslems, the rest Copts and Syrians, with one or two little negro slaves or bronzed Nubians. Many were very poor, but some belonged to the middle classes, and there were even a few from wealthy families, who would ride to school on donkeys from distant quarters of the town. The two brothers Shakoor devoted much of their time to the superintendence of the school, and taught all the higher branches, being assisted in writing, spelling, &c., by several native teachers. The girls' school advanced less rapidly, because of the early marriages, which usually withdrew the pupils about the age of twelve, and because girls were more wanted at home than boys. In 1870 there were about a hundred names on the roll, with an average attendance of seventy or eighty.

It was long Miss Whately's desire to acquire a piece of land on which to build suitable school premises. Her desire was gratified when in 1869 the Khedive, Ismail Pasha, at the kind suggestion of the Prince of Wales, made her a grant of the freehold of nearly an acre of land, just outside the old wall of Cairo, the only condition being that the building erected on it should have a handsome front, as it would face a main road. Considerable delay was experienced in getting the necessary papers for making the possession secure, and it was not till 1871 that the building was erected. Mansoor Shakoor, who had considerable knowledge of architecture, designed it, and superintended all the details of its erection. By its side, and separated from it only by a garden, Miss Whately put up a house for herself, that she might be always close to her work. About one fourth of the cost was contributed by those who in Cairo and in England took an interest in the work of the school, but Miss Whately herself contributed the remainder of the outlay, amounting to about four thousand pounds.[1]

In consequence of the extension of the work, and because this large outlay had seriously diminished her resources, Miss Whately depended largely on the gifts of others for means to carry on her work. After the addition of a medical mission in 1879, the expenses of the work amounted to some £1200 or £1300 a year, a sum which, of course, it was quite out of her power personally to provide. £200 of this was derived from an annual grant from the Egyptian, Government, and about £150 from paying pupils, while occasionally grants were received from several English societies. The new schools soon became one of the "sights" of Cairo, and the English and American tourists who visited them contributed considerably to the funds, while the rest of the money required was collected in England, mainly through the efforts of members of Miss Whately's family and the honorary secretary of her English committee. But the difficulty of securing sufficient funds to carry on her work efficiently was always one of Mary Whately's chief burdens, and she was often obliged to make up deficiencies herself. During her occasional visits to England, which latterly occurred only once in two or three years, she was largely occupied in addressing public and drawing-room meetings on behalf of her work.

But to return. The new school buildings were opened in January 1872. "All the friends and acquaintances who took any interest in education, whether natives or Europeans, were invited to be present. The school

---

1 Letter from Mary L. Whately, *The Christian*, June 15, 1882.

hall, a large and beautiful room, though very simple and without any architectural ornaments, was adorned for the occasion with wreaths of green leaves, berries, and flowers, such as an Egyptian winter offers in abundance; and a table spread in an inner room with fruit and sweets to regale the children, while coffee and sherbet were handed among the visitors. Mr. Shakoor then spoke to the parents and friends of the scholars, telling them how the building had been made for God's glory and the good of the children in time and in eternity, and that with a good secular education the knowledge of God's revealed Word in the Old and New Testament was given to all of them."[1] Four months later Mansoor Shakoor died, an irreparable loss to the mission, and four years later his brother Yousif followed him.

From the opening of the new buildings the schools advanced rapidly. It was soon found that the simple teaching of reading and writing to the boys would not attract scholars, but to secure the advantage of instruction in English and French, geography, history, and accounts, many parents would send their boys, who were thus brought under Christian influence. The extent to which this prevailed may be judged from the testimony of the schoolmaster, that "of the boys brought up under his tuition, not one had, so far as he could find, taken more than one wife," which showed a great breaking away from the traditions of Mohammedanism.[2]

The girls received a simpler education, but with both boys and girls the daily reading and explanation of the Scriptures in Arabic held a prominent position, the Bible being the principal reading book in use. "Nor is the teaching of those things that concern salvation confined strictly to the time spent in reading Scripture. A few questions, or a remark in the course of a secular lesson, often shows them what is the most important of all matters in our minds. Nothing positively controversial is taught; that is to say, no contemptuous expressions about the religion of any of the

---

1 *Life of Mansoor Shakoor*, p. 98.
2 *The Christian*, June 29, 1888.

children are allowed, and the plainest truths of the Gospel specially set forward; but occasionally something comes into the lesson which shows to an intelligent learner the vanity of the superstitions around them."[1]

The policy of employing Egyptians or Syrians as teachers was frequently challenged by people in England, and vigorously defended by Miss Whately. "The schools are under my personal superintendence," she wrote in 1885, "receiving not only daily supervision, but examination from me, and I never gave up the teaching of any part of Scripture into other hands, until I had truly converted as well as educated teachers as assistants."[2]

In 1879 pupils had to be refused for want of room, and from that time till her death the scholars numbered nearly seven hundred.

The period of the Arabi rebellion in 1882 was a severe testing time. Though deliverance came at the eleventh hour, and Cairo was spared, "the inhabitants," writes Miss Whately in her report for that year, "lived for months in a sickening anxiety which can hardly be realized by those who only know the general facts from the papers." Not only Jews and Christians, but Moslems who remained faithful to the Khedive were threatened with torture and death. Miss Whately stayed at her post long after nearly all the Europeans had fled, and only left when the English Consul informed her that he would be no longer responsible for her safety. "The superintendent of the Mission Boys' School remained in Cairo at great personal risk, to keep things together as much as possible. The schools were not closed till the bombardment of Alexandria, when the excited mobs in the streets made it unfit for children to be abroad, and it soon afterwards was necessary to take away the board with the notice of the 'British Schools,' &c." The school buildings were used as a refuge for the homeless and persecuted, both foreigners and Egyptians. A list of buildings doomed to pillage included the Mission House. "The second day after the entrance of the victorious army, the superintendent opened the

---

1 *Among the Huts*, p. 116.
2 *The Times*, Aug. 15, 1885.

school. The pupils flocked back by degrees. At first some of the children of *Arabists* hung back, but began to follow the rest after a time." Miss Whately had the joy of knowing that in the time of extremest danger many young Coptic girls, formerly her pupils, when urged to pretend to turn Moslems to save their lives, had replied, "No! if we die, we die in the faith of the Messiah."[1]

Yet the same year a night school for youths of the better classes was established. Several years previously Miss E.J. Whately had founded in connection with the school a branch for the education of the children of European parents in Cairo. After the rebellion these were much less numerous, and the branch, henceforth known as the Levantine School, was chiefly attended by Jewesses, Armenians, Syrians, and others of Eastern race, who paid for the education they received. Among them it did good service. Subsequently small branch mission schools were established in Gizeh and other places.

---

1 *Report of English Egyptian Mission for* 1882.

VI.

THE MEDICAL MISSION.

Sympathy with the sick poor around her for whom no medical aid was available, early led Mary Whately to dispense simple remedies and especially to distribute medicine to relieve the terribly prevalent ophthalmia. In this she attained considerable skill, and though her nerves were more susceptible than others often thought, she bore bravely the contact with dirt and the sight of suffering which these labours entailed. "She loved to relate," says her sister, "what affectionate gratitude was called out by these acts. The Egyptians are very sensible to kindness, and she never forgot how a poor mason, whose hand, injured by the fall of some part of a wall, she had daily dressed, afterwards recognising her as he passed by her garden railing, saluted her with the words, 'May Allah ever hold your hand, O lady!' This kindness it was that won her a way among the poor of the city. In lanes and streets where she had been met by pelting with dust and cries of 'Cursed Nazarene!' she was now met by the salutation, 'Blessed be thy hands and feet, O lady!' or similar words of welcome. 'Sitt Mariam' (literally Lady Mary) became a household word in many mouths."[1]

Miss Whately perceived that medical mission work—of which none whatever had been attempted in Cairo—would form an excellent introduction to Christian work among the adult population. In 1878 therefore she engaged Dr. Azury, a skilful Syrian doctor, who had

---

1 *Life of Mary L. Whately*, p. 62.

been trained in the American Medical College at Beyrout, and who had lately married Mrs. Shakoor's sister. Almost before the necessary premises could be secured numerous sufferers applied for treatment. At first a small wooden room was built by Miss Whately on her premises as a waiting room for the patients and dispensary for the doctor; and during the first three years over four thousand patients were cured or relieved, and many operations performed, some of which restored sight to the blind. In 1881 a suitable building for this branch of the Mission was erected, containing two airy waiting rooms, one for women and children and the other for men, a consulting room in which the doctor saw his patients, and two separate rooms, each containing a bed or two for the reception of cases that needed constant care. In the waiting rooms Mary Whately might be found almost any morning reading the Bible and talking to the patients waiting their turn to see the doctor. No compulsion was used, but an attentive hearing was usually obtained, while a psalm or some story from the New Testament was read and explained. As the same people would often come every day or two for several weeks, something like continuous teaching could be given. In this work Mary Whately greatly delighted. In any difficult case, says a friend *(Sunday at Home*, 1889, p. 406), "'Sitt Mariam' would take her place in the surgery, ready with a kind word and practical assistance." An instance of the good done by the mission is given by the same writer. "A young woman came one day weeping bitterly; she was one of the wives of a sheik of a village some miles away, and she was almost blind. Her husband had told her that she was no longer of use to him, and he should divorce her. She was in a pitiable state of distress. The doctor, by God's help, was able to cure the poor young wife completely. She returned to her village in deepest thankfulness, and was taken back into favour by her lord and master. Some time afterwards she returned again, this time bringing a tall turbaned man with her, who proved to be her husband; he was the sufferer this time, and the good and forgiving wife had persuaded him to come and see the doctor to whom she owed so much. After some time the man was cured, and during his bodily treatment we may be sure that his soul was not forgotten. He showed his gratitude by sending many from his village to the Medical Mission; so that the seed was sown broadcast."

VII.

LITERARY EFFORTS.

Mary Whately, though she belonged to a book-writing family, aspired to no literary fame. Her ten books were all the outcome of her work in Egypt, and were written to awaken interest in it, and in some cases to secure funds for it. She was, as a girl, the "story-teller" of the family, and among her companions secured a reputation for her powers of narration. This gift she turned to good account.

"It was at her father's suggestion and by his advice that her first book, *Ragged Life in Egypt*, was published. A friend staying in the house had been reading to him a series of letters Mary had written her, describing her first settlement for the winter in Cairo, the commencement of her school, her visits among the poor, etc. He listened with much pleasure and attention, and on his daughter entering the room a few minutes afterwards, he said, 'Mary, you ought to publish these papers!' Her first answer was, 'Oh! people are tired of Egypt! they have had so many books of travels there and so many details!' 'Yes,' he rejoined, 'but yours will be new; you have reached a stratum lower than any foreign visitor has yet done.' This determined her to publish; and the book was finished and brought out immediately. In 1863 the same friend read to the Archbishop during his last illness the manuscript of the second part, *More about Ragged Life in Egypt*. On the morning on which the reading was finished, he took his gold pen from his pocket, and giving it to her said, 'I shall never use this again, Mary; take it, and go on.'"[1]

In 1871 she published a further account of Egyptian life and of her mission work, under the title, *Among the Huts in Egypt*. Meanwhile in 1867 she had contributed to the *Leisure Hour*, and afterwards issued as a volume, *The Story of a Diamond*. Another story, *Lost in Egypt*, was written in 1881. In 1873 Miss Whately published a biography of Mansoor Shakoor, and in 1881 she wrote *Letters from Egypt for Plain Folks at Home*. In 1878 she published a story called *Unequally Yoked*, illustrating the miserable lives of English women who have been persuaded to marry Mohammedans, and in 1872 she wrote *A Glimpse Behind the Curtain*, a story of life in the harems of Cairo. Her last book appeared in 1888 with the title, *Peasant Life on the Nile*. With changed names and in a slightly veiled form, it recounts the history of some who received spiritual blessing through her mission work. All her books are written in a simple unaffected style, and reveal an unrivalled acquaintance with Oriental character and the Egyptian mode of life. Most of them are illustrated by engravings from her own sketches.

---

1 *Life of Mary L. Whately*, pp. 55-57.

VIII.

RESULTS.

Writing in 1861 Miss Whately said, "The reaping time is not yet."[1] Ten years later she writes: "It is a missionary's duty to sow beside all waters, and to lose *no* opportunity, even if his chance of doing good be but small. The sower of the seed has need of much patience; and though he need not actually be *expecting* and looking for disappointment, as that would paralyse his efforts for good, he must yet be prepared for it."[2] In this spirit of patience and perseverance Mary Whately carried on her work, and though her work was largely pioneering, she was not without encouragement. Her hand was the first to begin to break down the wall of ignorance, prejudice, and bigotry which had for centuries shut in the people of Egypt. She convinced thousands that the Christian book is a good book, and Christian men and women good people, despite the evidence to the contrary of so many in Egypt who bear the Christian name but do not live the Christian life. The sentiments of the people are leavened by thousands among them who in youth passed through her schools, and there acquired an acquaintance with Scripture truth. "Youths employed under Government, on the railways or in mercantile houses, who have received with the secular education which has secured their positions, a thorough knowledge of the Bible as its condition, continually

---

1 *More about Ragged Life*, p. 199.
2 *Among the Huts*, p. 151.

greet her after they have quite outgrown her recollection."[1] The teachers in later years were chiefly composed of those who had been pupils in the schools, and of whose conversion she had no doubt. Thousands of poor sufferers were relieved by the Medical Mission, thousands of homes made happier by the visits of herself and her assistants. Many of the Scriptures distributed on her Nile journeys were kept and read, and found afterwards in most unlikely places.

In 1870 Miss Whately was able to tell of the first of her scholars of whose conversion she could feel sure. In 1878 she writes of two little boys, pupils in her school, who read the Bible at home to their old nurse, a slave woman, during the illness which terminated in her death. So simply did she receive the truth, that she declined to see the Mollah or reader of the Koran, saying, "No, no, I want no one but Him whom the boys tell me about; the boys' Saviour is my Saviour."[2] In *Peasant Life on the Nile* Miss Whately gives several instances of Copts who through her efforts refused to turn Moslems, and of others who became Christians in deed and in truth.

Instances of blessing on the work of the Mission might be multiplied. Nevertheless the difficulty of bringing a Mohammedan to an open avowal of Christianity always remained extremely great. Converts to Christianity always incurred the risk of secret poisoning. Yet in the report for 1888, penned by Miss Whately only a few weeks before her death, she says, "The seed sown in past years is evidently taking root;" and the accounts for that year contain the significant entry, "Clothes for poor convert on his baptism, £2." She also gratefully acknowledged that the reading of the books of her lending-library, largely supplied by the Religious Tract Society, had reached more Mohammedans than any other Christian agency.

---

1 *Lost in Egypt*, preface.
2 *Letters from Egypt*, pp. 117, 118.

IX.

TWILIGHT.

Like the twilight in the land of her adoption, the twilight of Mary Whately's life was very brief. Her sun went down while it was yet day. Her last years were among her busiest. She would rise very early, often watching from her balcony the dawn break, and then would take a ride in the fresh morning air, or go out into her garden, for, as with her father, gardening was her delight. After a simple breakfast she would be usually found in the dispensary by nine o'clock, reading and talking to the patients. When they had all been cared for, she would teach her Scripture class in the Levantine school, and afterwards visit the other schools, or attend to some of her domestic duties. After a short rest in the heat of the day, the remainder of the afternoon would be occupied with receiving or paying visits, and the short evening before retiring early to rest, when free from various forms of mission work, with painting or reading. When burdened with the difficulties of the work, she would often exclaim, "Why tarry the wheels of His chariot?" and the coming of the Lord was ever the object of her lively anticipation.

In the summer of 1888 she paid her last visit to England, taking also a tour in Switzerland, which she greatly enjoyed. Early in the autumn she returned to Cairo, where she was joined by her elder sister, who frequently spent the winter with her. In February she made preparations for her usual Nile trip. After the boat had been engaged and paid for, she caught a cold, and was urged to defer the journey; but as this would have caused extra expense, she declined. The excitement of the work, which, on account of the doctor being unable through ill health to accompany her, was unusually heavy, kept her up for the time, but on her return to Cairo she had to retire to bed. Bronchitis set in, and in a few days the gravest was feared. A relapse discovered weakness of the heart, and on the morning of Saturday, March 9, 1889, her spirit fled. Then was there, as of old, "a grievous mourning" among "the Egyptians." No need was there to employ professional mourners to make a wailing; the teachers and scholars, and the hundreds of poor men and women who had learned to love her, wept aloud for her. Her body was laid to rest in the English cemetery in Cairo, but she herself rested from her labours among those of whom she wrote:—

> "Oh! they've reached the sunny shore
> >   Over there;
> They will never hunger more;
> All their pain and grief is o'er;
> >   Over there.
> Oh! they've done the weary fight
> >   Over there;
> Jesus saved them by His might;
> And they walk with Him in white;
> >   Over there."

W.R. Bowman

AGNES JONES[1]

CHAPTER I.

YOUTHFUL DAYS.

A chance visitor to the Liverpool Workhouse on Brownlow Hill might be lost in wonder at its vastness, as he looked at its streets of large buildings and was told of its more than four thousand inhabitants. He would scarcely imagine that those bare-looking groups of buildings possess an historic interest. Yet to the Christian philanthropist it is holy ground, for there, in willing sacrifice for others, were spent the last years of the life of that saintly woman who gave the death-blow to the old system of pauper nursing and all its attendant evils. But we are looking at the stream as it enters the limitless ocean of eternity. We can do that again by-and-by. Let us turn now rather to the beginning of that stream of life and trace it onwards.

Agnes Elizabeth Jones was born at Cambridge on the 10th of November, 1832, the 12th Regiment, of which her father was the lieutenant-colonel, having arrived there only a few days before.

When Agnes was about five years of age, her father's regiment, which had previously been quartered at Cork, was ordered to Mauritius. The wonderfully varied and beautiful scenery of this little island—a tiny

---

1 The extracts are made, by kind permission of Messrs. Nisbet & Co., from *Agnes Jones*, by her sister.]

gem set in the heart of the Indian Ocean—with its curiously shaped mountains, and tropical trees and plants, made a wonderful impression on the mind of the child, and although she was only eleven years old when she left, she always cherished the memory of it.

But it was not only that her mind was roused to a keen appreciation of the beauties around her during her residence in Mauritius. The higher part of her nature, chiefly through the faithful teaching of one of the French pastors on the island, was also touched, and in the young heart there arose the longing to be safely folded in the arms of the Good Shepherd. A sentence in one of his sermons haunted her night and day:—"And now, brethren, if you cannot answer me, how will you at the last day answer the Great Searcher of hearts?" An arrow shot at a venture, it pierced her heart, and although she did not yet yield herself fully to God, she never entirely lost the desire to be His, even when apparently outwardly indifferent. We may well thank God for His servant's earnest ministry, for had he been less faithful, the whole course of that life, which was to prove so valuable in the service of the Lord, might have been changed.

From Madagascar, five hundred and fifty miles from Mauritius, yet its next-door neighbour westwards in the silver sea, there came, when Agnes was yet but seven years old, the tidings of a fearful persecution of the Christians. The letters received at that time told of indescribably dreadful sufferings for Christ's sake, and the sight of the Malagasy refugees who fled to Mauritius, fired her young soul with the desire to become a missionary. This desire, however, in her exceeding reserve, she kept to herself. God had other purposes for her, and it was amongst her own country people, and not in the foreign field, that He called her to labour.

After the return of her parents from Mauritius, the greater part of four years was spent in a beautiful spot at the foot of the hills of the Donegal Highlands on the banks of Lough Swilly, one of the loveliest of the Irish lakes. This period is spoken of by her sister as one in which she appeared utterly indifferent to spiritual things, yet some entries in her journal indicate an intense longing after a higher life. They certainly show that she knew the sinfulness of her own heart and the weakness of her resolutions, and that, in common with so many reserved natures, while hiding the true state of her feelings from others, she was much given to introspection and inclined to magnify her faults. Such reserved natures do not "wear their heart on their sleeve," and it should be a comfort to parents and teachers who are anxiously watching children to know that "things are not always what they seem," and that many a child who seems altogether careless is in reality not far from the kingdom.

In January, 1848, when a little over fifteen, she was sent to school at Stratford-on-Avon, and remained there until her father's death in 1850. The good discipline of this school and the wise guidance of her teachers had a most wholesome effect on the development of her character, and the steady, indomitable perseverance in the face of difficulties which so marked her after-life distinguished her then. By her painstaking and close attention she made up for her want of quickness in learning. Hence she never forgot what she had once learned.

The actual time of her conversion seems to have been during the period that she resided with her mother and sister in Dublin. To the earnest man of God whose ministry they attended, the preparation of the younger members of his flock for admission to the Lord's Supper was no perfunctory task. He introduced her, with others of his candidates, to one of his helpers as "anxious inquirers." So shy and reserved was Agnes that she said but little, yet this lady remarked of her:—"In the class her intense appetite for the living bread was so apparent, that I often felt myself speaking to her only, her calm gentle eyes fixed on me, as God helped me to speak."

It is impossible for those who have definitely accepted Christ's salvation, and who truly realise His love to perishing sinners, to be idlers in His vineyard. We are therefore not surprised to find her soon at work, her own particular plot being in the ragged school. Her needy little scholars were a great interest to her. She always showed the greatest sympathy and devotion to them, and while caring for their souls did not forget their bodily needs. Even when on a holiday she sought and found work amongst the poor. Indeed, distress of any kind always appealed to her heart.

There are some Christians who are very active in the outside world, but who forget that the first duty of a child of God is to "show piety at home." It was not so with Agnes Jones, for it was in the home that the beauty of her life was most visible, and it was in the family circle that the affection and unselfishness of her character shone most conspicuously. Others, indeed, could plainly see the development of the Christ-life in her, but she herself, dwelling as she did in the presence of her Lord, was prone to judge herself harshly. Thus, with every moment occupied, she charged herself with being lazy and negligent.

The first step towards the great work of her life was taken while on a visit to the Continent in 1853. During the May meetings in Paris, there was one held on behalf of the Oeuvre des Diaconesses, one of the branches of the Institution at Kaiserswerth on the Rhine, founded by Pastor Fliedner. This she attended, and was then first made acquainted with that work, which became of great interest to her, an interest which was much strengthened by a visit to Kaiserswerth itself about two months later. "As we drove away," she writes, "my great wish was that this might not be my last visit to Kaiserwerth . . . That visit was, I believe, a talent committed to our care; may it not be buried."

So full was she of the conviction that by seeing more of the work at Kaiserswerth she would be the better fitted for her beloved work in Ireland, that she proposed that she should go there for a week. To her great joy her mother concurred in the proposal, and earnestly did Agnes pray that this visit might be blessed and sanctified by God to His glory.

She was charmed with all that she heard and saw at Kaiserswerth, with the love which was so manifest in all, with the intensity of purpose, the perfect obedience, the beautiful order, the incessant work without fuss or bustle, and above all with the spirit of prayer, which pervaded the whole institution. Her journals show how strong was her desire to return there for training, for she believed that "as we use means to fit us for any earthly profession, so are we bound to use every means which will enable us to adorn our Christian profession." Her friends, however, knew nothing of her wishes. They were told only in the ears of her God.

CHAPTER II.

AT WORK IN THE VINEYARD.

For some time after her return from the Continent, Agnes Jones resumed her former work in Dublin, labouring more energetically than ever. In 1856, however, she and her mother returned to Fahan, the old home on the shore of Lough Swilly, always a favourite spot with her, not only because of the beauty of its scenery, but also because her beloved father was there laid to rest.

To the Christian who is ever on the watch opportunities for service are never lacking, and Agnes soon found her hands full. Did a child fall into the fire—a very common accident in that district—she must be fetched, for so gentle yet so firm was her touch in dressing wounds that the fame of her skill had spread for miles, and she was sent for from far and near, to Protestants and Roman Catholics alike. Was some one dying, still it was she who must come to smooth the pillow and speak the words of life.

The spiritual side of her work she never lost sight of, but made the rest subservient to this, as a means to an end, always reading the Bible if allowed, and following the reading by a simple but practical and faithful explanation. She was indeed "instant in season" and out of season. In all weathers she might be seen speeding along the lonely mountain roads, setting off soon after breakfast, to be at work the whole day, with the exception of the early dinner-time, and often not returning until after dark. She was tempted, as every other worker is, to relax her energies and to stay at home if the weather were bad, or if she were not feeling well; but instead of yielding, she would, if a bad headache came on, start off the earlier, that she might not lose the chance of a visit through the pain increasing. Yet her duties at home were never neglected. Rather than omit them, she would rise at five, that she might anticipate the wants of others, and save her mother trouble.

Agnes herself, in her intense humility, considered that she was an unsuccessful worker, and was inclined to condemn herself for lack of zeal and earnestness. But her work was a great joy to her, and especially did she love her happy talks with some of the aged Christians amongst the sixty families she regularly visited.

He is a rash soldier who ventures into the battle without a weapon tried and proved, and he can only be an unsuccessful Christian worker who does not make the Word of God the rule and guide of his life. To Agnes Jones the Bible was a constant study. She was a most earnest student of God's Word, and delighted to meditate upon it. In her journal she writes:—"What should I be without my Bible?" And again, realising the truth of the promise, "He that watereth shall be watered also himself," she says:—"God's Word often comes home more strongly to my own heart as I read to the poor, and try to make a few simple remarks." Little wonder is it that, knowing and loving His Word as she did, Christ was to her a very personal Saviour and Friend. Her one longing was for more and more likeness to Him.

CHAPTER III.

FOREIGN TRAINING.

However strong and good our wishes may be, it is never safe to force on their accomplishment. They are never the losers who wait God's time, and the wisest course of all is the one which Agnes Jones pursued, of telling her wishes to God, and then, in perfect submission to His will, leaving the issue with Him.

It was not until seven years after her visit to Kaiserswerth that the way was made open for her to return there. This step had been suggested by her mother five years previously, but the filial spirit was so strong in her that, although she eagerly desired a more thorough training for God's service, she felt that her mother stood first, and refused to leave her alone. Now the case was different, and she gladly seized the opportunity. Still she was nervously fearful lest after all she should not be following the guiding pillar.

It was in the autumn of 1860 that she arrived at Kaiserswerth, where she immediately entered heartily into the work. Her intention was to stay for only a month, or at the most six weeks; but after she had been there but a short time, the pastor so strongly represented the great advantage it would be to her to spend the whole winter in the institution, that she felt constrained to write for her mother's permission to do so. As ever, she was full of prayer for God's guidance, and that whatever was done might be only for His glory. Her mother leaving the choice entirely with her, she decided to remain, believing that the training would be of inestimable use to her in her future work.

The Deaconesses' Institution at Kaiserswerth had a very small beginning. Pastor Fliedner, having heard of Mrs. Fry's work amongst female prisoners, was filled with longing to follow her example, and received two discharged prisoners, whose friends had refused them, with the object of giving them the chance of retrieving their character. He set them to work under the personal supervision of himself and his wife. The work soon increased, and assistance was needed. To the penitentiary were added an orphanage, a training-school, a hospital, and a lunatic asylum. More and more workers were drawn in, and at the time of Agnes Jones's first visit there were fifteen branches of the institution in different parts of the world. This number by the time of her second visit had increased to fifty.

The deaconesses as novices passed through every department of the work, and received a thorough training in both nursing and household work, the pastor wisely considering that if, when in visiting the poor, they could render them practical help, their words would prove far more effective. Much was made of Bible study, both public and private, and this, as well as the *Stille Stunde* (quiet hour), a half-hour daily set apart for prayer and meditation, could not but tend to give a spiritual tone to the whole work. Agnes revelled in all this, and found great happiness in the daily routine, in spite of much which was, perhaps, somewhat needless drudgery, such as sweeping and dusting her room, washing up after meals, and even black-leading stoves. She had, however, well learned the lesson that no action can be mean to the Christian if it come in the way of duty. Sometimes, indeed, it seemed a waste of strength to spend so much of the day in manual work, especially work which so injured her hands that for some time she was obliged to keep them poulticed, and was thus unable to assist in the hospital. Still she was, as she said herself, "as happy as the day is long, and it does not seem half long enough," in spite of a longing sometimes "for home sights and voices."

Soon after her arrival at Kaiserswerth, fourteen sick boys were given into her care for twelve hours a day. This was no easy task, particularly when she was left in sole charge of them, some being too far recovered to lie in bed, and needing to be kept at lessons or work. As the weeks rolled by, her work was changed, and in addition to other employment, she instructed a number of classes in English, both in the training-school and among the deaconesses. As for herself, she was daily becoming more proficient in German, and in a very short time was able easily to follow the sermon. This was a great enjoyment to her, as she much valued the truly evangelical teaching at Kaiserswerth.

At the end of three months of steady work, she spent a few days with an uncle and aunt who were staying at Bonn, but the gay boarding-house life contrasted so unfavourably with the happy Christian fellowship at Kaiserswerth, that she was thankful to return to her duties, playfully writing:—"The nun will not soon again leave her cell, for it was with very nun-like feelings she met the world again." Yet she was no misanthrope. She did not bring to God a heart which had tried earth's pleasures and had found them wanting, nor a life jaded with pursuing them. From the first, she had cast aside the love of worldly things, and had chosen to be wholly the Lord's.

During the latter part of her stay at Kaiserswerth, her duties lay entirely in the hospital. In January she wrote:—"My duties are in the children's hospital, all ages from two to twelve. It is a new life for me in a nursery of sick children, and a busy one too, for every moment they want something done for them."

A month or so later she was appointed superintendent of the boys' hospital, a post of peculiar responsibility and difficulty. It was one, too, from which she shrank, holding the mistaken idea that she possessed no powers of government. Certainly it was a position to tax the patience, for the children were not too ill to be noisy and disobedient, or even sometimes to unite in open rebellion, while the task was not rendered easier by the necessity of speaking in a foreign tongue.

Altogether she had a very busy life. She rose at 5.O A.M. every day, and kept hard at work, with the exception of the intervals for meals and the *Stille Stunde* (quiet hour), until night. "The cleaning and keeping my dominion in order is such a business," she writes. "Sweeping and washing the floor of the three rooms every morning, two stoves which must be black-leaded weekly, each taking an hour, weekly cleaning of windows, tins, dinner-chests, washing-up of bandages, &c., besides the washing-up after each of our five meals, keeps one busy." She must have been strong in those days, for she wrote:—"I come over from the other house every morning at six, the ground white and windows frozen over; often at three in the afternoon the water outside is still frozen, yet night or morning I never put on bonnet or handkerchief, unless when I go out for a walk."

From the first the hospital patients with their varied needs were a great interest to her. Now it is a dying man, beside whom she has to watch, longing to minister words of comfort, yet unable to do so, fearing that her then want of fluency in the language might trouble him in his weakness. Yet as she heard the poor man's cry, "Lieber Heiland, hilf mir" (Dear Saviour, help me), her prayers, too, rose for him to the compassionate Saviour. Now it is a little boy with a bad back, terrible sores, and a racking cough, who would let no one else touch him. "Every night," she says, "I used to pray with Otto after they were all in bed, and he used to put his poor little arm round my neck as I knelt beside him; but last night (the night before he died) he said of himself, 'I will only now pray that Jesus may take me to heaven, and that I may soon die,' and as I had put my face near him to hear, he said, 'Lay your cheek on mine, it does me so much good.'"

We have seen quite enough of Agnes Jones by this time to know that she never shrank from a duty, however repulsive. Her love for her Master, and her desire to serve others for His sake, preserved her from any fastidiousness. In spite of her sensitive and sympathetic nature she could bear to witness the most painful operations without flinching, for she kept before her mind the ultimate good which would accrue from the present suffering.

One day news reached Kaiserswerth of the deplorable condition of one of the English hospitals in Syria. Sick and well, it was stated, were crowded together in a place where rubbish of every kind was thrown, an insanitary condition anywhere, but especially so in an Eastern climate. Helpers, they said, were much needed. Agnes longed to step into the breach, and in a letter to her mother she says:—"The English send plenty of money, but hands are wanting. It is no new thought with me that mine are strong and willing; I would gladly offer them. Could my own mother bear to think of her child for the next few months as in Syria instead of Germany? It is but temporary, and yet an urgent case. My favourite motto came last Sunday, 'The Lord hath need;' if He has need of my mother's permission to her child He will enable her to give it. This is but the expression of a wish, and if my own mother were to be made too anxious by the granting it, let it be as if unasked by her own Agnes."

Her standard of filial obedience was indeed a high one, though no higher than the standard of God's Word. Before this, in asking permission to remain longer at Kaiserswerth, she had written to her mother:—"Your wishes shall be my guide, now and for the future, as long as I am blessed with such a loving counsellor. I trust my present training in obedience will not be lost in reference to home."

Although she thought the whole training at Kaiserswerth invaluable she wrote long after:—"I believe all I owe to Kaiserswerth was comprised in the lesson of unquestioning obedience." Those who would rule must first learn to obey, and certain it is that she would never have been fitted to be afterwards the head of a large institution hundreds to care for and govern, had she not so truly imbibed the spirit of obedience.

While she had a profound admiration for Kaiserswerth, she could still see that the life of a deaconess, shielded though it is from the world, is not exempt from danger. Some fancy that the life of a deaconess, or of any one similarly set apart, must be much more free from temptation than that of any ordinary person. "I think," she wrote, "every one is as much called on as a deaconess is to work for Him who first loved us; but if this does not constrain us as Christians, neither will it as deaconesses, and certainly the 'Anstalt' (Institution) is a world in which the Martha-spirit may be found as well as in the outer world. There are many most deeply taught Christians here, many whose faces shine, but I should say, comparing my home life (but few have such a home) with that of the deaconesses here, I should say that, in many positions here, there are more, not only daily but hourly temptations."

The fact that nursing was her vocation had for a long time been dawning on her mind, but the way to go to Syria did not seem open, and the Lord had other work for her. Almost by the same post there arrived two letters, one from Mrs. Ranyard, so well known as the originator of the London Bible Mission, suggesting that she should go and help her in the great work of superintending and training the Bible women, the other from a philanthropic gentleman, unfolding a plan for a proposed nurses' home in connection with an infirmary, and asking if she, after a few months' special training, would become its superintendent. Thus, while one door was shut, two others unexpectedly opened to her.

But which should she enter? This was the question which she prayerfully debated. She wished to lay out her life to the best interest for God, and both schemes had special attractiveness to her; the one, because of its intensely spiritual work; the other, because of her love for nursing, and the boundless possibilities for good there might be in training nurses. She feared, however, that as superintendent of the nurses' home she might be fettered in more definite Christian work. She felt she must be left in no uncertainty on this point. In her letter replying to the gentleman who had written to her, she said:—"You sent me the ground plan of the building, but I would ask, is its foundation and corner stone to be Christ and Him crucified, the only Saviour? Is the Christian training of the nurses to be the primary, and hospital skill the secondary object? I ask not that all should be of one Christian denomination, but what I do ask is that Jesus, the God-man, and His finished work of salvation for all who believe on Him, should be the basis, and the Bible the book of the institution. If this be your end and aim, then will I gladly pass through any course of training to be fitted to help in your work."

Soon after writing this letter she bade farewell to Kaiserswerth. Her plan was to go first to London to consult with Miss Nightingale and other friends as to her future. The seven months in Germany had been most happy ones, and she was ever thankful for the time she had spent there. She fully saw the great need of Christian training institutions. In those days the Evangelical Protestant churches, unlike the Romanists, who for many centuries had largely availed themselves of it, were not alive to the importance of the ministry of women. There were no institutions in England where Christian women could be trained to work for Christ, that work of all others the most important, and some, to secure the training they longed for, and could not get elsewhere, had even entered Roman Catholic sisterhoods. Times are changed now, thank God, and although there is still the need of more, there are many institutions where Christian women can be thoroughly and efficiently trained for service of different kinds at home and abroad.

CHAPTER IV.

IN LONDON SLUMS.

As we have already seen, Agnes Jones distrusted her power to rule. This fact, added to her mother's dislike to her entering a hospital determined her, for the present at least, to join Mrs. Ranyard in the work of the Bible Mission, for she knew that while she would be relieving her friend of some of the burden of her work she would have ample opportunities of discovering whether she were fitted to govern.

She was soon busy in many ways, in mothers' meetings, Bible classes, industrial kitchens, dormitories, refuges, and in visiting with the Bible women. In every department of that varied work she was most helpful to Mrs. Ranyard, even taking the whole charge of the mission for two months while the latter was absent in Switzerland. She found her knowledge of German very useful, and turned it to the best account on several occasions when she met with German immigrants.

In the narrow courts and lanes of London, unthought of and unheeded by the busy throng, she found many of the Lord's jewels who, though poor in this world's goods and sick in body, were yet rich in faith and strong in soul. One of these, a woman who for thirty-two years had been a terrible sufferer, would whisper, "Blessed Jesus, in everything suitable. Just the Saviour suitable for me." Another, whom she several times mentions in her letters, and to whom she delighted to minister as a nurse, a poor cripple who had only the use of her thumb, and who from lying eighteen years in one position had terrible bed-sores, could yet say, "I am ashamed to talk of my suffering when I think of all Jesus suffered for me."

Her happy work in London was brought to a premature conclusion by a telegram announcing that her sister was ill of fever in Rome, followed by another begging her to go to her at once. A journey thither was not such an easy one then as it is now, but, after arranging all her work so as to give Mrs. Ranyard as little trouble as possible, Agnes bravely undertook it. A heavy storm was encountered at Marseilles, where she embarked for Italy, and this delayed her arrival in Rome, so that on reaching there she found her sister out of danger. A cousin, however, who had formed one of the party, had fallen ill of the same fever, and needed careful nursing, so that she found her hands full, and, as the recovery of both invalids was slow, she determined to give up her London work, and devote herself to them.

Some months were spent in Italy; but her strength, which had been greatly tried by the work in London, again becoming enervated, and her nursing duties being at an end, she proposed that she should go to Switzerland and visit the deaconesses' institutions there. This plan she carried out, and visited several of the Swiss institutions, which she considered compared unfavourably with Kaiserswerth, both in organisation and spiritual tone. She visited besides some of those in Germany, and at Mannedorf had the joy of spending several days with that wonderful woman of faith, Dorothea Trudel.

All her experience had now gone to prove that her special gift was hospital work, and on rejoining her mother she definitely laid before her her wish to devote herself to the work of nursing, and with her consent entered into a correspondence with Miss Nightingale with the idea of entering St. Thomas's Hospital as a Nightingale probationer.

It is very clear that all through her life she was satisfied to be doing the "next thing," whatever that next thing should be which was pointed out to her by the guiding of God's Holy Spirit. She never ran counter to her mother's wishes, knowing that no blessing could be expected when the command, "Honour thy father and thy mother," was not observed; but when home no longer needed her, she was glad to enter the larger field to which God had opened the way.

CHAPTER V.

HOSPITAL WARDS.

It has been said that "every woman is by nature more or less a nurse," but like most sayings it is by no means always true. Many who possess the gentleness and sympathy which are so necessary in nursing the sick, yet lack the ready nerve, deftness, and promptitude. Who has not beheld the sad spectacle of women anxious to help, yet helpless because of their ignorance and want of training? That will be a happy day when a course of training in nursing, though it be but a short one, is considered a necessary part of every woman's education. Miss Nightingale truly says, "There is no such thing as amateur nursing... Three-fourths of the whole mischief in women's lives arises from their excepting themselves from the rule of training considered needful for man."

Agnes Jones was a "born nurse;" but although she had had many opportunities both at Fahan and at Kaiserswerth of developing her talent, she would not attempt to teach others what she had not thoroughly grasped herself. The post in Liverpool, of Superintendent of the Training School of Nurses for the Poor, was still open to her and, in spite of her fear that she lacked the capacity to govern, had many attractions for her, and so she said, "I determined at least to try, to come to St. Thomas's Hospital, and to see whether in so great a work as that of training true-hearted, God-fearing nurses, there were not some niche for me. If every one shrinks back because incompetent, who will ever do anything? 'Lord, here am I, send me.'"

Let no one think that the resolve cost her nothing. As a matter of fact it meant giving up a great deal, but to follow in the steps of Him who freely gave up all for us, she cheerfully surrendered her lovely Irish home for the dreary walls of a London hospital, where her companions were, as a rule, neither Christians in the true sense of the word, nor her equals in society. Yet who that knows the Lord Jesus as "a living bright reality" can talk of sacrifice? To know the need of the Lord's poor was sufficient for her, and she counted nothing too much to give up joyfully for Him and His. Nor was this choice, which she felt to be a life-choice, a thought but of yesterday. Not long after she went to Kaiserswerth she had, as she herself writes, "much watching of a poor dying man; sitting alone by him in that little room, day after day, it went to my heart to hear some of his requests refused, and to see the food given him, so unfitted to his state. And I sat there and thought, 'If these be the trials of the sick in an institution conducted on Christian principles, oh, how must it be in those institutions in our own land, where no true charity is in the hearts of most of the heads or hands that work them!' and I then and there dedicated myself to do what I could for Ireland, in its workhouses, infirmaries, and hospitals." She felt too, that although she could do good service for her Lord in ordinary Christian work, she could do still better if, possessing as she did a God-given talent for nursing, she could, like her Master, both speak a "word in season" and minister to the needs of the body.

So St. Thomas's was entered, entered with the hope and prayer that both amongst nurses and patients God would use her. And use her He did, as He does all who cry, "Lord, what wilt Thou have me do?" and then watch for the opportunity to do it. It was not long before she sought and gained permission to establish a Bible class for the other Nightingale nurses, which proved a great blessing to several of them. In her ward, too, she was often able to speak a word for Christ to the patients.

She was very happy in her busy life, writing, "I am so growingly happy in it, and so fond of nay work." Of its importance she became more and more convinced, and in a letter written from Barnet, where she was spending a few happy days with her friends, Mr. and Mrs. Pennefather, she says:—*"My work*, I more and more feel it, for the worst things only make me realise how Christian and really good nurses are needed."

But it was to Ireland that her thoughts ever turned, and it was of work in Ireland that she was thinking even while training in London For by this very training she hoped to be the better fitted for work in her own beloved country. "Ireland is ever my bourn," she wrote. And again:— "My heart is ever in Ireland, where I hope ultimately to work."

After a year at St. Thomas's, and a short visit home, she returned to London to take the superintendence of a small hospital in connection with the Deaconesses' Institution in Burton Crescent. Here she had all the nursing to do, as there were but few patients, and she had great joy in ministering to them. "I trust," she writes in a letter to her aunt, "I am gaining a quiet influence with my patients; they are my great pleasure." And again: "I am very happy here among my patients, and often feel God has sent me here; I have two revival patients; one had found peace before she came, the other is seeking it, and to both I can talk. Then I have a poor woman with cancer, who likes me to speak of Jesus, whom I believe she truly loves; so you see I am not without work."

A short time at this hospital, and a few months as superintendent at the Great Northern Hospital, ended her work in London. The work at the latter tried her much both in body and mind, for not only did the whole responsibility of it rest upon her shoulders, but owing to the inexperience of her assistants, most of the nursing devolved on her as well. One patient who was critically ill she was obliged for six weeks to nurse entirely both by night and day. Nervous debility was the natural consequence of such overwork, and a deafness from which she had suffered at Kaiserswerth so much increased that the doctor ordered her to rest. That was not immediately possible, as there was no one to take her place, and when at last a successor had been found, and she was able to return home, she was so weary both in body and mind that she failed to find her usual delight in the loveliness of Fahan. A few weeks' stay, however, in the bracing air near the Giant's Causeway restored her to her wonted health.

The winter was passed at her home, resting quietly in preparation for the work in Liverpool, of which the offer has been already mentioned. In the spring of 1865 she left for ever the old familiar spot with its beautiful hills and glens, and its cottages, to many of whose inmates she had been the means of bringing comfort and peace; Liverpool, with its needy poor and its many difficult problems, claiming her for the last three years of her life.

CHAPTER VI.

AMONGST THE PAUPERS.

In the year 1698, William III. stated in a speech that:—"Workhouses, under a prudent and good management, will answer all the ends of charity to the poor, in regard to their souls and bodies; they may be made, properly speaking, nurseries for religion, virtue, and industry." But could the good king who anticipated so many advantages from workhouses have only seen our poor law institutions a hundred and fifty or sixty years later, he would have been pained to learn how far they had fallen short of his sanguine expectations. The sick and helpless were entrusted to the care of women who, being paupers themselves, and of a low class, and being for the most part in the workhouse through loss of character, were found to be almost incapable of training. Rough they were, and in many cases brutal as well, while their roughness and brutality were intensified by the free use of intoxicants. Their language was terrible, and not only did they quarrel constantly amongst themselves, but fights were of frequent occurrence.

To endure such treatment and to witness such scenes was the daily lot of a sick pauper, who knew also that when dead he would have little better than the burial of a dog, since it was the common custom in many workhouses to bury corpses naked, with no covering but a few shavings thrown over the body. Little wonder was it that the poor, when overtaken by age or disease, shrank from the thought of entering a place which to them seemed worse than a prison, choosing rather to die without attention than to be treated in such a barbarous manner.

It seems strange that it was so long after a great reformation had been wrought in the management of our prisons that any one was found to lift up a voice in behalf of the much enduring inmates of our workhouses. There seemed to be no one who could spare a thought for the thousands of sick and poor in these institutions. But it was the old story of "out of sight, out of mind," for if only the evil had been apparent our English nation with its love of justice would have seen it righted long before. Workhouses were to be found all over the land, yet the public seemed not at all curious, much less interested, in the question whether they were properly managed or not. The guardians were often ignorant men, and were very slow to admit visitors, perhaps from a foreshadowing suspicion of the exposure which was in store for them, and the consequent necessity and expense of change, so that we need not wonder that the opposition which was called forth when first the evils of the workhouse system were exposed was tremendous, and that the task of awakening real interest seemed well nigh hopeless.

In the Liverpool Workhouse the state of things was no worse than in many others, and in many respects it was not so bad. There was a good committee, and therefore there was nothing like the wholesale starvation and cruelty which existed in too many other workhouses There was also some measure of thoughtful care for the sick ones, for Agnes Jones in a letter written after her first visit, says:—"There seemed care for the patients too; a few plants and flowers, *Illustrated News* pictures on the walls, and a 'silent comforter' in each ward, not the utterly desolate look one often meets in such places." Still, there were no trained nurses, and it was impossible for any committee, however zealous, to counteract all the evils of pauper nursing. The need for reform was great, and happily for Liverpool and for the country at large, there were not only eyes to see the need, but a mind which had grasped the only solution of the difficulty, and a large and sympathetic heart which prompted the hand to open wide the purse to accomplish it, for Mr. William Rathbone, ever foremost in all schemes for ameliorating the condition of the poor and needy, had long been alive to the necessity of substituting for pauper nurses trained paid ones. He it was who not only suggested the change, but offered himself to bear the whole expense of the scheme for three years, feeling assured that by that time the guardians would be so convinced of its practical good that they would adopt it permanently.

Having obtained the committee's consent to the trial of his plan, Mr. Rathbone offered the post of lady superintendent to Agnes Jones, then at the Great Northern Hospital in London. After consultation with Miss Nightingale and Mrs. Wardroper, the Lady Superintendent of St. Thomas's Hospital, and receiving their approval and also the promise of twelve Nightingale nurses from St. Thomas's for her staff, she accepted it. Still there was a delay of some months, which was partly due to the nurses' need of further training, and partly to the imperative necessity that she should have entire rest in order to recruit the strength which had been so sorely overtaxed at the Great Northern Hospital. She did not therefore enter on her duties until March 31, 1865. Even then she began her new and untried work in much trembling and with great distrust of herself, though her trust in her Saviour never failed. "It often seems strange," she wrote, "that I, who have so little self-reliance, and would like every step directed, am obliged to take such an independent position; and yet I have been so led that I could not help it, and I only trust I may be more and more led to look to the guidance of the ever-present and all-wise Heavenly Friend."

After her arrival she was still obliged to wait some weeks for the advent of her staff, consisting of twelve Nightingale nurses and four probationers. But although she was not yet in possession of the reins of government, and so was debarred from doing anything in the way of nursing, she was yet allowed free access to the wards, being only prohibited to speak on religion to the Roman Catholic patients. So the intervening time was not lost, for she found many opportunities of bringing cheer and comfort to sad and weary hearts and of pointing lost ones to the sinner's Saviour. Agnes Jones was not one of those who are always

"Seeking for some great thing to do,"

and ignoring the many small opportunities of service which lie ready to hand. She was quite content, since the larger field was not yet open to her, to occupy a smaller one. In a letter to her aunt she wrote very characteristically:—"I am trying and succeeding more and more in fixing my eyes on all the little things we shall be able to do. I believe in this is our safety, doing the daily *littles* as opportunity is given, and leaving the issue with God. It is the *individual* influence we shall have, the individual relief and the individual help for mind and body, that will be ours. If it is His will, He can make others see the many littles as one great whole, or they may see nothing done, while we have the comfort of the littles we know have been done."

The nurses and probationers arrived in the middle of May, and then work began in good earnest. The post of lady superintendent was by no means a sinecure. At 5.30 every morning she might have been seen unlocking the doors for the kitchen-women. She was often round the wards at 6.0, and all through the busy day until 11.0 at night she was kept fully employed, giving out stores, superintending her nurses, presiding at meals, and visiting patients, besides all the hundred-and-one duties and calls which fall to one in the like position. Her unselfishness was as conspicuous as ever, and she never thought of sparing herself in any way, her joy being to make the lives of others bright and happy.

The patients were quick to discover the benefits of the new *régime*. Instead of the old system of roughness and neglect, they found now a very different order of things, as nurses, perfectly trained, with soft voice and gentle footfall, passed from bed to bed, ministering to the sick and dying. Interesting and helpful books for those who were well enough to read found their way into the wards. Flowers—for Agnes Jones, who loved intensely all God's works in Nature, had great faith in the ministry of flowers—were there to give brightness in the midst of depressing surroundings. Visits from friends were rendered more easy. Christmas was made happy with special festivities. Indeed, she seemed always to be planning something to cheer the sick under her care. She very soon began Sunday evening Bible readings in the wards where there were only Protestant patients. Many crowded in, even Romanists, whom she was not allowed to invite, and listened with rapt attention, the late-comers slipping off their shoes, lest they should disturb her. After nearly two years' work, she commenced daily evening Bible readings, having an attendance of from twenty to thirty, while on the Sunday evening there were often more than a hundred.

It was no wonder that such devotion met with a ready response from the sad and friendless, and that her loving sympathy evoked love from the seemingly unloving.

Let us follow her as she passes through the wards. A thorough lady, quiet and self-possessed, she commands respect from even the roughest, and all look up with eager expectancy, hoping for just one word from her. Here is an old man, whose brightening face shows how welcome are her visits. As she stops we hear him murmur, "I never had a friend in all my life till I came here. You are my only friend." Another, who is drawing very near to the gates of death, taking her hand in his, says:—"I want to take leave of you—I never told you before, but do you remember speaking of the 'Gift of God is eternal life through Jesus Christ our Lord?' I got that gift then." And when she has gone, a poor man may be heard saying to the nurse:—"The lady can never know what she has done for me . . . I think I am in heaven when she comes."

Her nurses were thoroughly one with her. How could they be otherwise when she was so thoughtful and considerate for them? Before introducing them to their wards, she commended them to God in prayer, asking His blessing on them and their work. She had a Bible reading for them, but, not content with speaking to them collectively, she would frequently talk to them individually of the Saviour she so loved. Although she never passed over their faults, they were sure of her ready sympathy in their troubles, and as they poured them into her ear she would say, "Have you told Jesus so?"

The success of the work was an astonishment to all. The patients could at first scarcely understand why the nurses did not swear at them like their former ones. The police wondered as they saw women able to deal with those whom they had found utterly untameable; while the committee were so pleased with the success of the experiment, that, a year before the specified time, they decided permanently to adopt the system of trained nurses.

But such work was not without its trials. During the first year there was great difficulty with the ex-pauper women who were being trained, many who seemed to be doing well returning to their drunken habits. Dirt, disorder, insubordination, and grumbling had to be contended with. The vilest sins were practised even by children, and so shameful was the conduct of many of the inmates that Agnes Jones said, "I can only compare it to Sodom, and wonder how God stays His hand from smiting."

The isolation from home and friends was a trial in itself, while her anxiety about her work was so great that she scarcely allowed herself a holiday. A further trouble was that from morning till night she was never alone. It is small cause for wonder that with such a terrible strain, overtaxed nerves and strength should result in depression, a fact only revealed by her journals, for to others she was ever bright, and it was often said of her, "She is like a sunbeam."

A life lived at high pressure cannot long continue without failing partly or altogether, and the end came at last. In the beginning of 1868 there was much fever and sickness of various kinds, there being three hundred patients above the normal number, while the nursing staff was reduced by illness. A nurse, who had been ill with bronchitis, developed symptoms of typhus, and Agnes Jones, fearing that her life might be sacrificed, were she removed to the fever wards, gave up her bedroom to her, sleeping herself on the floor of her sitting-room. She was soon attacked by the same disease. For a week she progressed very favourably. Then dangerous symptoms showed themselves, and finally inflammation of both lungs.

Many were the touching inquiries from the patients of "How is the lady?" Nurses and friends watched anxiously the terrible progress of the disease. Much prayer was made, but the Lord had need of His servant, who had been so faithful to the trust committed to her here, for a more perfect service; and at the age of thirty-five she passed away peacefully into the brightness of His presence in the early morning of February 19, 1868, the beginning to her of a glorious day which should know no twilight gloom.

On the following Friday, when the coffin was carried into the hall, and placed in its case ready for removal across the Irish Channel, the landing and stairs were filled with patients who had crept there from the wards to see the last of one who had brought so much happiness into their wretched lives. And when she was carried to her last resting-place in the picturesque churchyard of Fahan, within sound of the rippling waters of Lough Swilly, she was followed, as was fitting, by nearly the whole population, many of whom could thank God for blessing which she had been the means of bringing to them.

Until the resurrection morning she might be hidden from the eyes of those who loved her; but none who knew her could ever forget her. Hear the testimony of one of the workhouse officials to the writer, more than twenty-five years after, when the question, "Do you remember Miss Jones?" was asked. "Remember her? I should think I do. I could never forget her. She used to have a Bible class on Sunday afternoons and on a week-day evening in that little vestry belonging to the church. She began it for the nurses, but there were only about fifteen of them then, and so she used to let us officers go as well if we liked. I used to love it, for it was beautiful to see her sitting there so homely and nice, and then she used to pray with us and expound the Scriptures. Oh, it was a real help, I can tell you! But it was a wonder to me how she lived those last few weeks of her life. You see the cholera broke out, and there was a lot of fever besides, typhus and different sorts, and she could never rest for looking after and caring for them all. Why, I've seen her in those wards there myself between two and three o'clock in the morning. Ah! she was a Christian, she was. Saint was the word for her, for if ever there was a saint upon this earth, it was Miss Jones. She seemed to me to live in heaven, and heaven was in her and about her and all around her."

"Only a tender love,
 Stilling the restless moan,
Soothing the sufferer,
 Cheering the lone.

* * * * *

Only a woman's heart;
 Yet she forgot her care,
Finding on every side
 Burdens to bear.

* * * * *

Humbly she walked with God,
 Listening to catch His voice,
And 'twas His work for her,
 Not her own choice.

And when that work was done,
 Life's quiet evening come,
What then awaited her?
 Only a tomb?

Nay, but a mansion fair
 Near to the great white throne,
And the dear Master's word
 Saying, 'Well done.'"

ELLEN L. COURTENAY.

ELIZABETH, DUCHESS OF GORDON.

I.

EARLY DAYS.

Just a hundred years ago there was born one who in a marked degree endeavoured to do her duty in that state of life to which it had pleased God to call her. That state of life was a very exalted one, with many opportunities of doing good. The Duchess of Gordon had many talents given to her for improvement, and she was not unmindful of the stewardship with which she was entrusted. Her rank and wealth were held as trusts for her Master's use.

Dr. Moody Stuart tells us in his interesting and graphic memoir of the last Duchess of Gordon[1], from which the following incidents are taken (by kind permission of both author and publishers), that Elizabeth Brodie was born in London on the 20th of June, 1794. Her father was Alexander Brodie, a younger son of Brodie of that ilk. Amongst her ancestors there were many remarkable men, some remembered for their faithful service of their heavenly as well as of their earthly King. The memory of one has passed down to posterity in the phrase "the Good Lord Brodie." His diaries reveal a life lived in great humility and special nearness to his Lord. Those around him found in him not only a benevolent neighbour

---

1 *Life and Letters of Elizabeth, last Duchess of Gordon*, by Rev. A. Moody Stuart, D.D. Messrs. J. Nisbet & Co., London.

but also a faithful instructor in the highest learning. His delight was to visit the sick, and to declare the love of Christ whenever he had the opportunity. He longed for his children to be great in grace, rather than in worldly distinction. His wish for them is expressed in the words he left on record, that he would not be detained "one hour from glory, to see those come of him in chief honour and place in the world."

The mother of Elizabeth Brodie was a member of the family of Wemyss, a granddaughter of the Earl of Wemyss. Her father had acquired a large fortune in India, and returned home to the large estates in Kincardineshire which he had purchased. The little girl had soon to experience the greatest loss that can befall a child. When she was only six years old her mother died, leaving her alone with her father. The next two years were spent with maiden aunts at Elgin, where she enjoyed a liberty which was bracing to both mind and body. School life began early. When she was only eight years old, she was sent to a boarding school in London, one special object being to eradicate the broad Scotch from her lip and thought. At school she became a great favourite with both teacher and companions, already exercising that power of winning attachment which was a feature all through her life. At the same time she is described as having "a very independent spirit." In matters indifferent she was ever yielding in her disposition; but it was impossible to move her from any principle she had deliberately adopted. Courage was another characteristic that early manifested itself. Her groom, who had served her forty years, delighted to recall instances of her fearlessness. On one occasion, when her party were crossing the Spey in a pony-chaise in a boat, the bridge having been carried down by the floods, her companion asked, "Isn't this dangerous, duchess?" "I never see danger," was the quiet reply.

When she was about sixteen Miss Brodie left school. The winters were now spent in Bath, the summers in Scotland. She had launched into the society of the world, and to a great extent she did as they did. One reproof she received made a lasting impression. It was from the lips of a little child who was exceedingly fond of her. Miss Brodie had joined others in playing cards on the Sabbath. The next day, contrary to all custom, the child kept away from her, and when asked to sit on her knee, gave a flat refusal, adding the reason, "No, you are bad; you play cards on Sunday." Her answer and resolution were ready: "I was wrong, I will not do it again." And those who heard her and knew her character were quite sure she would not do it again.

II.

MARCHIONESS OF HUNTLY.

Elizabeth Brodie was still very young when she entered upon the duties and trials of married life. Between the house of Brodie and the house of Gordon there had been a standing feud. About the middle of the seventeenth century the youthful and impetuous Lord Lewis Gordon had made a raid upon the property of the Laird of Brodie. He burned to the ground the mansion and all that was connected with it, the family escaping to the house of a cousin. This Lewis Gordon became third Marquis of Huntly, and was the ancestor of one who made a better conquest, the gallant Marquis of Huntly, who sought and won the hand of Miss Brodie. They were married at Bath on the 11th of December, 1813. The union thus formed was never afterwards regretted. When, fifteen years later, he experienced great losses of property, his sorrow found expression in these words, "All things are against me: I've been unfortunate in everything, except a good wife." What that wife did for him in spiritual as well as temporal comfort, the sequel will show.

The Marquis of Huntly was a thorough man of the world at the time of his marriage. And for a time his wife joined him in the fashionable circle in which he found his chief pleasure. Both in London and in Geneva, where they spent the greater part of the first portion of their married life, she became very popular. But she soon realised that true joys were not to be found in the mere attractions of society. For some years her life cannot be described otherwise than as unprofitable. One instrument used by God for her awakening was a Highland servant. This girl was grieved to see that the interest of her mistress was absorbed by the things of time, which left no room for the contemplation of the things of eternity. She ventured to make a wise and well-weighed remark. It was a word fitly spoken, and did not fail in its purpose. The young lady's eyes were further opened by what she saw of the sins of the worldly circle in which she moved. She began to realise the sentiment of her ancestor, the good Lord Brodie:—"God can make use of poison to expel poison: in London I saw much vanity, lightness, and wantonness." His aspiration was also soon echoed from her own heart—"Oh, that the seeing of it in others may cure and mortify the seeds of it in myself!" She could not help observing the shameless vice that passed unrebuked, by many hardly noticed. The observation gave a shock to her sensitive soul. Her distress was great, and in her distress she turned to the right quarter. She sought solace in the Bible. That hitherto neglected Book enchained her attention, and she became a most diligent searcher into its hidden truths. Some of the gay friends of the society in which she moved found her occupied in this Bible reading. It supplied them with a new amusement, telling how the attractive marchioness had become a "Methodist." Hers was not the nature to be turned aside from its purpose by a taunt. "If for so little I am to be called a Methodist, let me have something more worthy of the name." Such was her reflection, and her Bible reading was continued with renewed earnestness.

In the course of that reading the work of the Holy Spirit was impressed upon her attention. The promise met her eyes, "If ye, being evil, know how to give good gifts unto your children, how much more shall your Heavenly Father give the Holy Spirit to them that ask Him?" "From that time," she records, "I began to pray for the Holy Spirit." To the end of her life she increasingly realised and brought others to realise the paramount importance of the personal work of the Holy Spirit. Lady Huntly could not now join in the pursuits of the world as she had formerly done. Her husband did not fully sympathise with the change in her views, but he saw enough of the sinful emptiness of mere gaiety to make him refrain from insisting upon her taking part in its pursuits. More than this, he gave every facility to her for carrying out her wishes, even when he could not understand the spirit which was their motive.

When in Geneva, after her Bible reading had begun, she found a very helpful friend in Madame Vernet. "If any one is to be called my spiritual mother," she said, "it is Madame Vernet of Geneva." That good Christian unfolded to her plainly the plan of salvation, showing her first her lost condition, and then the way of redemption by Jesus Christ. Lady Huntly was also helped by her intercourse in Paris with Lady Olivia Sparrow and others who frequented her house for the sake of the religious society.

On her return from Paris the winter was passed at Kimbolton Castle, the seat of her brother-in-law, the Duke of Manchester. That place was memorable in her spiritual history. "I knew Christ first," she afterwards said, "if I really know Him, at Kimbolton; I spent hours there in my dressing-room in prayer, and in reading the Bible, and in happy communion with Him." Lady Huntly referred to this period of her spiritual life in these terms, some one having made the remark that deep conviction of sin is almost invariably the beginning of the work of God in the soul: "I did not quite agree with that statement, and do not think it is by any means always the case. In my own case I believe that for two years I was a saved sinner, a believer in Jesus Christ, and yet that during all that time I did not see the exceeding sinfuluess of sin. I believed in a general way that I was a sinner, who deserved the punishment of a righteous God; I believed that whosoever came to Jesus Christ should he saved; but I had no deep sense of sin, of my sin. Since then I believe that I have passed through almost every phase of Christian experience that I have ever read or heard of; and now I have such a sight of my own utter vileness and unworthiness, that I feel that the great and holy God might well set His heel on me, so to speak, and crush me into nothing." This sense of absolute unworthiness was always a feature of her life. "A useless log" was the term she applied to herself.

One means of profit which Lady Huntly much enjoyed was her intercourse with a friend of bygone days, Miss Helen Home. They were now both walking in the same way. The Bible readings at the house of Miss Home were felt to be of great service.

Lady Huntly soon introduced family prayer in her home. She felt that if God was to be heartily served, His altar must be set up in the house. At first she gathered together her servants and any lady visitors in the house. But later, as we shall see, the whole establishment took part.

III.

DUCHESS OF GORDON.

The old Duke of Gordon, Lord Huntly's father, died in the summer of 1827. The subject of this biography became Duchess of Gordon, a title which involved increased responsibilities and increased anxieties. Happily she realised her position, and determined, by the help of God, to show more clearly that, in whatever rank of life she was, she was striving to be a faithful servant of her Heavenly Master. She felt that she must confess Christ more boldly, that she must be more decided for Him, however much this profession might appear singular in her recently-acquired rank.

A short time before leaving Huntly for Gordon Castle, she explored the old Huntly Castle with a party of friends. The duchess was at the time greatly bowed down by a sense of the responsibility of her changed life. There were certain inscriptions round the ceiling of a great hall in the old castle. No one could make them out. But whilst the duchess was standing alone in deep thought, her companions having gone off to examine other curiosities, the sun burst out from a cloud through one of the broken window mullions and shone brightly on the opposite wall, and in the light of his rays she read:—

TO. THAES. THAT. LOVE. GOD. AL. THINGIS. VIRKIS. TO THE. BEST.

"It was," she used to say, "a message from the Lord to my soul, and came to me with such power that I went on my way rejoicing." Ever after this text was a favourite one. She always looked upon it as peculiarly her own. Very practical was her reading of God's Word. She, indeed, expected to find in it a word from Him. Just at the time of her setting out for her new home she read as usual her daily portion in Bogatsky's *Golden Treasury*. Through two leaves of the book being stuck together, she had missed the portion appointed for the day before. But now it presented itself to her eye—and no less surely to her heart: "Have not I commanded thee? Be strong and of a good courage; be not afraid, neither be thou dismayed: for the Lord thy God is with thee whithersoever thou goest." Her comment was, "That was another message from the Lord, that put strength into me."

Many years afterwards she wrote: "It was this day sixteen years that the text in Bogatsky was given to me from Joshua 1. 9, and truly I have found the goodness of the Lord with me, and everything temporal that I committed to Him He has indeed kept. It is really most wonderful when I see trials and trouble all around me, to see how everything I prayed for regarding my own home has been accomplished; and shall I not trust Him for my soul, and for all that guidance I so greatly need in all that He would have me to do? Surely He will guide me in spiritual as well as in temporal things; and the more I cease from man, and from any child of man, the more I shall be enabled to live simply to His glory." Another sixteen years passed. The duchess was within a few days of her death. She heard that a young man was in anxiety about his preparation for the ministry. "He looks to difficulties; give him for a New Year's message from me, Joshua 1. 9: 'Have not I commanded thee? Be strong and of a good courage; neither be thou dismayed.' These words were given to me after Duke Alexander's death, and from that day onward they have been a help to me."

IV.

GOOD WORKS AT GORDON CASTLE.

The duchess did not write a regular diary. But for one week in the first year of her residence at Gordon Castle such a record was kept. Extracts from it may serve to give some insight into her thoughts and life. The reader will be struck with the marked self-humiliation which was so characteristic of this child of God. "I desired to have resolution to commence and continue a journal, that I might obtain a clearer view of my own heart, which I know, alas! to be deceitful above all things and desperately wicked. Well may I say with Job, 'I abhor myself and repent in dust and ashes.'" "A day lost though well begun; more peace, more clear belief, but, alas! not less indifference, not less hardness of heart; great idleness; after breakfast little or nothing done. O Lord, deliver me from pride and vanity, and make me a humble and devoted follower of the meek and lowly Jesus. He indeed is our peace." "Another unprofitable day; but when, alas! is any day otherwise with me?" "Sins of the week: unbelief proceeding from pride of reason, selfishness, carelessness, hardness of heart, vanity, evil speaking." These extracts are sufficient to show that there was a very severe introspection—a very real shrinking from sin, and sense of unworthiness. Some of the faults she lamented seemed to others remarkably absent in the duchess Evil speaking, for example, was about the last thing she could be accused of. There was no one more careful of the character of those with whom she had to do.

This short diary also shows her busily occupied in attending to members of her household, ministering to one maid, who was sick, instructing another in the *Shorter Catechism*. Happy was the household that had such a mistress at its head!

In 1830 William IV. came to the throne. The Duchess of Gordon was selected by Queen Adelaide as Mistress of the Robes at the Coronation. The Queen bestowed upon her many marks of favour and friendship. But the promotion to the highest honours of the Court was not allowed to militate against her soul's welfare. The service of the King of kings was always put first.

It is needless to say that the duchess was always a regular attendant at God's house. For thirty years she made a practice of taking copious notes of the sermons. The notes were copied out carefully during the week. This note-taking—sometimes a slight embarrassment to the preacher—was a great help to the hearer. As at least two sermons a week were thus noted, there must have been a great mass of manuscript before the thirty years were expired. Amongst those whose sermons she much enjoyed were Mr. Howels of Long Acre, Mr. Harington Evans, and Mr. Blunt, of Chelsea.

Good works were promoted by the duke and duchess at the cost of much self-denial. The duke's predecessor had left the estates heavily burdened. The consequence was that they were put under trust, only a limited income being allowed to the duke. This made contributions to charitable objects less ample than they would otherwise have been. But generous help was bestowed that cost the givers something to give. The duchess set her heart on building and endowing a chapel in connection with the Church of England. To render this possible the duke proposed to sell some of his horses. For the same purpose the duchess left a golden vase valued at £1200 to be sold. To quote her own words to explain what resulted from this charitable idea: "The Duchess of Beaufort, hearing of my vase, thought of her diamond ear-rings, which she got me to dispose of for a chapel in Wales, and her diamonds made me think of my jewels; and as the duke had always been most anxious for the chapel, he agreed with me that stones were much prettier in a chapel wall than round one's neck, and so he allowed me to sell £600's worth, or rather what brought that, for they cost more than double. The chapel is going on nicely, and I have still enough jewels left to help to endow it, if no other way should open. I do think I may with confidence hope for a blessing on this. It is no sacrifice to me whatever, except as it is one to the duke, who is very fond of seeing me fine, and was brought up to think it right."

The strict observance of family prayer has already been referred to. A room had been fitted up in the castle as a little chapel. The duke was always present, and now, in the absence of the chaplain and the duchess, used to conduct the prayers himself. In later years, when the widow returned to Huntly Lodge, exactly at half-past nine in the morning and evening the household assembled for prayers. Both indoor and outdoor servants were first gathered together. The butler then came to the duchess, and in words which we are assured were never varied by one syllable or accent during the twenty-seven years of her grace's widowhood and his own stewardship, announced, "They're all assembled." A brief blessing was asked, a psalm or hymn read, the organ led the voice of praise, a passage of Scripture was read and frequently explained. A prayer followed, in which the duchess wished that the Queen should never be forgotten.

Very faithfully the duchess sought to do her duty in bringing the interests of religion before those with whom she had to do, especially those of her own household. "But you do not know the difficulty I have in speaking to any one who does not meet me half way. I think if I could see my way clearly, I might get over this painful shyness, which I then know would be want of faith. But I cannot see that, situated as I am, it is my duty; and moreover, I *fancy* I have not the talent, and it is not one which I have to account for; for I have so often done more harm than good, even when I have prayed to be directed; indeed, I trust I have not often had to speak without that prayer . . . Oh! I do pray for more zeal for souls, more true sense of their infinite value; for I think if I felt it as I *see* it, I should do more."

V.

THE HEAVY BLOW.

In the summer of 1835 the duke and duchess made a tour on the Continent. Even amidst all the movements and difficulties connected with hotel life, family prayers were not neglected. Every morning before starting they assembled together to ask God's blessing. The duchess on this tour had daily opportunities of reading the Bible with her husband. She was very anxious about his soul's welfare. His testimony to his old friend, Colonel Tronchin, at Geneva, was very significant. "Tronchin, I am a very changed man to what you once knew me, and I owe it all to my dear wife." She herself writes with reference to the duke—"He has done and said many things since he came here which almost give me hope that the Spirit of God is really at work, and that he begins to experience something of the blessedness of those who fear the Lord."

The greatest trial in her life was now approaching the duchess. He who had been her support and joy for so many years was to be taken from her. On the 27th of May, 1836, she was told by the doctors that the duke had only a short time to live. The terrible news was of course overwhelming, but she knew whither to turn. "I had not realised till then the hopelessness of the case. I retired to another room and fell on my knees; and as if they had been audibly uttered, these words were impressed upon my heart, 'Thy Maker is thy Husband; the Lord of hosts is His name; and thy Redeemer the Holy One of Israel; the God of the whole earth shall He be called,' and I rose up to meet the trial in His strength." The next day the duke died. Full proof was given of the sufficiency of God to support His servants in their darkest hours. Two days afterwards she wrote—"I must tell you of the blessed consolation I have in thinking of the perfect peace which my beloved husband enjoyed uninterruptedly, and the presence of the Comforter from the Father and the Son to my own soul. Pray for me. Although I feel indeed in the wilderness, yet like her who was led there, I would desire to lean on the arm of the Beloved One, who has truly given to me 'the valley of Achor for a door of hope,' and who is a very present help in time of trouble. The comfort I have is at present almost without alloy. It is only when earthly things pull me from my resting-place that I see the desolation of all earthly joys; and yet I am not excited, out as the Lord has enabled me to stay my mind on Him, He has kept me in perfect peace." When the beloved remains were removed into their last resting-place in Elgin Cathedral, she dedicated herself afresh to God. "When the coffin was lowered into that vault, I felt as if God had shoved under my feet all that was most dear to me, the only one on earth to whose love I was entitled, and that now I must live to Himself alone."

After her husband's death her wish was to return at once to Huntly Lodge, where she had spent the first years of her married life, and which was now hers by the marriage settlement. But a lease which the tenant was unwilling to resign prevented this for a time. Accordingly she made up her mind to travel abroad for some months. During the winter of 1836 she lived at Pau. The return home was made the following summer. Naturally she dreaded coming back to the now desolate home—the same place, but all so changed. But God was good, and the grace sufficient for the day was given. *"Huntly Lodge, 31st August*, 1837.—The Lord has been better to me than all my fears. Wagstaff (the duke's factor), accompanied by both Mr. Bigsby (of the English Chapel at Gordon Castle) and Mr. Dewar (minister of Fochabers), received me. My heart was so full of the Lord's goodness, that there was no room for bitterness; and after a few moments alone, I could not rest till we had thanked our tender Father; Mr. Bigsby was the organ of our thanksgiving. The three gentlemen, Annie (Sinclair), and I joined in prayer then, and at night with all the people of house, stable, and farm; this morning Mr. Dewar's prayer was very much what I needed. My blessed Lord Jesus is very present, and I know I cannot come to my Father without Him. Oh, pray that I may be more and more awakened, and never fall asleep again. Oh, for the quickening grace of the Holy Spirit to realise continually that blessed presence! 4th *Sept.*—My heart is full of thankfulness and wonder as to myself. I dreaded above all things the bitterness of desolation on my return here; and behold the Lord made His presence so manifest that I am now, as in times past, rejoicing in His unmerited love."

VI.

WIDOWHOOD AT HUNTLY LODGE.

The arrangements at Huntly Lodge were now, of course, entirely in the hands of the widowed duchess. Essentially the motto which was the principle of the establishment was, "As for me and my house, we will serve the Lord." It was a matter of some doubt with her whether she should keep up the style natural to her rank, or let the Lodge and retire into a humbler life. After carefully and prayerfully weighing the matter, her decision was that "position is stewardship," and that it was her duty not to despise the high estate to which God had been pleased to call her, but to consecrate it to His service. This determination was a wise one. Her light was placed so that many could see its steady and bright burning.

The whole house was ruled in strict order, marked quietness and simplicity prevailing. We are told that everything throughout the day was conducted with the exactness of clockwork. The duchess rose soon after six o'clock. The family met at breakfast at nine. Exactly at half-past nine, as we have seen, both morning and evening, the house assembled for family prayers. After breakfast one of the first occupations of the duchess was to visit her old bedridden maid, to minister to her in things both temporal and spiritual. At noon she had a daily reading of the Bible in her room. The reading was interspersed with conversation, and followed by prayer. She seemed to be never tired of these spiritual exercises. The later hours of the day were occupied with reading and other pursuits until five o'clock, when she would again visit her invalid maid. In dealing with the poor the duchess was not only generous but discriminating. She spared no trouble in inquiring into the cases of distress before her. We are told that the list of two hundred persons whose families she regularly relieved had before her death increased to three hundred. The post was also often used as the means of dispensing her anonymous charity. One reason why she was so anxious to have a thoroughly capable chaplain was that he might thoroughly examine into the deserts of applicants for help. It was not pecuniary assistance only that was sought from the duchess. Her kindly counsel was much valued. To quote her own words, "Though I do so need advice and wisdom in my own matters, the most extraordinary people think proper to consult me about the most extraordinary things, and I cannot lose the opportunity of giving the only Christian advice they may be in the way of receiving. May the Lord help me; oh, how constantly do I need help!"

The Sabbath day was indeed a holy day at Huntly Lodge. Everything that could be done the day before was done. No fire was lighted in the drawing-room on the Sunday, with, as we are informed, the double object of saving unnecessary labour, and "to present no inducement for visitors to meet together for idle conversation." The doors of the house were locked during the hours of service, one, or at most two, servants staying at home. No letters were received or posted on the Sabbath. There were no arrivals nor departures of guests on that day. On a certain Sunday morning at breakfast the duchess was surprised to hear a carriage-and-four brought round to the door. Her immediate "What is that?" was answered by the appearance of a young English nobleman who had come to bid her good-bye. "Oh no," she said, "not on the Sabbath." Affectionately she persuaded him to remain until the next day. Away from home, on the Continent and elsewhere, she was careful that the day should be strictly observed. So great was her interest in Sabbath observance that she wrote a little tract on the subject.

The duchess used to delight in surrounding herself at Huntly Lodge with those who were specially set apart for the service of God. The ministers from time to time assembled there, first gathering together for prayer and conference, and then in a more open meeting, at which the duchess and her friends were present, and finally at family worship.

Schools for the poor were munificently founded by the Duchess of Gordon. The schools at Huntly, which were commenced in 1839, were finished in 1843. They consisted of infant schools, schools for older boys and girls, and also an industrial school for training fifty girls for service. When living in Edinburgh, she built large schools in the destitute district of Holyrood. The lady of Huntly was indeed a worthy precursor in the great work of general education. One excellent plan of religious instruction she adopted in her own household. A weekly class was formed of her female domestics, She had prepared a large number of questions. To each of the class she gave each week a slip of paper containing one question. This was to be answered before the next meeting. There was no one in the establishment who could help feeling that the mistress took the deepest interest in him or her.

VII.

ANXIETIES AND REST.

The Duchess of Gordon had been brought up an Episcopalian. But when in May, 1843, the great Disruption took place, when four-hundred and seventy-four ministers of the Church of Scotland took up their cross for Christ, resigning their earthly livings for conscience sake, the duchess was deeply moved by this heroic act of self-denial, and eventually, after much thought and prayer, she joined the Free Church, becoming a member of Free St. Luke's Church. She had left the Church of England, but she loved and honoured it to the end of her life. "I have not time for entering into my reasons for separating from the Church of England, but they were purely conscientious; and I believe I could never be a blessing to the little body of English Episcopalians, if acting against my conscience. They want God's blessing, not man's help; the latter without the former is a curse. Put not your trust in any child of man. But I am not against those dear friends, and can feel myself more at liberty to help them now than before, because I am now acting openly in all things. May the Lord Jesus enable you to look to Him, and to feel and say with Luther, 'Lord, I am Thy sin, Thou art my righteousness.'"

The first occasion on which the duchess partook of the Communion in connection with the Free Church at Huntly was a memorable event. The people assembled in large numbers. By the kindness of the Lady of Huntly provision was made for the visitors within the precincts of the old castle, military tents being erected for the purpose. Her own account of the scene may well be given. *"Huntly Lodge, Aug.* 5, 1847.—Now to tell of a time I hope never to forget. Friday was the fast day; Professor M. Laggan preached in the morning, and Mr. Moody Stuart in the evening. For Sabbath, Dr. Russell, who arrived on Friday afternoon, assisted to arrange a pulpit and two tents in the court of the old castle, one for the elements, the other for our party. Oh! it was indeed a communion: the Lord was there evidently set forth before us, and not only set forth, but present. God the Sovereign and Judge, God the Creator, without whom nothing was made that is made, is God the Saviour, Immanuel, the Lamb slain from the foundation of the world. There seemed truly nothing of man's making between us and the living God; a realisation of being God's creatures, God's redeemed children, formed for Himself, for His own glory. Mr. Dewar preached the action-sermon, after which Mr. M.S. fenced the tables, and addressed us, and served the first table. He told me he never so realised the oneness of Jehovah in Three Persons. If we had seen the Heavenly Dove overshadowing us, and heard the voice saying, 'This is My beloved Son, hear ye Him,' we should have been doubtless overwhelmed; but could hardly have had a more real sense of the presence of Him who made the heavens and the earth, the trees, the grass, and the new creature in Christ Jesus. Mr. Dewar served two tables and gave the concluding address; and Mr. Moody Stuart again preached in the evening on Isa. 1. 18: 'Though your sins be as scarlet, they shall be as white as snow.' Many were much affected, and the place was so beautiful! I hope the weather will permit our having the tents pitched again."

VIII.

GOOD WORKS ABROAD.

After the duke's death, his widow paid frequent visits to the Continent. Pau was a specially favourite resort. There she found both English and French Protestants worshipping in places utterly inadequate for the purpose. She generously purchased a site for a church to be used by both congregations, the lower storey being fitted up for a French Protestant school. She also liberally subscribed towards the erection of the church. Her good works at this place were not few. Having heard that a man living near had broken his leg, she drove off at once to visit him, and repeated her visits weekly. A Bible was given to him, and the result was that his first journey on his crutches was to the Protestant service at Pau. He was convinced that in the teaching of the Protestants alone there was safety. The next day the children were withdrawn from the Roman Catholic school. The excitement was great, and no little persecution and pecuniary loss ensued to the new converts. The duchess began her Protestant school at Pau with eight pupils. She also had Bible classes from time to time, one being for Roman Catholic girls. A Sabbath evening service was held by the duchess for her French servants.

The story of Manuel Fuster, a Spanish refugee, is an interesting one. He had been destined by his parents for the priesthood. But having fallen into destitute circumstances, the duchess's butler had shown him kindness and given him some work to do for the house. Full of gratitude, when her grace passed through the courtyard, he fell down on his knees to thank her. She told him that that homage should be paid only to the Most High. At this interview and at many others she spoke to him about his soul's salvation. A French Bible was given to him before she left. On her return to Pau the next year, he was found breaking stones by the roadside, a conversation proving that he was quite a changed man. In the end he did good Christian service as a colporteur in France.

In 1847 the duchess was advised to winter in the south of Europe. Frequent attacks of bronchitis had made this course advisable. She took up her residence at Cannes, having prospects of being useful there. And her hope of being useful was very substantially realised. *"Cannes, Dec. 1847.*—Constant occupation, and many, many new opportunities of meeting with the Lord's people, and speaking of the glad tidings of great joy, have caused the delay in writing. I now know what fine climate is, and the country and views are beautiful; but above all there is a field of usefulness that we could not have at Nice, and an open door for the Gospel. Altogether, no tongue can tell the goodness of the Lord to us. He is letting me get glimpses both of His love and His glory in the face of Jesus Christ, such as I have never had before; and all this with such peace in outward circumstances! Is it not marvellous? You need not be alarmed about my 'exposition' on Saturday; I feel too deeply my own incapacity to attempt anything beyond what I should say to an infant school at home. The people who come to it are either the families of the servants I employ, or of the children taught by Annie Sandilands. We live as quietly as possible; Lord Brougham sends me the newspaper and bouquets of flowers; other friends lend Caroline their ponies, and do all kind things. Some young English girls come here once a week to a Bible class, and we have meetings every other evening at the chapel at home." The parting from her little flock at Cannes was a painful experience. "Our children were first broken-hearted, and after we were gone were roaring so that nothing could pacify them but Monsieur Bettets taking them all into the drawing-room and praying with them. Those chiefly affected were little Italians, and indeed they seem to have much warmer feelings."

The course of events in the life of the duchess in Scotland seems to have been very even and not very full of startling incidents during the last years of her life. Her personal piety was matured, and her works of usefulness were multiplied. She much delighted in the ministry of Dr. Rainy, who left Huntly in 1853, after a sojourn there of four years. "I wish much you had heard our three last sermons from Mr. Rainy; I never heard any more useful, striking and impressive. I was particularly struck by the way he brought out the necessity of taking up the cross in these days, in a real giving up of self, self-love, self-righteousness, self-pleasing."

IX.

QUICKENED SPIRITUAL LIFE.

The year 1859 is remembered as a season of remarkable quickening of spiritual life in America and Ireland, and later in Scotland. Such a movement could not fail to attract the attention of the Duchess of Gordon who, living so entirely in the presence of the Spirit, was able to realise the workings around her. Huntly Lodge was always ready to receive any who were busied with the spread of the good tidings. Mr. MacDowall Grant, Mr. Brownlow North, and Mr. Reginald Radcliffe were amongst the evangelists who were welcome visitors, as they went about their work of love. In January, 1859, and in the following months, there were impressive gatherings of ministers who met to bring themselves to the attainment of a nearer walk with God, and to strive for the awakening of their people. In January, 1860, there was a conference on a still larger scale, twenty-four ministers staying at the Lodge, whilst others found hospitality elsewhere. There was an unmistakable quickening on all sides. It was suggested to the duchess by Mr. Duncan Matheson, who had been her missionary in the district for some years, that a great assembly might be gathered together for two or three days in one of her parks. The matter was carefully weighed by one who shrunk from anything like undue novelty or unsound sensationalism. But when once she was convinced that it was God's way she hesitated no longer. What the world would think was a light consideration with her. Invitations were sent by the duchess to ministers and laymen of all denominations in England and Scotland.

The spot chosen was the Castle Park; the date, the Wednesday and Thursday of the third week in July. There was provision made for accommodating the expected guests in the Lodge itself and all the adjoining houses. The duchess filled her schools with stores for the ministers and their families, and all whom they might choose to invite. No expense of thought or labour was spared. But there was one thing that might have rendered all the careful arrangements of no avail. The rain had been falling for weeks, and there seemed no prospect of its cessation. Happily the fears were disappointed. From the time the people began to assemble until after the forenoon train on the last day had carried away the last of those who had lingered to the close of the assembly, there was not a drop of rain. The great day of the gathering was especially bright. It seemed as if God the great Creator were specially smiling on this effort for His glory and the everlasting welfare of His creatures. The place chosen for the gathering was most suitable, there being two or three places like amphitheatres on which the hearers could sit. Everything had been arranged so carefully by those whose hearts were thoroughly in the work that the duchess was able to note after the great gathering was over—"Truly there was not one thing out of place or unseemly." Eternity will unfold the results. The assembly was characterised "by much freedom and power in the speakers, by refreshing and lively joy and thanksgiving in the Lord's people, by the awakening of many of the dead, and by holy liberty granted to those that were bound." The number at this meeting in 1860 was about 7000. Meetings of a similar character were held in the three following years. In one or more of these the number reached 10,000. About the last of the great assemblies, the duchess wrote—" *August,* 1863. I cannot but wonder to see these meetings increasing in numbers and interest every year; not as a rendezvous for a pleasant day in the country, but really very solemn meetings, where the presence of the Lord is felt, and the power of His Spirit manifested. I trust that I have been somewhat awakened by the preaching of our own minister, which has been very striking indeed."

X.

THE END IS PEACE.

At the beginning of 1861 the duchess was brought almost to death's door. To use the words of her biographer, "She was visited with a severe and all but fatal illness, which was inscribed by the Lord's own hand with all the characters of the believer's death-bed, except that He brought her up again from the gates of the grave, and prolonged her precious life for three years more." So alarming was the illness that she made all arrangements for her departure hence. Various remembrances were set aside for her relatives and friends, and directions were given that certain letters should be written for the promotion of the welfare of some whose interest she had at heart.

On the evening of her attack she asked her friend to repeat the hymn

> "One there is above all others,
> Oh, how He loves!"

She then observed that she had been depressed for some time with a sense of her many sins, but that the Lord was now giving her tranquil and joyful rest. She often spoke of the manner in which her soul was comforted, and that never-forgotten night. It is thus described by Dr. Moody Stuart, who was for many years her close friend: "There was nothing of the nature of a dream or trance; but as she lay sleepless, there appeared as if really before her eyes a white scroll unrolled, glistening with unearthly brightness, and with floods of vivid light ever flowing over it. Written at the head of the scroll, in large bright letters of gold, she read this inscription:—'THE LORD OUR RIGHTEOUSNESS.' All her darkness was dispelled in a moment; with the glorious words, the Spirit imprinted on her heart and conscience the fresh seal of the pardon of all her sins; she believed and knew that the Lord Jesus Christ was of God made unto her 'righteousness,' and that His blood had made her whiter than snow. Her soul entered in a moment into perfect rest; the peace of God that passeth all understanding now kept her heart and mind through Christ Jesus; and she rejoiced in the full assurance that for her to die that night was to depart and be for ever with the Lord."

Day after day passed on, and she still lived. All her thoughts and words were about her Lord and the spiritual welfare of those around her. Her servants were a special care to her. As she was not allowed to see them individually, she sent them a message that they must not be content with trusting in a general way to the mercy of God, but that each of them must be found in the Lord our Righteousness if they would be saved. Throughout the illness her mind was kept in perfect peace, being emphatically stayed upon her Lord. One can well understand how prayers would be offered up for her by many that the valued life might be spared, if it were God's will.

During the time of her slow and partial recovery she occupied herself with learning hymns. She laid up a store which became in later months a great source of comfort to her. The hymn which she first committed to memory was one of her chief favourites:—

"A mind at perfect peace with God."

The second verse she specially valued:—

"By nature and by practice far,
   How very far from God;
Yet now by grace brought nigh to Him,
   Through faith in Jesus' blood."

As we have said recovery was only slow and partial. She tried to learn the lesson designed in this lengthening out of her earthly sojourn. "I thought my life was spared," she said, "to give the opportunity of devoting for a longer period my influence and substance to the cause of Christ, but I see now a deeper meaning in it. There is more personal holiness to be attained, more nearness to Christ, and more joy hereafter through a deeper work here in my heart."

Her old habit of early rising had of course to be abandoned. But the hours of the early morning were well spent, especially in meditation and intercessory prayer. As an example of the things that occupied her mind, we may quote words spoken to her maid as she entered the room: "I awoke very early this morning, and have been very happy and busily engaged. My thoughts have been much occupied with three things all so different, yet each needing God's help to-day. The first is the Queen's visit to Aberdeen to inaugurate the Prince Consort's memorial; the second is Mr. M.'s prayer meeting in London in a hall that had been a dancing-saloon in his parish; and (referring to a young man formerly in her service, but then studying for the ministry) the third is John's College examination."

At the end of 1863 the duchess expressed a strong wish that the ministerial conference at Huntly Lodge should be resumed. A meeting was held on the 13th of the following January. As she heard what had transpired she remarked, "I liked the meeting, and had only one thing to find fault with: some of the gentlemen prayed for me as if I was something, and I am nothing. I must speak about that before the next meeting." She invited all to meet again on the 10th of the following month. She little thought that they would indeed meet on that day, but only to lay her remains to rest. The 10th of February was to be her funeral day.

The fatal illness was of very short duration, and gave her little opportunity of thought. She was sorrowing over her inability to think when the words were given to her: "I am poor and needy yet the Lord thinketh upon me." "Yes, that's it," was her reply; "In Thy strong arms I lay me down." She was quoting from the following hymn, which she frequently repeated to her friends, and which she said more than any other expressed the present state of her feelings:—

"I only enter on the rest,
  Obtained by labour done;
I only claim the victory
  By Him so dearly won.

And, Lord, I seek a *holy* rest,
  A victory over sin;
I seek that Thou alone should'st reign
  O'er all, without, within.

In quietness then, and confidence,
  Saviour, my strength shall be,
And '*take* me, for I cannot *come*,'
  Is still my cry to Thee.

In Thy strong hand I lay me down,
  So shall the work be done;
For who can work so wondrously
  As an Almighty One?

Work on, then, Lord, till on my soul
  Eternal Light shall break;

> And in Thy likeness perfected,
>   I 'satisfied' shall wake."

On the evening of the 29th of January the duchess attempted to ask for something. Miss Sandilands repeated the words, "My Beloved is mine, and I am His." "Yes," she answered. This emphatic token of assent to a truth which was essentially her own by appropriation was the last attempt she made to speak. She fell asleep at half-past seven on the Sabbath evening, the 31st of January, 1864. She went to the land where time is no more, in her seventieth year, just reaching the allotted term of life, as she had certainly in no ordinary degree performed its allotted work.

There was no need of hired mourners at her funeral. The depth of real grief was unprecedented. The sad procession was composed of many hundreds of mourners, and of nearly seven hundred children from her schools. The whole district was desolate and bereaved. The man was only speaking what many another was thinking when he said, "This is the greatest calamity that ever befell this district; of a' the dukes that reigned here there was never one like her; there's none in this neighbourhood, high or low, but was under some obligation to her, for she made it her study to benefit her fellow-men; and what crowds o' puir craturs she helped every day. And then for the spiritual, Huntly is Huntly still, in a great degree, but the gude that's been done in it is a' through her."

All that was mortal of this mother in Israel was laid to rest in Elgin Cathedral. That noble fane contained the remains of no one more loved than she. "I can't understand how people should love me," she used to say. Others could understand it. And now that they could love her in person no longer, they love her memory.

S.F. HARRIS, M.A., B.C.L.

CPSIA information can be obtained
at www.ICGtesting.com
Printed in the USA
LVHW081929200622
721688LV00001B/26